Hacking
del.icio.us™

Hacking
del.icio.us™

Leslie Michael Orchard

WILEY

Wiley Publishing, Inc.

Hacking del.icio.us™

Published by
Wiley Publishing, Inc.
10475 Crosspoint Boulevard
Indianapolis, IN 46256
www.wiley.com

ISBN-13: 978-0-470-03785-0
ISBN-10: 0-470-03785-7

Manufactured in the United States of America

10 9 8 7 6 5 4 3 2 1

For general information on our other products and services or to obtain technical support, please contact our Customer Care Department within the U.S. at (800) 762-2974, outside the U.S. at (317) 572-3993 or fax (317) 572-4002.

Library of Congress Cataloging-in-Publication Data

Orchard, Leslie M. (Leslie Michael), 1975–
  Hacking del.icio.us / Leslie Michael Orchard.
    p. cm.
  Includes index.
  ISBN-13: 978-0-470-03785-0 (paper/website : alk. paper)
  ISBN-10: 0-470-03785-7 (paper/website : alk. paper)
  1. Internet programming. 2. Web sites—Management. 3. File organization (Computer science) I. Title.
QA76.625.O736 2006
006.7'6—dc22
                        2006014068

About the Author

Leslie Michael Orchard is a hacker, tinkerer, and creative technologist working in the Detroit area. He lives with two spotted Ocicats, two dwarf bunnies, and a very patient and understanding girl. On rare occasions when spare time comes in copious amounts, he plays around with odd bits of code and writing, sharing them on his Web site named 0xDECAFBAD (`http://decafbad.com/`).

Credits

Executive Editor
Chris Webb

Development Editor
Tom Dinse

Copy Editor
Nancy Rapoport

Editorial Manager
Mary Beth Wakefield

Production Manager
Tim Tate

Vice President and Executive Group Publisher
Richard Swadley

Vice President and Executive Publisher
Joseph B. Wikert

Compositor
Maureen Forys,
Happenstance Type-O-Rama

Proofreader
C. M. Jones

Indexer
Johnna VanHoose Dinse

Cover Design
Anthony Bunyan

Acknowledgments

Alexandra Arnold, Science Genius Girl Extraordinaire, said "Yes!" about a year ago, and we're likely to have just returned from our honeymoon shortly before this book hits the shelves. How did I get so lucky?

Joshua Schachter built del.icio.us on a simple concept — and he's somehow managed to keep it built on a series of simple yet powerful concepts as it has bloomed, growing exponentially. Congratulations on your amazing success in doing something you love!

Chris Webb gave me the opportunity to combine two things for which I've got a lot of love — del.icio.us and writing. He and Tom Dinse kept me on track for this project, despite an unexpectedly turbulent span of months. Thank you

Contents at a Glance

Contents

Part III: Beyond del.icio.us

Chapter 10: Exploring Open Source Alternatives 275

Introduction

When Joshua Schachter invited me to try out del.icio.us in the latter half of 2003, I was already playing with a set of my own blogging-by-bookmark tools. I did some convoluted things with browser bookmarks, processed by scripts I'd written to post quick items to my blog. I thought these were pretty cool — so, my initial reaction to del.icio.us was something like, "This is really nice, but I've already got one."

Keep in mind that I'm a tinkerer who very much enjoys doing it myself — so when I admit that del.icio.us made me happily ditch all my own work, it's just about the highest praise I can give. Very shortly after I discovered del.icio.us, Joshua's clean and well-considered incremental improvements got me hooked and made my scripts look like the awkward hacks they were.

Convenient bookmarklets, XML data feeds, and the del.icio.us API have made use of the service frictionless — and yet, counter-intuitively, these things have also made the site incredibly sticky. Personally, I progressed from having my programs carbon-copy browser bookmarks to del.icio.us, to eventually abandoning my own code and switching to exclusively using del.icio.us for bookmarks. After a few redesigns at my site, I dropped publishing link blog posts to my site and simply pointed my links to their new de facto home at del.icio.us. All the while, I've known I could leave and take my bookmarks with me at any point — but I've never had any reason to do so.

When Joshua introduced tagging features, the powers of social bookmarking really bloomed and the benefits of sharing bookmarks became readily apparent. More than just simply a service to manage a collection of bookmarks or maintain a "remaindered links" blog, del.icio.us morphed into a powerful hub for the aggregation and annotation of resources on the Web, filtered by the valuable attentions of real people.

Although the phrase "Web 2.0" has reached a cringe-worthy critical mass among veterans weary of buzzwords in general, it's not hard to say that del.icio.us is at the vanguard of what prompted the term's coining. Many of the site's basic features and concepts have been cloned elsewhere in part or whole — with tagging in particular causing a stir in both academic and entrepreneurial circles.

Furthermore, through XML feeds and its Web-based API, del.icio.us has encouraged the growth of a rich ecosystem of Web- and desktop-based tools for managing, enhancing, and analyzing social bookmarks. This pattern has been repeated at other sites, in both independent inventions and inspired imitations — spawning cross-fertilized hacks and a whole new mashed-up Web of interrelated data and content.

Whom Is This Book For?

I wrote this book with tinkerers in mind — that is to say, tinkerers of various levels of familiarity with del.icio.us in particular and Web development skill in general. Whether you're just getting on your way to being a power user at del.icio.us, or whether you're a hardcore Web development guru who's running your own hand-built blogging package, I hope you'll find something of interest within these pages.

For some of the more in-depth programming examples provided in this book, you'll need to have Web hosting or a server of your own — preferably one that includes hosting basic HTML with JavaScript and CSS includes, serving up PHP scripts, and possibly running Python programs. I've tried to keep the requirements light, so in general you won't need access to a database. So, for instance, if you've been able to run your own installation of WordPress or Movable Type for your personal blog, you should have everything you need.

Otherwise, you should be fine with just a Web browser — my favorite is Firefox — and an interest in exploring del.icio.us and the universe of social bookmarking.

What's in This Book?

The chapters in this book are organized into three parts. The first is intended as a general introduction to del.icio.us and to offer some tricks for power users; the second delves into more in-depth programming and hacks that use the del.icio.us API and XML data feeds; and the third part of the book examines a few of the options offered by clones and competitors.

Part I: Exploring del.icio.us

To kick off the book, Part I is devoted to introducing the basics of del.icio.us, after which the more advanced tricks and tips for using the service are explored.

- **Chapter 1: "What Is del.icio.us?"** This chapter presents an overview of what del.icio.us has to offer to a new user. Here, you'll get an illustrated guide walking you through features available to registered users and visitors in general, as well as a few pointers to further discussion about the site.

- **Chapter 2: "Enhancing Your Browser."** Now that you've gotten the hang of the basics, this chapter guides you into some more expert tricks available to del.icio.us users. You are shown how the official bookmarklets for easy posting to del.icio.us work, and how to improve them. A few of the extensions available for Firefox, Safari, and Internet Explorer are introduced as well — all with the goal of helping you become a power user.

- **Chapter 3: "Seasoning Your Desktop."** As del.icio.us users have sought to further integrate the service into their daily habits, desktop applications using the site's API have begun to spring up. This chapter offers a peek at a handful of these programs you can install for ubiquitous access to del.icio.us bookmarks outside the browser.

Part II: Remixing del.icio.us

Once you've gotten the hang of being a del.icio.us power user, you might get the itch to start digging under the surface and see just how the open APIs and XML data feeds provided by the site can help you build interesting things. This part of the book should help you out with that.

- **Chapter 4: "Exploring del.icio.us APIs and Data."** This chapter gives you a very hands-on perspective, using HTTP requests and XML to directly explore the API and data feeds available at del.icio.us. In the latter part of the chapter, a few packages available in various languages and environments are introduced in order to ease the process of implementing applications on top of del.icio.us services.

- **Chapter 5: "The What and How of Hacks."** Before we get into the thick of things with the del.icio.us API and data, however, this chapter presents a quick survey of the tools and technologies available that make remixes and mashups possible with a site like del.icio.us.

- **Chapter 6: "Tagging Hacks."** One of the most significant features of del.icio.us — tagging — is described in this chapter. After a survey of important aspects of tagging, the chapter presents examples of the varied ways in which bookmarks annotated by tagging can be searched and visualized.

- **Chapter 7: "Mashups and Enhancements."** Some people have their own ideas on how to make del.icio.us a better service. Thanks to the API and data feeds, however, tinkerers need not wait for the developers at del.icio.us to agree and implement new features. This chapter is all about how third-party sites offer new ways to view, analyze, and extend del.icio.us bookmarking. Toward the end of this chapter, an original mashup implemented in PHP — the TechnoFlickrDeli — is offered and discussed.

- **Chapter 8: "Getting Your Links Out of del.icio.us."** Not everyone is comfortable with completely relying on del.icio.us as their exclusive provider of bookmarks and link sharing. This chapter offers a variety of ways to get your bookmarks out of del.icio.us — from simply displaying them on your own site, to getting a complete export of your bookmarks and navigating them in an alternative interface.

- **Chapter 9: "Getting del.icio.us into Your Blog."** On the other hand, some del.icio.us users look for ways to more deeply integrate the service into their site or blogs. This chapter covers ways in which you can better integrate the display of bookmarks on your site, as well as providing links and buttons to encourage visitors themselves to post bookmarks to your content.

Part III: Beyond del.icio.us

As you may know, del.icio.us isn't the only game in town. There were bookmarking sites before it came on the scene, and others have sprung up since. This part of the book takes a look at a few open source clones and other direct competition for del.icio.us.

- **Chapter 10: "Exploring Open Source Alternatives."** Some tinkerers take do-it-yourself so much to heart that they'd rather build their own version of del.icio.us than entirely rely upon it. Others had their own ideas for Web-based bookmarking before del.icio.us was born. This chapter takes a look at a handful of Web-based bookmarking projects.

- **Chapter 11: "Checking Out the Competition."** In the field of social bookmarking, del.icio.us is not alone. Whether they achieved the same level of success, other people have had and executed very similar ideas as del.icio.us. Some of these sites have been around longer than del.icio.us, and others have sprung up since. Some are almost identical clones, while others have tried striking off on their own with new and unique features. This chapter offers a look at a handful or two of these sites.

This book also has a single appendix, entitled "Site URLs, Feeds, and API Methods Reference." As you explore building your own hacks, mashups, and remixes from the technology offered by del.icio.us, this appendix should serve as a useful cheat sheet and reference to the URL structures in use, API methods available, and XML data feeds provided by the site.

Source Code

As you work through the programs and hacks in this book, you may choose either to type in all the code manually or to use the source code files that accompany the book. All of the source code used in this book is available for download at the following site:

```
www.wiley.com/go/extremetech
```

Once you've downloaded the code, just decompress it with your favorite tool.

Hacking
del.icio.us™

Exploring del.icio.us

What Is del.icio.us?

On the site's About page, you'll find that del.icio.us is described as a "social bookmarks manager." But, unlike many of the early social software offerings that have peaked in popularity over the past few years, del.icio.us wasn't created just to help you find a job or hook you up with a date for Saturday night. Instead, del.icio.us is all about links: bookmarking, describing, tagging, sharing, and discovering things on the Web.

Now, at first glance, you might wonder what del.icio.us has over the bookmarks menu in your browser. Well, just for starters, links posted to del.icio.us are available from pretty much anywhere in the world. And, you'll never need to import or convert bookmarks between Web browsers again — unless you really want to, that is.

But here's where the social aspects start to come into play: Every time you add a bookmark to your del.icio.us collection, the site tells you about other people who've posted the same link. From here, you can dive into others' collections. After awhile you'll discover people who tend to link to the same things as you — and in exploring their collections, you just might stumble upon interesting things you wouldn't have found otherwise.

Another socially enhanced feature that's central to the del.icio.us experience is tagging. A tag on del.icio.us might best be described as a freeform cross between a keyword and a category. Like a keyword, a tag is meant to be short and sweet — one word, maybe a tiny phrase or WikiWord. But, like a category, a tag is used to group bookmarks together. Where the benefits of tagging begin to emerge is when many people converge on the same tags for similar topics. Tagging becomes very powerful when it's turned into a multiplayer game.

And finally, del.icio.us has its doors thrown open wide to welcome tinkering and remixing. Bookmarks listed by user and tags are available as XML feeds right alongside the HTML meant for human consumption. Most major features of the site offered for use within a browser are made available to scripts and third-party tools via a simple HTTP GET and XML-based API. By eschewing zealous restrictions on access to achieve user lock-in, del.icio.us has become even more popular and relied-upon than it might've otherwise.

in this chapter

☑ Signing up and getting started

☑ Sharing links

☑ Making bookmarks social

☑ Exploring tags

☑ Subscribing to bookmarks

☑ Programming with the del.icio.us API

☑ Joining the community

Signing Up and Getting Started

Taking advantage of what del.icio.us has to offer requires audience participation, so why not start off by getting yourself signed up for an account? Open up a browser window and pay a visit to the del.icio.us home page, shown in Figure 1-1. Oh, and in case it's at all confusing: The site's title is also the URL (`http://del.icio.us`).

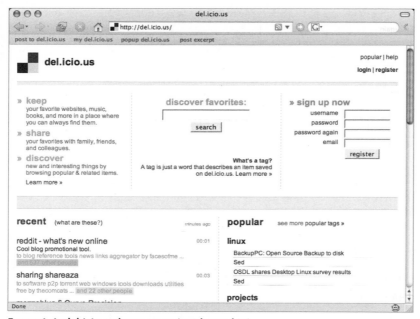

FIGURE 1-1: del.icio.us home page (not logged in)

This first page welcomes you with a bit of introductory text to explain the site. If you like, click around and read more about the site. Eventually, however, you'll want to sign up for an account. This is easy to do — use either the form presented on the home page or click the register link in the site's upper navigation bar. Click here, and you'll be presented with a form to create a new account for yourself.

On the registration page (shown in Figure 1-2), you'll find a form asking for a username and password alongside optional fields for your name and email address. Even though the email address is optional, you really should provide it if you'd ever like to recover a lost password. A more recent addition to the form is the use of a *CAPTCHA*, an attempt to foil automated account creation by robots. This is one of the few spots where automation isn't welcome — the creators of del.icio.us do want to know who's to blame when a robot runs amok, after all.

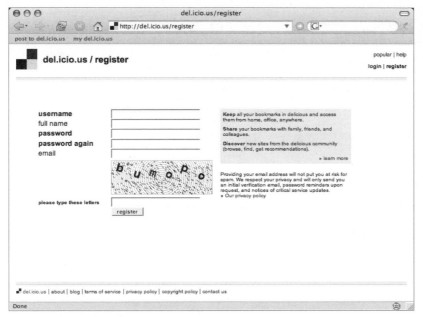

FIGURE 1-2: Registering to create an account

On the Web

CAPTCHAs — or, "completely automated public Turing test to tell computers and humans apart" — are a growing practice on modern Web sites. But, if you've never seen one before or are just curious about them, here are a few pointers to follow for more information:

The CAPTCHA Project: www.captcha.net/

Wikipedia: http://en.wikipedia.org/wiki/Captcha

Anyway, you know what to do: Fill out the form, make sure you pass the Turing test, and click the register button. You should be given a page something like Figure 1-3 in response, unless you happen to run into a problem — such as attempting to claim a username already registered, or if you happen to fail the CAPTCHA test.

Note

If you supplied an email address when you registered an account, you'll be informed about a verification email that's on its way. This message will contain a link you'll need to click in order to verify that the address you've given is correct. This is just one more way to ensure you're a live human being.

Immediately after successfully creating your new account at del.icio.us, you're greeted with an initial page of instructions (refer to Figure 1-3). The primary way to interact with the site is via "bookmarklets," which are small capsules of JavaScript code executable as bookmarks. As the instructions suggest, you should probably use your browser's Links (on IE) or Navigation (on Firefox) toolbar as home to these bookmarklets, where they'll be within easy reach. What you're looking at are the first steps toward replacing your old browser bookmark habits.

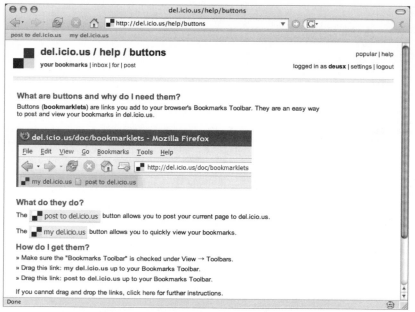

FIGURE 1-3: Post-registration help with del.icio.us bookmarklets

Once you've created an account successfully, you'll find that you're automatically logged into the site (see Figure 1-4). The introductory material that was shown in Figure 1-1 has gotten out of your way, and now you see the site's front page view. This page offers a sort of two-pronged fire hose of links, giving you the most recent links to be posted to the site alongside the moment's most popular links.

If you hadn't noticed before, you can see that this site is obsessed with links: Nearly everything on this page is a hyperlink to somewhere else — and links to within del.icio.us itself are in the minority!

Sharing Links

Now that you've gotten yourself an account on del.icio.us, and you've successfully installed the bookmarklets, you're ready to start sharing links.

Browse to a site — any site besides del.icio.us itself — and click the "remember this" book-marklet. You should shortly see a page like Figure 1-5. Thanks to the JavaScript code in the bookmarklet, this page comes pre-populated with the URL and page title found from the pre-vious page. From here, you can optionally supply a bit of extended description for this URL — some people fill this in with a quote lifted from the page, while others supply their own com-mentary or witticisms.

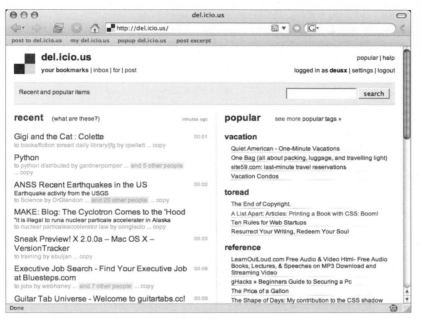

FIGURE 1-4: del.icio.us home page after login

FIGURE 1-5: Posting a link

The other field available on this form allows you to associate tags with this link. You can enter these manually, one after another, separated by spaces. You can also take advantage of whatever tag suggestions appear associated with this link by clicking on one or more, which automatically appends them to the tags field. I'll get into this a bit more in a minute, but it's useful to pay attention to these recommendations. They'll help you take advantage of consensus built among other del.icio.us users.

Finally, once you've reviewed everything to your satisfaction, go ahead and click the "save" button. Alternately, most browsers allow you to simply hit Return in one of the form fields to submit the form, shaving seconds off your posting time. Shortly after submission, del.icio.us takes you right back to the URL where you started.

Congratulations! You've just posted your first bookmark to del.icio.us. Now, check out your personal collection. To get there, just add your user name after `http://del.icio.us/`.

For example, my own collection can be found here:

```
http://del.icio.us/deusx
```

Figure 1-6 gives you a look at what my bookmark collection looked like just after posting the link from Figure 1-5. The newly posted link appears at the top of the list because the collection is presented in reverse-chronological order. You should be able to see the extended description I added, as well as the collection of tags I selected. Note, also, that there are links to edit or delete each bookmark.

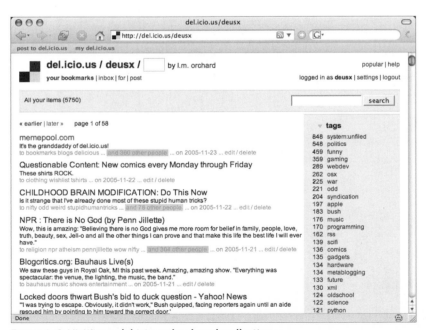

FIGURE **1-6:** Visiting a del.icio.us bookmark collection

Making Bookmarks Social

Now that you have gotten a start on your collection of links, it's time to take a deeper look into just what it means to use a "social bookmarks manager." You might want to post a few more links of your own before reading on, especially if those links have appeared somewhere such as a popular news site. Alternately, you can visit someone else's bookmark collection (e.g., `http://del.icio.us/deusx`), which might have a few more posted links.

What you should be looking for is visible in Figure 1-6: Each bookmark has an indicator of how popular the link has become, with a color-coded count of other users who've posted the same link. This is more than a simple indicator, however — these are links that, when clicked, will result in something like what's shown in Figure 1-7.

The page in Figure 1-7 is a listing of notes posted by users who all bookmarked this URL. Here you'll find variations in how people have edited the title or extended descriptions for a particular link, as well as what collection of tags others have chosen to attach.

You can also see a ranking of common tags users have attached to this particular URL, in order of their popularity. This should give you a taste of how del.icio.us attempts to provide a rough view of the consensus among its users.

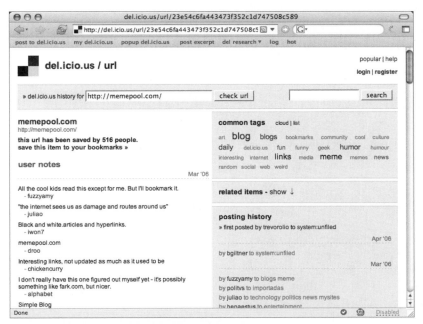

FIGURE 1-7: Viewing common details on a bookmark

Another feature on the page shown in Figure 1-7 is in the sidebar and rather understated: the "related items - show" link: Check out what happens when you click this link (see Figure 1-8). Because providing this display takes a relatively large chunk of processing, it's not done by default. But, if you click here, you'll get a list of recommended URLs that may be similar to the bookmarked URL you're currently viewing. This is based on analyzing the postings of other users and similar tags used for other bookmarks.

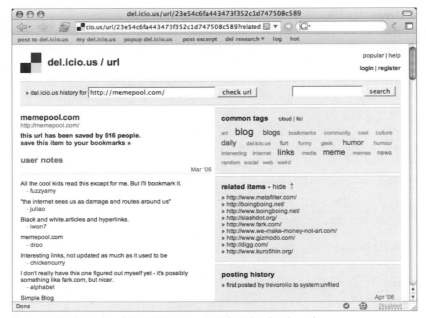

FIGURE 1-8: Viewing related URLs associated with a bookmark

Speaking of URLs

Although it might not mean much to you until you start getting into some deeper hacking with del.icio.us, there's one more not-so-obvious feature to these pages in Figures 1-7 and 1-8. If you've been watching so far, you may have noticed that most of the URLs used to navigate the features of del.icio.us are very straightforward and simple — except for this one. This URL contains a string of apparently random letters and numbers reminiscent of opaque session tracking used in many "Web 1.0" applications.

Continued

Well, as it turns out, this string is an MD5 hash of a bookmarked URL. This technique is used to sidestep any issues involved in referring to a URL as a query parameter in another URL. Given any URL, run an MD5 hash on it, and you can find it on del.icio.us — provided that someone, somewhere has posted a bookmark to it. In the coming chapters, you'll see a few hacks that make use of this little trick.

Not sure what an MD5 hash is? Basically, it's a way to produce a consistent 128-bit fingerprint of any given collection of data. When expressed in hexadecimal, MD5 hashes come out to 16 characters in length no matter what the content of the original data, thus making them convenient and predictable digests for data. Here are a few pointers to more information:

- **Wikipedia on MD5:** `http://en.wikipedia.org/wiki/MD5`

- **RFC 1321:** `www.faqs.org/rfcs/rfc1321.html`

Exploring Tags

You've already been exposed to tags so far in your exploration with del.icio.us — both in supplying them when you post a bookmark and as links associated with displayed bookmarks — but now it's time to check them out in detail.

Since the feature was introduced on del.icio.us, many articles, papers, blog entries, and inspired implementations have been devoted to tagging. Tags are like categories turned inside out: Instead of meticulously placing bookmarks into a carefully arranged hierarchy of folders, you attach the tags to bookmarks. And rather than use a taxonomy of topics well considered and agreed upon in committee, the design of del.icio.us encourages the use of tagging in a flat namespace somewhat akin to word association — just fire off a handful of words you might vaguely consider in characterizing the link you're posting and submit.

It might sound hasty and sloppy, but it works. In fact, it works because it's hasty and sloppy: Because you don't have to put much effort or thought into the process, you're more likely to actually do it — as opposed to many well-intentioned and richly expressive approaches to metadata and classification that never actually see use by real people on a daily basis.

For a start, you might want to check out the master list of tags in use on the site. You can see what this page looks like in Figure 1-9, and you can visit it for yourself at the following URL:

```
http://del.icio.us/tag
```

This sort of tag presentation has often been called a "tag cloud." The tags all appear as links in a big visual jumble, with more heavily used tags appearing in more emphasized and larger fonts. This particular page is arranged alphabetically by default, but you can click the "by size" link to see the tags sorted in order of popularity. If you click any of these tags, you'll find a page listing links from anyone who chose to attach that particular tag to their posting.

FIGURE 1-9: Viewing overall tags in use

For example, if you were to click "osx" — one of my favorite tags — you'd see a page similar to Figure 1-10. This is again just a reverse-chronological presentation of links with descriptions, along with their attached tags and an indication of popularity. The important thing to notice, however, is that every one of these links has had the "osx" tag attached.

It's when you've got many people tagging similar links that the social aspects start to bear fruit: People tend to attach similar tags to similar things. And, even where people tend to differ slightly in their choice of tags (e.g., "osx" versus "mac"), del.icio.us can make attempts to present similar tags together. It's a fuzzy process, but it hits a sweet spot between laziness and utility.

As you can see in Figure 1-10, the "osx" tag offers you what amounts to a decently topic-focused linkblog, thanks to the fact that most people use this tag when posting links related to Apple's Mac OS X operating system. On the other hand, notice the "related tags" listing in the upper right. If you haven't found what you're looking for on this tag display, try one of those — these have been assembled after an analysis of what other tags tend to appear in the same context as the current page's tag.

Using something akin to peer pressure, the site can gently nudge people toward more popular — and therefore more agreed-upon — tags through examples and recommendations. Over time, shared tagging forms a sort of ad hoc and emergent classification scheme, which, although vague and fuzzy, is in many ways superior to more intentionally planned schemes — if only by virtue of its actually being useful and subject to constant updates.

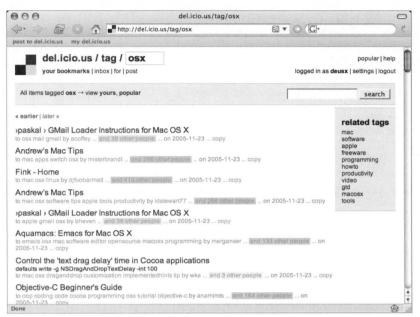

FIGURE 1-10: Checking out links under the "osx" tag

Note Besides viewing single tags, you can also check out tag intersections by tossing a few tags separated by "+" into your URL. This shows you links that have all of the specified tags. For example, the following URL displays links tagged with both "apple" and "css":

```
http://del.icio.us/tag/apple+css
```

These links might help you sort out some details specific to developing Web pages using CSS on Apple's Safari Web browser.

Now, after all this talk about the social aspects of tagging, it'd be nice to see some of the personal benefits of tags. I mean, these are your bookmarks after all; what about your tags? Well, try this URL on for size:

```
http://del.icio.us/deusx/osx
```

If you like, substitute your own user name for the *deusx*. Either way, you should find a page that looks like Figure 1-11. Here you'll see just the bookmarks you've posted with this tag attached. And also notice that, because the results have been focused down to your own collection, there are some richer options for further search: A list of your own related tags is available for tag intersection drilldown, as well as the master list of your other tags in use. Also worth noting is that there's a link back to the shared tag, but you've already seen that page in Figure 1-10.

FIGURE **1-11: Viewing bookmarks under a user's personal tag**

Something else to notice on the page shown in Figure 1-11 is the option to view recommendations. This is just another example of the social intelligence del.icio.us offers. Check out Figure 1-12 for an example of what these recommendations look like. Here, you'll find pointers toward other people who've turned up as statistically like-minded, at least with respect to what you think this particular tag means.

Keep in mind, however, that these recommendations aren't magic: This feature will reward you to the degree that you've loaded your account up with bookmarks. The more you post, the better your results.

Subscribing to Bookmarks

Once you've had a chance to wander around a bit, you might start finding people whose collections reliably turn up interesting items for you. Or, you might discover that you've got friends already on del.icio.us who'd like to post links directly intended for your attention. You will probably also discover combinations of tags that perfectly suit your interests — wouldn't it be nice to be kept in the loop on all the new bookmarks that show up there?

Well, although exploration and browsing are activities that the del.icio.us user interface invites, it also offers a few options to keep you updated with less manual effort.

FIGURE 1-12: Viewing recommendations associated with a user's tagged bookmarks

As a registered del.icio.us user, you have an inbox at your disposal. With this tool, you can register interest in other users' collections and maintain a socially focused aggregated page of their bookmarks. Also, as you discover friends with del.icio.us user names, you can apply a special for: tag to your bookmarks to catch their attention — and vice versa. And, finally, so many of the lists and pages on del.icio.us offer RSS feeds you can pull into feed readers and aggregators so that you can be truly kept up-to-date.

Tracking Others' Bookmarks with Your Inbox

What would a socially oriented site be without a friends' list or a buddy network? Well, that's not quite what the inbox on del.icio.us is for, but it does let you gather up other users' collections into a single aggregated view where you can more easily keep updated on their new bookmarks. Figure 1-13 offers a peek at what this page looks like once you've started adding a few users' names.

You can access your own inbox from the prominently placed "inbox" link right next to "your bookmarks" in the top-of-page site navigation. Unlike many social software services, however, your collection of inbox subscriptions is private and not readily viewable by other users. This isn't so much a popularity contest as it is a tool to help you stay fed with interesting things from like-minded people. The list management page, shown in Figure 1-14, is accessible via the "edit inbox" link in the "subs" box on the right side of the inbox page.

FIGURE 1-13: Viewing a populated del.icio.us inbox

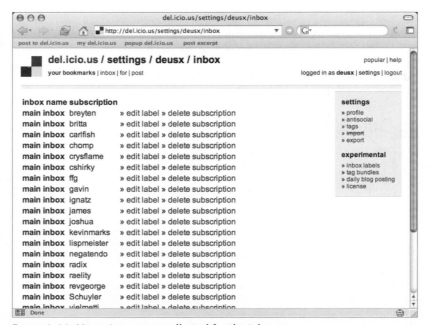

FIGURE 1-14: Managing names collected for the inbox

The interface here is very simple and to the point: In Figure 1-15, you can see a form at the bottom of the page you can use to add a user's bookmarks to your subscriptions list. You can also specify a tag, in case you'd like to narrow your attention down to a particular topic covered by an individual's bookmarks. You can also remove existing subscriptions, as well as rename them using some label more meaningful to you than a username or tag.

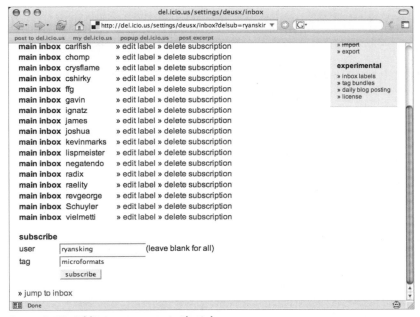

FIGURE 1-15: Adding a new user to the inbox

Sending and Receiving Bookmarks Using Tags

While you can keep tabs on individual people with your inbox, your friends and colleagues can take a more direct route to get your attention using the `for:` tag prefix. Any time you tag a bookmark using a del.icio.us user name prefixed by `for:`, that bookmark appears in the user's "for" collection. This page is available as a link right next to the "inbox" link in the top site navigation.

So, for example, if someone were to tag a bookmark with `for:deusx` when posting, I'd see that link appear in my personal "for" list in Figure 1-16. You can tag a bookmark using any user name, and anyone on del.icio.us can tag a link intended for your attention. It's worth noting that while the bookmark itself is not private, the `for:` tag is hidden from public view along with your aggregate collection of these tagged links.

Taken together, the `for:` tag prefix and private collection form a sort of messaging system you and your colleagues can use to share links and bring interesting things to each others' attentions.

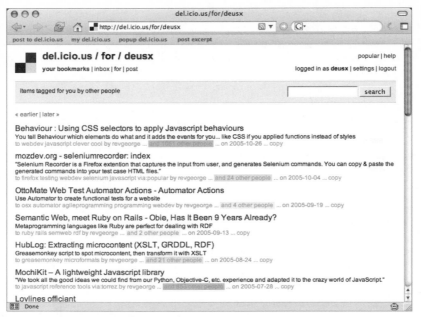

FIGURE 1-16: Viewing bookmarks tagged with for:deusx

Discovering del.icio.us RSS Feeds

As I mentioned before, del.icio.us provides many ways to get information into and out of the service. Besides bookmarklets and browser-viewed pages, del.icio.us also offers RSS feeds for many of the more interesting views on links posted to the site.

For an introduction to the various feeds offered by del.icio.us, check out the help page on the subject (shown in Figure 1-17):

```
http://del.icio.us/help/rss
```

In a nutshell, RSS feeds at del.icio.us are machine-readable XML documents that provide updated views of the lists of links you've been browsing throughout the site so far. Rather than remembering to visit del.icio.us to look for updates, you can use a feed reader or aggregator to keep tabs on these RSS feeds so that interesting new links will come to you.

Are you new to RSS feeds? These feeds aren't an original del.icio.us invention — if you're interested, you can find more reading on RSS with this Wikipedia article:

```
http://en.wikipedia.org/wiki/RSS_(file_format)
```

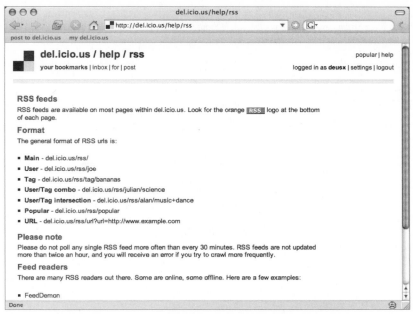

FIGURE 1-17: Documentation on finding and using del.icio.us RSS feeds

Reading the help pages at del.icio.us, you can see that several forms of RSS feeds are available, such as:

- Links that have been recently posted

- Links that have recently become popular

- Links posted by an individual user

- Links posted with a particular tag or combination of tags

- Links posted by an individual user with a particular combination of tags

And there are quite a few more streams of links from del.icio.us that have corresponding RSS feeds — keep an eye out for them. You should be able to see the familiar orange RSS icon appearing in the footer of many pages, as well as when these icons are called out elsewhere in the page.

Also, many feed aggregators and Web browsers are capable of "sniffing out" available RSS feeds when they've been included in a Web page's metadata.

For example, most of the screenshots in this chapter were taken using Mozilla Firefox (www.mozilla.org/products/firefox/). If you look back through the figures provided so far, you may notice a special "transmission wave" icon appearing in the location bar on many occasions. This is an indication that the pages displayed have corresponding RSS feeds. You can see this feature yourself, if you visit del.icio.us with Firefox.

Other browsers, such as Apple's Safari, offer similar RSS autodiscovery features. Also, some feed aggregators use this technology to let you simply provide the human-readable URL for a Web site, which will then be used to discover the machine-readable version. The end result of all of this is that del.icio.us makes it easy for both human beings and machines to gain access to bookmarks flowing into the site.

If you don't already have a feed aggregator that you use regularly, you may want to check out Mozilla Thunderbird (`www.mozilla.org/products/thunderbird/`). This is an open source application that offers email and feed aggregation features all in one place. Plenty of commercial and shareware options are available, but I use Thunderbird here for demonstration purposes.

In Figure 1-18, you can see a subscription to links tagged with `delicious`, as well as popular links and links that have been posted by others for my viewing with a `for:deusx` tag. Viewing links in an aggregator is just the start of where RSS feeds from del.icio.us become useful, however. These feeds, as well as their uses beyond feed aggregators, will come up again and in more detail in the coming chapters.

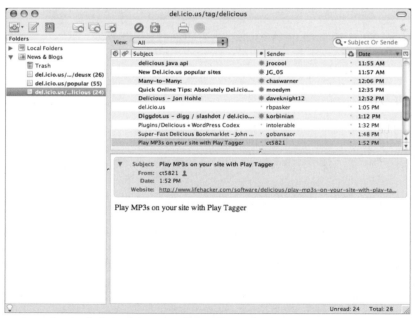

FIGURE 1-18: Feeds from del.icio.us in Mozilla Thunderbird

Programming with the del.icio.us API

Through machine-readable RSS feeds, del.icio.us provides a way to get bookmarks out of the system and into other applications. But wait, there's more — the site also offers a rich Web-based application programming interface (or API) that enables you to develop your own scripts and software wrapped around del.icio.us functionality.

This API goes beyond simple timely updates of links: You can make custom queries of your bookmarks by time and tag — as well as request a full dump of your data in case you ever want to back it up or switch services. Furthermore, you can post new bookmarks via the API, as well as perform a few tag maintenance functions.

This is just a quick summary of what capabilities the API provides. You can start digging into some details about the del.icio.us API in Appendix A. You'll also get a chance to see the API put through its paces in future chapters, both in your own code and in other programs that extend and enhance the functionality offered by this social bookmarking service.

Joining the Community

In addition to fostering a community based on bookmarks shared between friends and like-minded strangers, there's also a meta-community surrounding del.icio.us itself. You can keep up-to-date with updates and changes made to the service, as well as catch announcements and discussion about new software and third-party services under development by others.

The del.icio.us team maintains a blog located at this address:

```
http://blog.del.icio.us/
```

Here, you'll be able to catch new features and official announcements by the developers working on the site daily. Occasionally, you may find things such as tutorials on how to use the service or details on events and conferences where del.icio.us team members appear.

If email threads are more to your liking, there's also a long-running mailing list you can join for discussion and details about del.icio.us and other related developments. You can find archives and subscription details here:

```
http://lists.del.icio.us/pipermail/discuss/
```

And finally, if you'd like more immediate contact with del.icio.us fans and developers, there's a live Internet Relay Chat (or IRC) channel located here:

```
irc://irc.del.icio.us:6667/delicious
```

If your IRC client doesn't support URLs such as the one provided, try connecting to the server `irc.del.icio.us` on port 6667 and joining channel `#delicious`.

Don't have an IRC client? Here are a few free clients you may want to check out:

Windows, Linux: XChat at `www.xchat.org/`

Mac OS X: Colloquy at `http://colloquy.info/`

Summary

This chapter's whirlwind tour of features available at del.icio.us didn't even touch experimental features — and I'm sure to have missed a few more updates by the time you read this. But you should now at least have a taste for what's possible with this social bookmarking service.

On the surface, this site offers an easy way for you to move your bookmarks out of your browser for access from anywhere in the world, where you can share them with friends. And once you've started sharing your bookmarks, a payoff comes in the form of recommendations and the opportunity to find other like-minded link gatherers. Then, when you're ready to dive deeper, there are RSS feeds and an API to explore for hacks and tweaks, which you'll see in the coming chapters.

But, you're not quite ready to close your browser yet: In the next chapter, you see that there's a lot more to it than the starter set of bookmarklets you were given when you first signed up.

Enhancing Your Browser

Because del.icio.us offers a Web-based user interface meant to plug into your daily hunting and gathering habits, the first place where you can start hacking is in your Web browser.

And depending on your browser of choice, you've got a few options: First, you can use bookmarklets added to your Navigation toolbar. These are JavaScript-loaded bookmarks that can interact with the current page you're viewing. Second, some modern browsers support rich plug-in interfaces, allowing access to the browser's own bookmarks as well as even greater integration with del.icio.us via the API.

In this chapter, you're going to get a chance to play with some of the more advanced bookmarklets available, as well as see what makes them tick. Then, I'll take you on a tour of a few browser-based plug-ins and extensions you'll find for your favorite browser.

Tinkering with Bookmarklets

Bookmarklets are the easiest way to integrate del.icio.us into your daily browsing habits. When you signed up for an account, you were sent to a quick help page describing a few useful buttons for you to drag onto your bookmarks toolbar (see Figure 1-3). I breezed past them pretty quickly in the previous chapter in order to keep the tour moving along, but now we're going to circle back around for a closer look.

In a nutshell, bookmarklets are a bit of an unholy union between bookmarks and JavaScript. Since the early days of Netscape Navigator, most modern Web browsers have understood URLs starting with a `javascript:` prefix. At first, these URLs were mostly used as the HREF targets of hyperlinks within pages in order to fire off functions and events scripted with JavaScript in response to user interaction.

But then, one day, someone figured out that `javascript:` URLs can be bookmarked. What this means is that you can pack a string of JavaScript code into a bookmark as a `javascript:` URL. When you click that bookmark, the JavaScript code executes in the context of the page you're currently viewing. The end result is that you can compose and fire off JavaScript code that has access to the data of the page in your browser, without ever needing to modify the original page.

This discovery has led to all sorts of interesting little mini-applications: Some bookmarklets have been helpful in Web development, tweaking the size of a browser window or changing CSS style sheets on the fly. Other bookmarklets can customize pages more to your liking by switching all links on the page to open in a new window, or by automatically sending the page through a translation service. And, when these JavaScript-enriched bookmarks are added as convenient and easy-to-reach buttons on the Navigation or Links toolbar, it's kind of like having the power to add new features to your browser without writing full plug-ins or extensions.

 If you've never played with bookmarklets before now, you're missing out on a great way to expand your browser's capabilities. Check out these resources for further reading:

Wikipedia article on bookmarklets: `http://en.wikipedia.org/wiki/Bookmarklet`

Bookmarklets home page: `www.bookmarklets.com/`

Tantek's Favelets: `http://tantek.com/favelets/`

Web development bookmarklets: `www.squarefree.com/bookmarklets/`

Opening the Hood on the Official del.icio.us Bookmarklets

Now, there are plenty of pre-cooked bookmarklets available out there to keep you busy for quite a long time. But, in this chapter, I'm going to focus on getting under the hood of del.icio.us bookmarklets. When you're done, you should have picked up some hints on how to customize and tweak them to do just what you want.

So, let's get right down to business. When you signed up, you were offered a starter set of bookmark buttons. As I mentioned earlier, you can see these in a help page pictured back in Figure 1-3:

- **My del.icio.us:** This offers a quick link to your own bookmarks page.
- **Post to del.icio.us:** This scoops up details about the page you're currently viewing and prepares a form to post the page to your bookmarks.

While the first of these buttons is a simple link, the second is a full-fledged bookmarklet. If you followed the directions after signup and added these buttons, you should try taking a look at those bookmarks now — in Firefox, for instance, you can do this using the Manage Bookmarks item under the Bookmarks menu. Check out Figure 2-1 to see what you should find in your Bookmarks Toolbar folder.

FIGURE 2-1: Bookmarks Manager in Firefox opened to the Bookmarks Toolbar folder

Dissecting the Standard del.icio.us Bookmarklet

The bookmarks with URLs prefixed by `javascript:` are the interesting ones. They're far too long to view all at once in the single line offered in the Bookmarks Manager — but if you were to copy and paste it into a text editor, you'd see something like this:

```
javascript:location.href='http://del.icio.us/deusx?v=3&url=
'+encodeURIComponent(location.href)+'&title='+encodeURIComponent
(document.title)
```

At this point, it would help if you had some familiarity with JavaScript to understand what's going on — although even for JavaScript gurus these things can be cryptic. By taking advantage of the `javascript:` URI scheme available in modern browsers, bookmarklets sneak functionality into a space really intended only for URLs. So, line breaks and common formatting conventions aren't allowed. Furthermore, some older browsers may allow only around 2000 or so characters into a bookmark. Thus, bookmarklets are an exercise in compression over clarity.

But as a starting point, this first bookmarklet is pretty simple:

1. First, it scoops up the URL (`location.href`) and title (`document.title`) of the current page.

2. Next, it encodes these into a form safe for inclusion in a URL (with a call to `encodeURIComponent`).

3. Then, the URL and title are themselves concatenated into a URL that will summon up a bookmark posting form.

4. Finally, the browser is sent to this URL (via setting `location.href`), and you end up with the form you saw back in Figure 1-5.

Now, take a close look at the URL this bookmarklet works to build. For example, if I were to try bookmarking my own home page (`http://decafbad.com`), my browser would take me to this address:

```
http://del.icio.us/deusx?v=3&url=http%3A%2F%2Fdecafbad
.com%2F&title=0xDECAFBAD
```

Notice that the URL to my home page has itself been URL-encoded via `encodeURIComponent`, thus explaining the `%3A`'s and the `%2F`'s. With respect to the query parameters used, this posting form URL is a bit of a mini-API all on its own. It's not quite documented, but as you'll see shortly, there are a few more parameters you can use with this URL.

Dissecting the del.icio.us Popup Window Bookmarklet

Deeper down the bookmarklet rabbit hole, you can find a popup-based bookmarklet available over at this page:

```
http://del.icio.us/help/morebuttons
```

Whereas the previous bookmarklet will cause you to leave the current page to arrive at a new posting form, this one simply produces a new little popup window with a minimal del.icio.us posting form presented (see Figure 2-2).

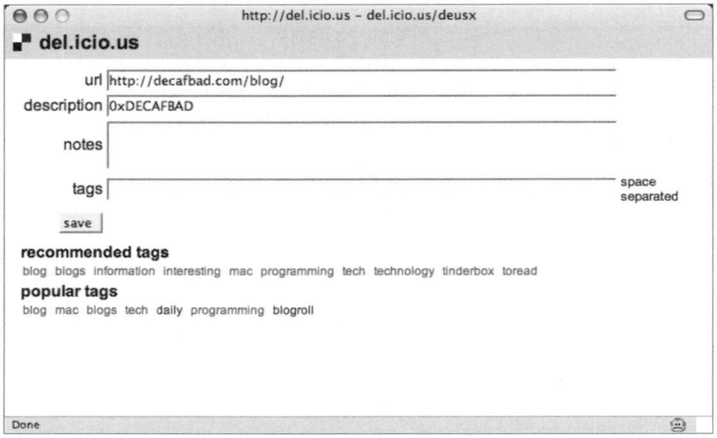

FIGURE 2-2: Posting a link using the popup window bookmarklet

It's a little more complex, but here's the source for the popup bookmarklet:

```
javascript:q=location.href;p=document.title;void(open('http://
del.icio.us/deusx?v=4&noui&jump=close&url='+encodeURIComponent(q)+
'&title='+encodeURIComponent(p),'delicious','toolbar=no,width=700,
height=400'))
```

Again, having a text editor on hand as a scratchpad can be very beneficial for developing and reverse engineering bookmarklets. If you enter the preceding URL into it, you can insert your own line breaks and formatting to make sense of it. With a little work, you can get it looking something like Listing 2-1.

Listing 2-1: Reformatted JavaScript source for the del.icio.us popup posting bookmarklet

```
q=location.href;
p=document.title;
void(open('http://del.icio.us/deusx?v=4&noui&jump=close'+
'&url='+encodeURIComponent(q)+
'&title='+encodeURIComponent(p),
'delicious','toolbar=no,width=700,height=400'))
```

So, most of the complexity in this new bookmarklet comes from the presentation of the popup window. Here's a breakdown, line by line:

- The page URL is captured in the variable q.

- The page title is capture in the variable p.

- The function call open() is short for window.open(), which is what will open a popup window. The void() function wrapper makes sure that the browser ignores the return value of window.open(), which would otherwise be displayed in the parent window in response to the bookmarklet click. The rest of this line is spent constructing the posting form URL prefix.

- The page URL in q is encoded for inclusion in the URL and appended as a query parameter url.

- The page title in p is encoded for inclusion in the URL and appended as a query parameter title.

- The call to window.open() is finished up with the name of the window, as well as a few options with which to build the window.

So now, that's two bookmarklets you've seen reverse engineered. That should give you a bit of a taste for it. One more thing to notice is that there's a new posting form URL used in the popup:

```
http://del.icio.us/deusx?v=4&noui&jump=close&url=
http%3A%2F%2Fdecafbad.com%2F&title=0xDECAFBAD
```

In the interest of tinkering, let's dissect this, too:

- http://del.icio.us/deusx: This is a URL to your page of links. I'll be using my user name (deusx) in examples, but you should remember to replace this with your own username that you used during the sign up process.

- v=4: This appears to be an indicator of the current user interface version.

- noui: This parameter indicates that a minimal user interface should be used, which is perfect for a popup window. If you compare the non-popup posting form with this one, you'll notice that a lot of the tag recommendation machinery is missing, as well as the general site navigation.

- jump=close: Once you've completed posting the link by submitting the form, the popup window will be closed.

- url=http%3A%2F%2Fdecafbad.com%2F: This is the URL-encoded link that you're about to post.

- title=0xDECAFBAD: This is the title of the page you were viewing when you clicked the bookmarklet button.

Improving the Bookmarklet to Include Selected Page Excerpts

What does all this dissection get you? It offers a peek into ways to customize the bookmarklet and the link posting form. Consider this, for a moment: There are URL and description fields in the posting form that are pre-populated with the `url` and `title` query parameters, respectively. I wonder if there might not be parameters to fill in the notes and tags fields, too?

Well, it turns out that there *are* additional query parameters you can use in pre-populating the bookmark posting form. For example, try typing in the following URL — remembering to replace *deusx* with your own del.icio.us user name:

```
http://del.icio.us/deusx?url=http%3A%2F%2Fdecafbad.com%2F
&title=0xDECAFBAD&notes=This+decafbad+guy+is+pretty+cool
```

You can also accomplish the same thing by using the basic non-popup bookmarklet to start posting a bookmark. You can then simply tack on a new notes parameter at the end of your location bar. Take a look at Figure 2-3 for an example of what you should see.

So, there's one new puzzle piece: Along with the URL and the title, you can also pre-populate the descriptive notes for a bookmark. And what can you do with this new discovery?

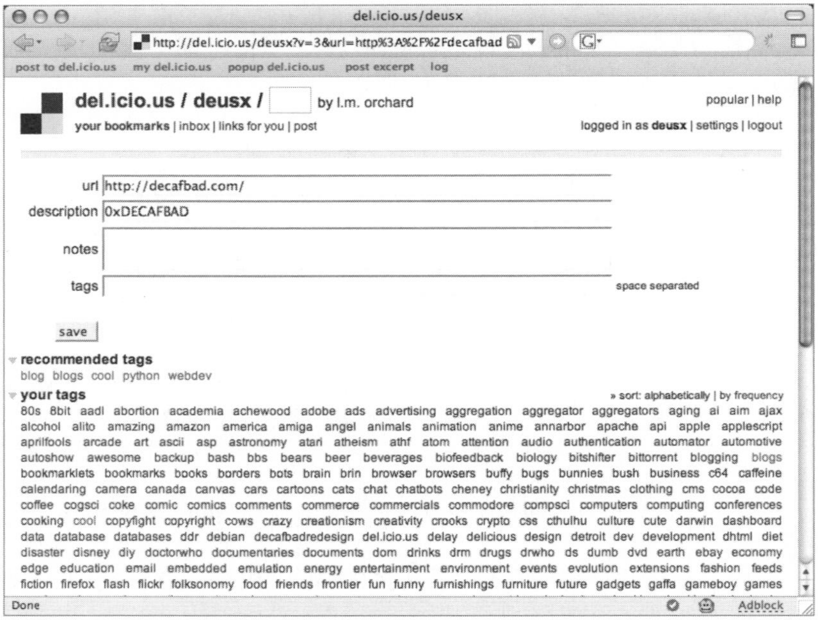

FIGURE 2-3: Posting a link with the notes field pre-populated

However, it turns out that JavaScript can access text you've highlighted on the page. With this piece of functionality, you can streamline the bookmarking process: Rather than copying and pasting by hand, you can simply highlight a bit of relevant text and then let an improved bookmarklet harvest the selection and pre-populate the posting form.

Excerpting Selected Text with JavaScript

Unfortunately, the code to grab the current selection from a browser window is not uniform between browsers. But despair not because Peter-Paul Koch of QuirksMode.org has pieced together a method that works in most browsers:

```
www.quirksmode.org/js/selected.html
```

At QuirksMode.org, you'll see a nicely formatted and cleanly formulated listing showing how to dig up the current text selection based on the existence of various browser environment features. Study this to see how it works and make sure you understand it — because in order to make it work for a cross-browser bookmarklet, you're going to have to mangle and compress it until it looks something like this:

```
''+(window.getSelection?window.getSelection():document.
getSelection?document.getSelection():document.selection.
createRange().text)
```

On the other hand, if you never plan to share this bookmarklet and you only ever spend your time in a single browser, check out the compatibility matrix at QuirksMode.org. You might need to use only one of the three techniques in your personal browser-specific bookmarklet:

- In Internet Explorer, try this: `document.selection.createRange().text`
- In Firefox and Safari, use this: `window.getSelection()`
- In Firefox (again) and a few other browsers, try this: `document.getSelection()`

Splicing Selected Text Excerpts into the Bookmarklet

Now, you're going to turn a single-line text field into a development environment, which can be trying on the patience. Be sure to mind your parentheses and other syntactic punctuation marks. Oh, and try to have some aspirin on hand because this will give you a headache to debug. But, it'll be worth it, and sometimes a little headache is the price of hacking.

One of the browsers I've found to be best at it is Firefox, with its helpful JavaScript Console that can feed you messages about syntax errors when you leave out a semicolon or parenthesis. You should also have a text editor scratchpad open as a "staging area," where you can piece together the code in a more readable form before removing all the formatting and line breaks. This is basically inverting the process you followed while reverse engineering a bookmarklet.

In that spirit, take a look at Listing 2-2 for a more readable presentation of JavaScript code intended for Firefox that will construct a posting form URL with the notes field harvested from the current highlighted text selection.

Listing 2-2: Prototype JavaScript code to pre-populate from text selections

```
username = 'deusx';
url      = location.href;
title    = document.title;
notes    = window.getSelection();

post  = 'http://del.icio.us/';
post += username;
post += '?v=3';
post += '&url='   + encodeURIComponent(url);
post += '&title=' + encodeURIComponent(title);
post += '&notes=' + encodeURIComponent(notes);

location.href = post;
```

While the code in Listing 2-2 can't be used in a bookmarklet directly, composing it this way at first can help you get your ideas in place. Then, you'll need to compress and mangle until the code looks like this:

```
javascript:un='deusx';u=location.href;t=document.title;n=window.
getSelection();p='http://del.icio.us/'+un+'?v=3&url=
'+encodeURIComponent(u)+'&title='+encodeURIComponent(t)+'&notes=
'+encodeURIComponent(n);location.href=p
```

Notice that I've gotten rid of all spaces and all line breaks, and that I've reduced all variable names to one- or two-character abbreviations. Also, I've turned the posting form URL construction into one long concatenation. I did all of this in my text editor right alongside a copy of the original code for comparison.

And, one last time: Be sure to replace *deusx* with your own del.icio.us user name. There's a reason I broke it out into its own variable — it ends up being a common pitfall for del.icio.us bookmarklet authors.

Trying Out the Improved Page Excerpt Bookmarklet

At this point, you're all ready to use this new bookmarklet. First, create a new bookmark in your toolbar using the Bookmark Manager (or your browser's equivalent), as shown in Figure 2-4. This time, you don't have a Web page from which to drag a link onto your toolbar, so you'll need to paste in the tweaked `javascript:` URL by hand from your scratchpad.

Next, find your way to an interesting Web page somewhere. In Figure 2-5, I've humbly chosen my own blog for this task (`http://decafbad.com`). Drag and highlight some text on the page that you'd like to appear in your bookmark. Then, click the toolbar bookmarklet — I've named mine "post excerpt."

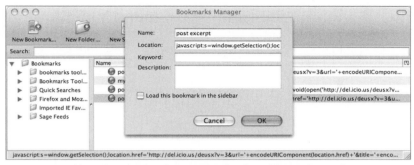

FIGURE 2-4: Adding the improved excerpting bookmarklet to the toolbar

FIGURE 2-5: Selecting some text on a Web page in preparation for using the bookmarklet

At last, Figure 2-6 shows you what the end result should be: a del.icio.us bookmark posting form with the URL and title filled in just like before. But this time, the notes field has also been pre-populated with the text you'd selected on the page before firing up the bookmarklet.

It's all about efficiency: With one small tweak to a bookmarklet you can now capture a link, a title, and an excerpt from the page you're viewing simply by highlighting and clicking a button. It took a little explaining to get here, but you should have a better feel for what a bookmarklet is and how one can interact with the del.icio.us bookmark posting form.

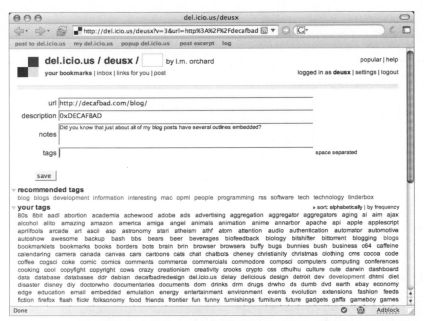

FIGURE 2-6: Posting a link with the notes field pre-populated with a page excerpt

Simplifying the Bookmark Posting Form

Pre-populating the notes field of the bookmark posting form added a bit of efficiency to the process. Is there more you can do?

Well, if you use del.icio.us for any length of time, you might start to have a pretty good idea of what tags you'd like to use whenever you post a link. So, the tag selection and recommendation interface that appears on the posting form (see Figure 2-6) may start to lose its usefulness. Many people love it, and it's a pretty slick addition — but it can slow things down and make your bookmark posting feel less efficient.

You've already seen the noui parameter used by the popup form to strip the site navigation (see Figure 2-2), but this still leaves some of the tag assistance machinery in place. Is there a way to get just a plain and simple posting form?

As it turns out, that undocumented UI version parameter found in the posting form URL comes in handy here. Try this URL to the posting form:

```
http://del.icio.us/deusx?v=3&noui&url=http%3A%2F%2Fdecafbad
.com%2F&title=0xDECAFBAD
```

Notice that this URL contains v=3, rather than v=4 as used so far in this chapter. Take a look at Figure 2-7 to see what effect this has on the posting form.

FIGURE 2-7: Posting a bookmark using version 3 of the form

As you can see in Figure 2-7, the link posting form has been stripped down to basics: just the URL, description, notes, and tags field along with the submit button. Because it's just a change to the posting URL, this is a quick tweak to make if you'd like to make your customized bookmarklet leaner. Simply swap v=3 for v=4, and you should see the simpler form in your popups and in-browser bookmarklets.

Note The effect generated by using v=3 appears to depend on pairing v=3 with the noui parameter. This is probably fine because if you're looking to have a simpler posting form, you won't miss all of the site navigation. But it's good to keep this in mind, just in case you were to try using the v=3 parameter without noui and got stumped as to why you weren't getting a simplified form.

Making Bookmark Posting Super-Fast

The main goals in the bookmarklet enhancements presented so far in this chapter are to streamline the process and make it faster and less obtrusive to post your bookmarks. The less these things get in your way, the more likely you'll use them and really see the benefits of social bookmarking at del.icio.us.

So, as I continue with that theme, are you finding that all this button clicking and form filling is trying your patience as you quickly try to fling bookmark after bookmark into your collection? Maybe not, but just in case: The Super-Fast Delicious Bookmarklet by John Resig could be just the thing for you.

The Super-Fast Delicious Bookmarklet is a Firefox-only bookmarklet that takes advantage of a feature called Smart Keywords to reduce your bookmarking process down to a couple of quick steps that never even touch the standard del.icio.us posting form.

You can find the original blog post about this bookmark variant here:

```
http://ejohn.org/blog/super-fast-delicious-bookmarklet/
```

Read this post to learn how to properly set up this bookmarklet.

Explaining Smart Keywords

With Smart Keywords, you have the ability to assign a short keyword to any bookmark. This, then, allows you to navigate to this bookmark simply by typing that keyword into the location bar and hitting Return. Where the "smart" part comes in, however, is that you're able to type other things after the keyword and have them inserted into the bookmark URL before making the request.

So, as shown in Figure 2-8, suppose you bookmarked the following URL with an assigned keyword of g:

```
http://google.com/search?q=%s
```

FIGURE 2-8: Creating a bookmark using the Smart Keywords feature in Firefox

Now, if you type g super fast bookmarklet into the location bar, you'll navigate immediately to a Google search results page for the phrase "super fast bookmarklet" (see Figure 2-9).

It's the %s in the bookmark URL that makes the magic happen. Anything after the bookmark keyword and a space is scooped up and inserted in place of the %s in your bookmark's URL. You can now load up your bookmarks folder with all sorts of interesting canned searches and fire them off without ever needing to submit a form. Just figure out where the desired parameter is in the search URL, and turn it into a Smart Keywords bookmark template with a %s.

On the Web   You can read more about Firefox Smart Keywords here:

```
http://kb.mozillazine.org/Using_keyword_searches
```

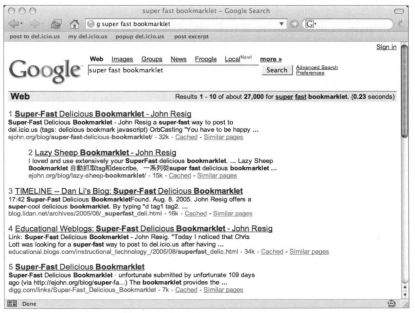

FIGURE 2-9: Smart Keywords used to facilitate a Google search

Using Smart Keywords to Make a Super-Fast Bookmarklet

Here's the payoff: Combining this feature with a bookmarklet's `javascript:` URL offers a powerful way to get user input into the JavaScript code. You can stick a `%s` anywhere in the `javascript:` URL and it will be replaced by the post-keyword text supplied when you trigger the Smart Keyword, thus allowing you to parameterize the bookmarklet in a pretty flexible way.

John Resig's bookmarklet takes advantage of this to allow you to specify tags you'd like attached to your bookmark posting. This is combined with using the current highlighted text in the notes field, a hack you saw explained just a few pages ago.

Taken all together, your bookmark posting process is reduced to just two steps with this bookmarklet:

1. Highlight some text on the page that you'd like used for the bookmark notes.

2. Type **d** in your location bar, along whatever tags you'd like used for the bookmark, and hit Return.

You can see this in action in Figure 2-10. After you highlight the text and then enter the keyword and tags into the location bar, the bookmark is posted to del.icio.us and the window closes — all without your ever seeing the posting form or needing to click "submit."

The idea is that, after you've had time to read through the page and you're ready to bookmark it, you're probably ready to close the window or tab anyway. So, if you use this bookmarklet, you can excerpt, tag, bookmark, and dispose of the page all in one quick shot.

FIGURE 2-10: Using the Super-Fast Delicious Bookmarklet

Slowing Down the Super-Fast Bookmarklet

For some people, this super-fast bookmarklet is *too* super-fast. That is, the tagging and excerpting features of the bookmarklet are great — but it'd be nice to have a chance to edit the bookmark, rather than just have it automatically post and close the browser window or tab.

At this point, it's useful to note that this bookmark takes advantage of a subtle feature of the del.icio.us posting form machinery: If all of the fields are populated and a `jump=doclose` parameter is included in the posting URL, the posting form never makes an appearance. That is, all of the supplied information is used to automatically submit the bookmark, and the window is closed without ever displaying the form.

Well, after some experimentation with this feature, it appears that auto-posting requires this exact set of parameters: `tags`, `url`, `description`, `extended`. However, some of the parameters in the posting form URL can be supplied using two different names. For example, `description` and `title` both work to supply a title for a bookmark. Similarly, `extended` and `notes` both work to fill in the fuller notes or excerpt field.

So, if you substitute a synonym for one of the parameters, it turns out that the auto-posting feature no longer works. Thus, you are presented with the form and given an opportunity to edit the bookmark before it's submitted.

To implement this tweak, take a look at the Super-Fast Bookmarklet's source code:

```
javascript:u="deusx";q=location.href;e = "" + (window.getSelection
? window.getSelection() : document.getSelection ?
document.getSelection()   :
document.selection.createRange().text);p=document.title;window.
location.href="http://del.icio.us/"+u+"?jump=doclose&tags=
"+escape("%s")+"&url="+escape(q)+"&description="+escape(p)+
"&extended=" + escape(e).replace(/ /g, "+");
```

This bookmarklet, in particular, is fairly complex because it's rolling the cross-browser code for capturing the current text highlight in the browser. Here's a modified version of the bookmarklet that's not so super-fast:

```
javascript:u="deusx";q=location.href;e = "" +
(window.getSelection ? window.getSelection() :
document.getSelection ? document.getSelection()   :
document.selection.createRange().text);p=document.title;window.
location.href="http://del.icio.us/"+u+"?v=3&noui=1&tags="+escape
("%s")+"&url="+escape(q)+"&title="+escape(p)+   "&extended=" +
escape(e).replace(/ /g, "+");
```

The following two changes were made:

- The `jump=doclose` parameter is replaced by `v=3` and `noui=1`, which will give you a simple posting form and return you to the original page after posting the bookmark. If you'd like the page to still close after submitting the bookmark, just leave the `jump=doclose` intact.

- The `description` parameter has been replaced with the `title` synonym, which seems to be enough to short circuit the auto-posting feature yet still pre-populate the form with the page title.

You may want to have both the original bookmarklet around, along with this tweaked version, so you can have a choice of what happens when you're done with a page.

Finally, this particular method of short-circuiting the auto-posting feature — as well as the feature itself — is left undocumented, in order to steer people wishing to automate things toward the documented and scriptable API. This means that, someday, this whole thing might start behaving differently after an update or two to the del.icio.us service. But, until then, enjoy!

Posting Bookmarks without Ever Leaving the Page

The final bookmarklet I'll introduce is from Andrew Sutherland. You can find the original page explaining it here:

```
http://code.jalenack.com/archives/new-delicious-bookmarklet/
```

You'll see that this bookmarklet is delivered to you via a quick "wizard" that customizes it to your del.icio.us user name, which saves you from needing to edit it after you've dragged it to your toolbar. But what really makes this bookmarklet special is that it employs a few tricks to present you with a fully styled custom posting form overlaid atop the page you're currently viewing. Check out Figure 2-11 to see it in action.

FIGURE 2-11: Using the in-page posting form bookmarklet

This functionality is a bit beyond the scope of your typical bookmarklet, however. Take a look at the source code:

```
javascript: z = document.createElement('script'); z.src =
'http://code.jalenack.com/delicious/delicious.php?username=deusx';
z.type = 'text/javascript'; void(document.body.appendChild(z));
```

As you can see, the bookmarklet itself is pretty simple. It's a bootstrap that uses the browser DOM to create a new <script> tag in order to inject some additional JavaScript into the page. This allows the actual implementation of the bookmarklet to live at the author's site — where it can be maintained in a form that's much friendlier to develop.

Fully explaining how this bookmarklet works is beyond the scope of this chapter. But, it's a useful bookmarklet to know about, and I thought the script injection trick might be an interesting addition to your own bag of tricks.

Extending Firefox

Now that you've had a chance to really get up to your elbows hacking bookmarklets and JavaScript, I'm going to change gears a bit so you can check out what options are available for extending your browser via more direct channels such as extensions and plug-ins. However, because these options tend to be a bit more complex to develop, this will be less of a hands-on section and you won't spend as much time digging under the hood.

So, first on display is Firefox, possibly the world's most expandable and extensible browser ever made. Based on Mozilla platform technology, Firefox offers a great deal of flexibility thanks to its use of XUL, CSS, and JavaScript. The browser itself is constructed using these technologies, and modular extensions can be installed that can alter practically any aspect of the browser.

 Want to learn more about XUL and the technologies used in Firefox and its extensions? Pay a visit to this URL to start your reading:

```
http://kb.mozillazine.org/Dev_:_Extensions
```

Installing the Official del.icio.us Firefox Extension

The crew at del.icio.us has released an official Firefox extension that provides extensive additions throughout the Firefox user interface. You can install a copy for yourself from this URL:

```
http://del.icio.us/help/firefox/extension
```

Upon installation, one of the first things to notice is that the extension has added a couple of new buttons to your toolbar. You can see these toward the top of Figure 2-12. The first button, an icon of the del.icio.us logo, will take you straight to your collection of bookmarks. The second toolbar addition is a stylized tag that will give you a popup form to bookmark and tag the current page — not unlike an enhanced version of the popup bookmarklet introduced earlier.

You can also right-click or control-click any link on a page to get a context menu, where you'll find that the extension has added a new Tag This Link item. This will allow you to instantly bookmark links you see on a page, without first needing to navigate to them. This can come in handy in many cases, such as when you'd like to bookmark downloadable files or media files such as videos or MP3 audio. This feature is also shown in Figure 2-12.

You should also notice a new application menu added to Firefox, as shown in Figure 2-13. This menu gives you quick access to a few different facets of del.icio.us: You can bookmark and tag the page you're currently viewing, or jump directly to view the descriptions and tags used by others in capturing the current page.

In addition, there are menu items offering shortcuts to your collection, links from people in whose collections you've registered interest, links intended for your attention, and your account settings. And finally, there are a few items leading to overall popular links and informational pages.

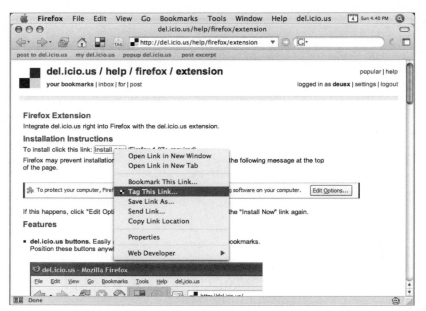

FIGURE 2-12: A demonstration of the del.icio.us extension's new link context menu item

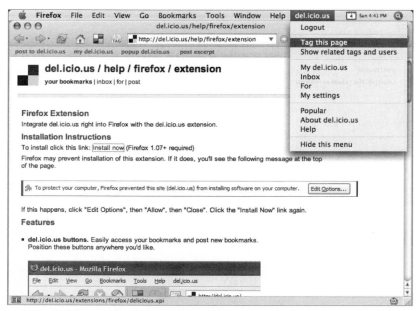

FIGURE 2-13: The del.icio.us extension adds a new application menu in Firefox.

Bookmarklets can offer you a lot of unexpected functionality, but there's nothing like a real extension to the browser to really integrate a service like del.icio.us into your browsing habits.

Using Live Bookmarks with del.icio.us Feeds

As part of the quick tour in the previous chapter, you were introduced to the RSS feeds del.icio.us has to offer. In particular, if you've been using Firefox as you explore the site, you have seen the orange "transmission waves" icon appear from time to time in the location bar. This icon is an indication that the page you're viewing is associated with an RSS feed — clicking it allows you to create a Live Bookmark, as shown in Figure 2-14.

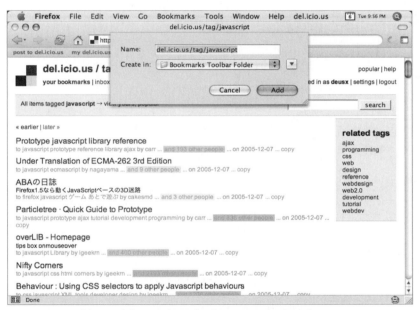

FIGURE 2-14: Adding a del.icio.us RSS feed in a Live Bookmark

You can read more about the Live Bookmarks feature in Firefox here:

```
www.mozilla.com/firefox/livebookmarks.html
```

In a nutshell, Live Bookmarks are a cool way to integrate updates from RSS feeds into your browser bookmarks. You can add a Live Bookmark by clicking the orange icon in the location bar. Live Bookmarks act a bit like bookmark folders, except that Firefox itself maintains them automatically. Periodically, the browser will check for updates in the feed: Whenever updates are found, the new links are added to the top of the folder. Figure 2-15 shows links contained in a Live Bookmark based on a del.icio.us RSS feed for the tag javascript.

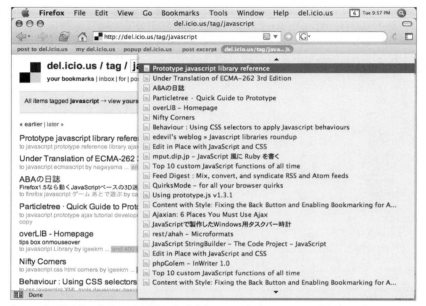

FIGURE 2-15: Viewing an RSS feed of del.icio.us links as a Live Bookmark

This feature gives you a direct way to integrate bookmarks from del.icio.us into your browser. You can put them into the bookmark toolbar, or just in the general collection in your bookmark menu. They'll always be up-to-date, loaded up with fresh links from your favorite users and tags. In addition to individual users and tags, you can subscribe to your del.icio.us inbox as a feed or the `for:` tag prefix associated with your user name.

Although you should find lots of pages on del.icio.us for which RSS feeds are available and the orange icon appears, you can also read more about specific feeds available here:

```
http://del.icio.us/help/rss
```

Synchronizing Your Bookmarks with Foxylicious

Although del.icio.us allows you to all but leave your bookmarks menu behind, some would prefer to have a little synchronization. While it's nice to have the remote and shared link collection that del.icio.us offers, it's still nice to have a local copy to manage and keep. If this is something you're interested in, then Dietrich Ayala's extension named Foxylicious is just the thing for you. Take a look at it over at this URL:

```
http://dietrich.ganx4.com/foxylicious/
```

After you've had a chance to install it, you can configure the extension (see Figure 2-16). Supply it with your account user name and password, as well as with a chosen bookmarks folder to be managed by Foxylicious. Along with these options, you can also opt for daily scheduled updates. Once configured, you can now go on using either your del.icio.us or local Firefox bookmarks, and the two will remain in synch.

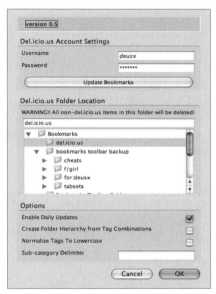

FIGURE 2-16: Configuring Foxylicious to synchronize bookmarks with del.icio.us

Exploring Greasemonkey and User Scripts

If you thought bookmarklets were powerful, just wait until you've had a chance to check out the Greasemonkey extension for Firefox.

Greasemonkey allows the execution of "user scripts" written in JavaScript that can do all the things bookmarklets can, and more. This extension makes functionality available to user scripts not ordinarily available to bookmarklets — such as cross-domain HTTP requests and local data storage. Also, user scripts execute automatically when pre-determined URL patterns are matched, rather than requiring you to click a button to run the code. This allows you to build up a set of regular customizations to sites you visit, without needing to remember to activate them.

You can install Greasemonkey from its home page here:

```
http://greasemonkey.mozdev.org/
```

And, once you've got the extension installed, you can start exploring available user scripts here:

```
http://userscripts.org/
```

This is a relatively new extension for Firefox, but tinkerers are already coming up with lots of user scripts to remix del.icio.us itself and together with other sites. In fact, you can check out the growing collection of scripts at userscripts.org here:

```
http://userscripts.org/tag/delicious
```

I'll highlight a few of these scripts here, just to give you a taste.

Newsmashing with the Monkey

One of the features introduced in Chapter 1 was depicted in Figure 1-7: Bookmarks posted to del.icio.us can be viewed by URL, showing you the collected notes and tags accumulated over time by the people who've posted the link. You can have these details just one click away on every page, using the Newsmashing user script demonstrated and available here:

```
http://blog.yanime.org/GreaseMonkey.htm
```

Once you've installed this user script, every page gains a link in the upper-left corner that you can use to summon up an overlay containing details of everyone's bookmarks related to the current page. In effect, this allows you to view many others' commentary on what you're reading. You can see a demo of this user script in Figure 2-17.

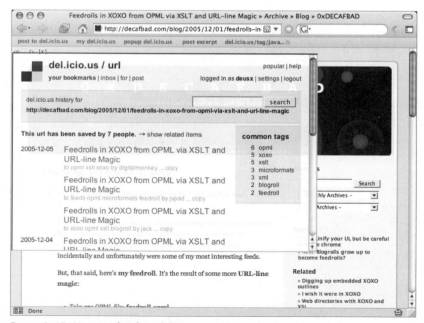

FIGURE 2-17: Viewing bookmark history on the current page

Experiencing Déjà Vu in Your Bookmarks?

Ever feel like you've bookmarked something before? If you try to post a link to del.icio.us that you've already posted before, you'll get a message telling you as much. You can edit the tags and notes if you like, but sometimes it's just the case that you forgot about your previous posting and didn't really intend to post it again.

So, for those cases, there's Familiar Taste. Check out the following user script:

```
www.blackperl.com/javascript/greasemonkey/ft/
```

Once Familiar Taste is installed, you should see something like Figure 2-18 whenever you visit a page for which you've already posted a bookmark in the past. This should help keep you from making duplicate bookmarks and remind you of what tags you used for the page.

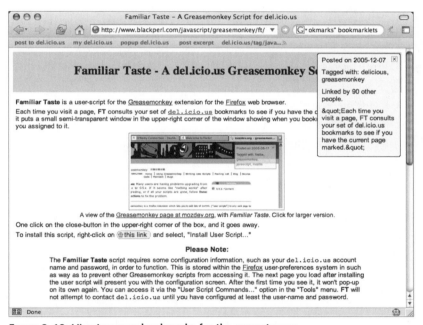

FIGURE 2-18: Viewing your bookmarks for the current page

Completely Revamping the UI with del.icio.us direc.tor

The previous two user scripts were pretty minor tweaks to pages you visit outside of del.icio.us, but this last user script implements a radical transformation on the del.icio.us user interface itself. Check out the del.icio.us direc.tor user script here:

```
www.joegrossberg.com/archives/002307.html
```

This script is based on code previously used as a bookmarklet, but combined with Greasemonkey, this version can "permanently" alter your view of del.icio.us — at least until you disable the user script. Check out Figure 2-19 to see what this user script does for you.

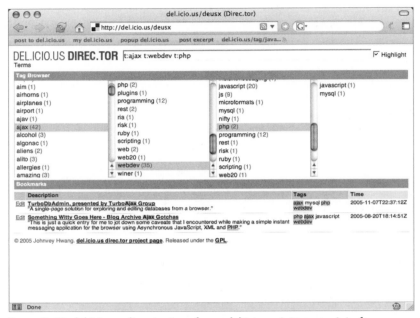

FIGURE 2-19: del.icio.us direc.tor transforms del.icio.us into a new interface

Tricking Out Safari

Safari is Apple's official Web browser for OS X. And while it isn't based in XUL and JavaScript technologies like Firefox, it does offer some opportunities for hacking thanks to the bundle and plug-in aspects of Cocoa applications in general.

Using Sogudi to Build a Faster Bookmarklet

Using Smart Keywords in Firefox to speed up bookmarking and tagging is a neat trick. If you're a regular Safari user, you might wish that your browser came with this feature. Well, actually, a Safari user first introduced that Smart Keywords bookmarklet trick. What you may be missing, however, is a freeware enhancement named Sogudi. You can find out more about it here:

```
www.kitzkikz.com/Sogudi
```

Sogudi is an InputManager bundle that imbues Safari with the same sorts of templated bookmark URLs as Firefox has with Smart Keywords. The only real difference is that instead of %s, Sogudi uses @@@ as the placeholder in the URL. That, and Sogudi's shortcuts are managed separately from Safari's normal bookmarks (see Figure 2-20).

You can read about the original Sogudi bookmarklet as well as improvements incorporated from the Firefox Smart Keywords version at this URL:

    www.zzamboni.org/brt/2005/08/07/52/

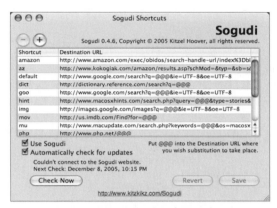

FIGURE 2-20: Managing templated URL shortcuts in Safari Sogudi

Uploading Your Bookmark Collection with Safarilicious

Have you already built up a large collection of bookmarks with Safari? Looking for a way to migrate them out to del.icio.us? You may want to check out Safarilicious, available here:

    www.stylemac.com/safarilicious

Safarilicious is a standalone application that can read from Safari's bookmarks and post them to your del.icio.us account. When you first launch the program (see Figure 2-21), you'll need to supply it with your user account details.

You can also supply a list of bookmark folders that should be ignored, in case you want to hide or hold back some bookmarks — such as your del.icio.us bookmarklets or other things not appropriate for del.icio.us. And there's one last option available on this first screen: You can compose a default set of tags to be assigned to each of these bookmarks as they're posted to your account.

Once you're ready, you can switch over to the Preview tab (see Figure 2-22). When you first click the tab, or when you hit the Refresh button, you'll get a list of what bookmark data will be posted to del.icio.us once you hit the Export! button. Use this to make sure everything's in order before you fire up the process.

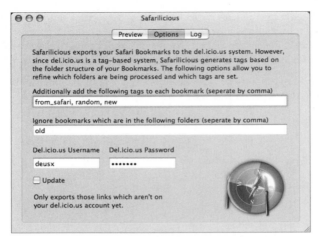

FIGURE 2-21: Configuring Safarilicious with account and tagging
details for export

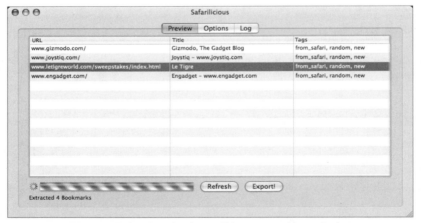

FIGURE 2-22: Previewing bookmarks that will be exported by Safarilicious

Using delicious2safari to Download Your Bookmarks

On the flipside, have you amassed a bit of a collection at del.icio.us that you'd like to pull back
into your Safari browser locally? You'll want to check out this open source application called
delicious2safari, found at the following address:

```
http://tuxtina.de/software/
```

This program has a very simple interface (see Figure 2-23): You enter your del.icio.us user name and password, select a destination for your bookmarks from one of three places, and then decide if you'd like the bookmarks placed into folders based on tags. Then, click the Get my bookmarks! button, and off you go. The application window will update a few times with messages telling you what's going on with the import process.

FIGURE 2-23: Getting ready to download bookmarks from del.icio.us with delicious2safari

When the import has wrapped up, you should then be able to see a new folder named "del.icio.us" in your chosen destination. Figure 2-24 shows you how the downloaded bookmarks are arranged, with subfolders named by tag.

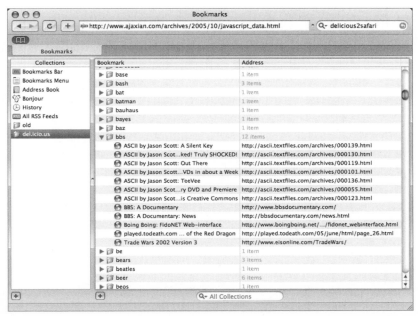

FIGURE 2-24: Viewing the end result of downloading del.icio.us bookmarks into Safari

Tweaking Internet Explorer

While not as open and flexible to hacking as Firefox, Microsoft's Internet Explorer still has a number of tricks up its software sleeves.

Posting Bookmarks from the Context Menu

One of the features that the official del.icio.us extension for Firefox adds is a context menu item on links that allows you to post directly from a right-click menu. Well, if you're a die-hard Internet Explorer fan, you, too, can have this feature. In fact, for what it's worth, this hack predates the official del.icio.us extension by a few years.

Steve Hatch put together a hack using JavaScript and the Windows Registry to create a pair of new right-click menu items in Internet Explorer for links. At first, this was a bit of a manual process to get working, but Dan Grigsby built a quick installer package that can give you this functionality with double-click ease. You can find details about this installer here:

```
www.unpossible.com/blog/archives/000086.html
```

Basically, once installed, you can right-click any link within a page and select "del.icio.us: post" to arrive at a pre-populated del.icio.us bookmark form with the URL and link title waiting for you. In addition, if you happened to have selected some text before triggering this menu item, it will be pulled into the notes field on the form as well. Check out Figure 2-25 to see this hack in action.

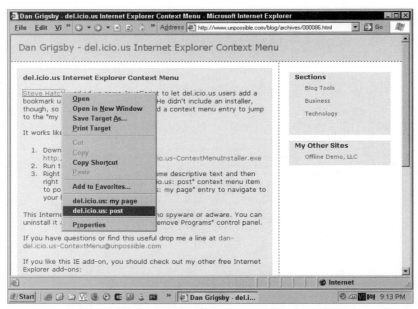

FIGURE 2-25: Posting a bookmark for the current page from the context menu in Internet Explorer

Downloading Your Bookmarks into Internet Explorer

Now that you're an avid del.icio.us fan, you should be celebrating your newfound freedom from your Favorites menu. But it's understandable that you may still have some attachment to it, and maybe you've got a smidgen of apprehension about your bookmarks living off in some stranger's hard drive. But fret no longer because there's the Bunnyhug Updater for del.icio.us, available here:

```
www.bunnyhug.net/blog/projects/deliciousupdater/
```

This small .NET application accepts your user name and password, and then runs off to download all of your del.icio.us bookmarks (see Figure 2-26). You can also specify a Favorites subfolder into which your bookmarks should be saved. When the process is complete, you'll have a newly updated local backup of your removed bookmarks under your Internet Explorer Favorites menu (see Figure 2-27).

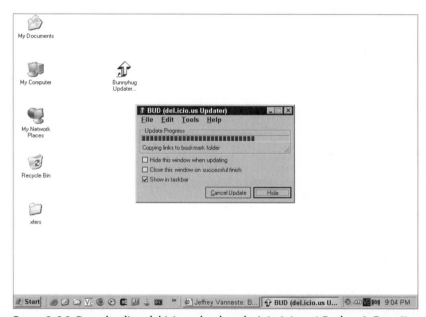

FIGURE 2-26: Downloading del.icio.us bookmarks into Internet Explorer's Favorites menu

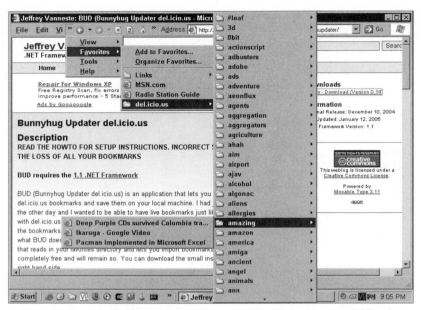

FIGURE 2-27: Bookmarks from del.icio.us are organized into Favorites folders by tag

Summary

The first part of this chapter was devoted to the del.icio.us bookmarklets and hacking some more enhanced functionality into them. Lots of hands-on attention was given here because bookmarklets are one of the easiest ways to get some new functionality out of a wide range of browsers.

The second part of this chapter briefly showcased a number of browser-specific extensions and add-on applications. The development of these tools can get quite a bit more involved, but you should have some pointers to chase now, if you'd like to learn more.

Next up in Chapter 3, we step out of the browser and onto your desktop. Here, you'll see what sorts of rich applications are available using the del.icio.us API, as well as a few other interesting integrations with other tools on your machine.

Seasoning Your Desktop

Because del.icio.us is all about bookmarks and links, it follows that most of the tools and interesting hacks you'll find tend to live on the Web or in your browser. In the previous chapter, you got a peek at what bookmarklets and browser-based tools have popped up to use and abuse what del.icio.us has to offer. In upcoming chapters, you'll see hacks and tweaks to take advantage of del.icio.us on the server side for your blog and Web site.

But in the middle, your desktop is probably feeling somewhat neglected in this brave new Web where you barely need to launch anything other than your favorite browser. There are advantages to leaving the browser and taking advantage of local resources, however.

The Web-based user interface at del.icio.us is a great study in minimal design and gets straight to the point, allowing you to manage your bookmark collection with ease. But for all the convenience of a Web site accessible from any browser in the world, it's nice to have a local desktop power tool to use in sorting through your links. Desktop applications can use the del.icio.us API to make local backups of your bookmarks, perform instant searches on your collection, and better integrate links into your desktop environment.

So, while the desktop itself is somewhat under-utilized with respect to del.icio.us, this chapter attempts to showcase a few of the tools that are available to help you squeeze a little more power out of your links.

Mac OS X

It seems like Mac OS X users and developers have really embraced del.icio.us and its API. You can find applications and enhancements that integrate your bookmarks into just about every major aspect of OS X — including the major new features introduced by OS X Tiger, such as the Dashboard and Spotlight searches.

Cocoalicious

First up is Cocoalicious, an open source del.icio.us desktop client for Mac OS X, written by Buzz Andersen and made available here:

```
www.scifihifi.com/cocoalicious/
```

The main window in Figure 3-1 shows off many of the key features of this application: There's a side pane listing all tags used in your collection, another pane listing bookmarks available in the collection or in any combination of tags selected, and a pane with an embedded Web browser in which any of the bookmarks can be viewed.

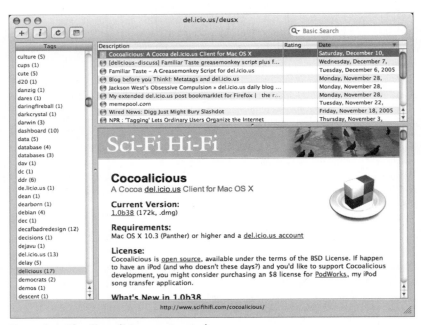

FIGURE 3-1: The Cocoalicious main window

You can also post and edit bookmarks using the dialog sheet shown in Figure 3-2. Here, you can fill out all of the standard bookmark fields. One neat feature in this dialog box, however, is that the tags field offers tag-completion when you hit F5, drawing from possible matches used in your collection.

There are also a few other nice features offered by this desktop client: Cocoalicious creates a local full-text index of all of your links, which gives you the ability to search your collection very quickly without needing to hit the del.icio.us servers. Also, you can drag and drop links from the list pane into other tags, thus attaching additional tags onto that bookmark.

FIGURE 3-2: Editing/posting a link in Cocoalicious

Delibar

If a full-blown desktop application is a bit too obtrusive for you, Delibar might be a little more your speed. Delibar is a small application that runs in the background as a menu bar icon, offering a hierarchical menu structure of your bookmarks and tags. You can download a copy of this desktop del.icio.us client here:

```
www.rknet.it/program/delibar/
```

Figure 3-3 offers a look at the features of Delibar: After starting it up and allowing it to grab a copy of your bookmarks, you can click the menu bar icon and start browsing. In addition to this new system-wide bookmarks menu, you can also call up a quick form to post a new bookmark to your collection. This form is available via an item under the Actions menu, as well as by hitting Control-⌘-D as a hotkey shortcut. This is a pretty nice feature because the hotkey works pretty much everywhere.

FIGURE 3-3: Browsing and posting bookmarks from the Delibar menu item

dashLicious

One of the most highly anticipated features of Mac OS X Tiger was the Dashboard. This is an overlay screen of widgets that remains hidden until the touch of a hot key or mouse gesture. These widgets are implemented using HTML and JavaScript and include things such as calculators, calendars, weather reports, and an array of toys and fortune cookies.

Now, alongside all these other marvels comes dashLicious, a Dashboard widget for Mac OS X Tiger that allows you to quickly post bookmarks to your collection. You can download it here:

```
http://protagonist.co.uk/dashLicious/
```

Once dashLicious is installed and you supply your user details via the form on the back of the widget (see Figure 3-4), this Dashboard widget will give you fast access to a link posting form (see Figure 3-5). This alone would be enough to recommend installing dashLicious, but there's more: If you use Safari as your regular browser, or the built-in browser in NetNewsWire, the widget will attempt to grab the URL and title of your currently viewed page when you activate the Dashboard.

Depending on your personal preferences, dashLicious can be a nice change from standard browser bookmarklets.

FIGURE 3-4: Setting up user account details in dashLicious

FIGURE 3-5: Using dashLicious to post a link

Spotlight and delimport

Another heavily hyped feature introduced by Mac OS X Tiger is Spotlight, the new system-wide search tool. Spotlight offers the ability to index files and documents found on your computer, using plug-ins developed by Apple and third-party developers. These plug-ins harvest descriptive metadata from the custom document types produced by the software you use, putting it all into a common format understood by Spotlight for indexing and search.

Written by Ian Henderson, delimport is a software package that does two things: First, it makes a regularly maintained local backup of all of your del.icio.us bookmarks as individual files in a folder located in your home directory. Second, it provides Spotlight with a plug-in that understands these bookmark files, thus allowing you to perform Spotlight searches on your bookmark collection from your personal machine.

You can download delimport from this URL:

```
http://ianhenderson.org/delimport.html
```

This package comes as an installer that will drop both the bookmark download tool and the Spotlight importer plug-in into their respective appropriate locations. You'll be asked initially for your username and password, and whether you want the bookmark downloader to start up every time you log in.

An initial flurry of bookmark importing and indexing activity will start, followed by updates every 30 minutes to grab new links from your collection. After the first download, however, you'll be able to fire up a Spotlight search and start seeing your bookmarks appear in the results. See Figure 3-6 for an example of what this will look like. After this first indexing run, the importer will start up every 30 minutes to grab updates from your bookmark collection.

FIGURE 3-6: Bookmarks downloaded by delimport appear in Spotlight searches

As you can see, these search results offer notes and tags in the expanded detail view of any particular item. If you double-click on any of the results in the Spotlight search, the link will be launched in your browser of choice.

Quicksilver

While Spotlight offers system-wide searches at the touch of a hotkey, Quicksilver offers searches and practically everything else within a few keystrokes. It's a very rich, modular desktop enhancement that gives quick keyboard access to open files and documents, fires off scripts, controls applications, and performs many other actions. And as it turns out, with a little help from a plug-in, Quicksilver can perform local searches of your del.icio.us bookmarks.

If you haven't ever run into Quicksilver before, why not grab a copy? It's easier to experience this tool than to explain it, so check it out here:

```
http://quicksilver.blacktree.com/
```

Download Quicksilver, install it, and spend some time playing around. It doesn't take long to get the hang of launching apps and opening documents with next to no effort. If you really start to explore this tool, you might find further useful capabilities — such as appending short notes to text files and moving files around with just a few keystrokes.

Eventually, you'll want to check out the plug-ins available in the Quicksilver preferences (see Figure 3-7). There's a ton of additional modules to add new abilities and search catalogs. And among these, you'll find the "del.icio.us Bookmarks" plug-in. When you click the checkbox, Quicksilver automatically downloads and installs it. After installation, check out the Catalog tab under preferences.

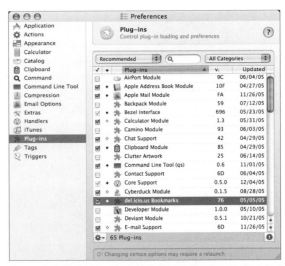

FIGURE 3-7: Selecting and installing plug-ins in QuickSilver

You can now add a "Del.icio.us bookmarks" catalog item (see Figure 3-8). After it's had a chance to run, all of your bookmarks will become available to Quicksilver searches. Just fire up Quicksilver via hotkey and start typing part of a tag or part of the title of one of your bookmarks. You should see results like Figure 3-9, with bookmarks mixed in with other files and documents.

FIGURE 3-8: Adding the del.icio.us bookmarks catalog item in QuickSilver

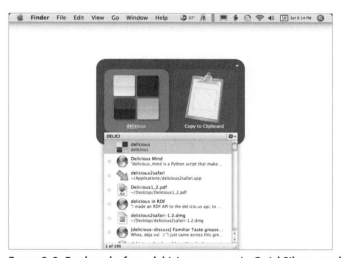

FIGURE 3-9: Bookmarks from del.icio.us appear in QuickSilver searches

Windows

In the Windows desktop world, it seems that there are far fewer del.icio.us desktop applications — at least in contrast to what's available on Mac OS X. Access to del.icio.us via bookmarklets in a browser is very powerful, so it may just be that tinkerers have yet to exhaust the possibilities enough to venture out onto the Windows desktop. That said, however, there are a few worthy applications to check out.

TagSense

If you're looking for a desktop client on Windows, tagSense.net seems like a good start (see Figure 3-10). Take a look at the application's home page, where you can grab the installer and get started:

```
http://tagsense.net/
```

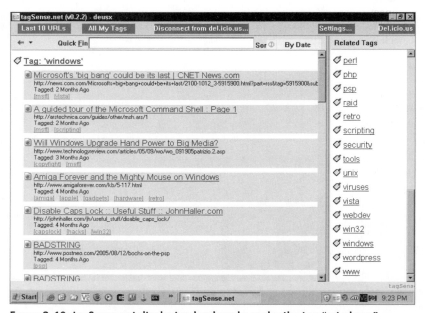

FIGURE 3-10: tagSense.net displaying bookmarks under the tag "windows"

You can use this application to download a local copy of your bookmark collection and perform lightning fast searches as you type. Also, this tool will allow you to explore your tags and navigate between related tags. Finally, when you've spent enough time with your bookmarks, you can minimize tagSense.net to your Windows notification center (or system tray), ready to be summoned up again at the touch of a hotkey.

At the time of this writing, this application doesn't yet offer the ability to post new bookmarks to del.icio.us — but it's possible this feature may be available by the time you read this.

Google Desktop

Google Desktop is another useful and free tool from the labs at Google — although unlike most of the Web-based services available via browser, Google Desktop is, oddly enough, a desktop enhancement application you can install under Windows.

The main idea behind Google Desktop is that it's an always-on, yet mostly unobtrusive information display. It can be used in a minimal configuration as a simple taskbar search form, or as a modular sidebar on your desktop. In the sidebar configuration, Google Desktop provides views on your email inbox, news and local weather, as well as a handful of tools such as a notepad and a to-do list.

You can grab a copy of Google Desktop for yourself at this URL:

```
http://desktop.google.com/
```

One of the more interesting features of Google Desktop is that it offers an SDK for developers to use in creating new plug-ins for search and modules in the sidebar. So, this is where Google Desktop connects to your bookmarks on del.icio.us: With the Google Desktop del.icio.us plug-in, you can add a sidebar module that will pull your top bookmarks into the Google Desktop sidebar. Check it out here:

```
www.manastungare.com/projects/google-desktop-delicious/
```

Figure 3-11 offers a peek at this plug-in's features. After installation, you can set your user name in the sidebar module's options, which will load it up with your top bookmarks. This module is adaptive: As you click these bookmarks, your most frequently used links will float to the top. Another feature showcased is the expanded view of bookmarks you can get by clicking the sidebar module's title bar.

And finally, although this plug-in provides convenient access to your bookmarks collection, it unfortunately doesn't offer the ability to add bookmarks to your collection.

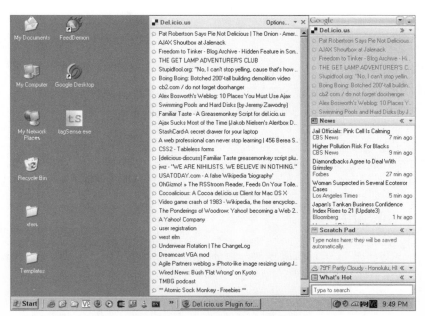

FIGURE 3-11: Bookmarks from del.icio.us in Google Desktop

Linux

Using del.icio.us under Linux also appears to be a mostly browser-driven affair. Because Firefox is available for Linux users, all of the hacks from the previous chapter will work under Linux. However, if you're a Gnome or KDE user, there are still a couple of applications for you to check out.

Gnomolicious

If you're a Gnome user, check out Gnomolicious. This is a panel applet that gives you fast access to posting links to del.icio.us, complete with tab completion drawn from regular updates it downloads from your collection. Check out Figure 3-12 to see this applet in action. You can download a copy from here:

    www.nongnu.org/gnomolicious/

FIGURE 3-12: Using the Gnomolicious panel applet

Konqueror Sidebar

For users of KDE 3.5 and Konqueror, there's to be a relatively new del.icio.us sidebar plug-in available (see Figure 3-13). I wasn't personally able to get this up and running on my own machine, but you might have better luck. So, I'll pass on the link here:

    www.kde-apps.org/content/show.php?content=26325

FIGURE 3-13: The Konqueror
del.icio.us sidebar

Cross-Platform

For the most part, del.icio.us itself is about as cross-platform as you can get. But, I've got one last trick left to show you using a powerful idea-organizing tool written in Java.

DeliciousMind

Mind maps are graphical representations of concepts and connections between ideas, often used as a tool during brainstorming and in organizing thoughts. For some people, mind maps are the best things since sliced bread. So, reflecting this, there are quite a number of books and tools available to help manage ideas in this form.

If mind maps are your cup of tea, then you may be interested in FreeMind. This is an open source application written in Java for composing and sharing mind maps. Pay a visit to the FreeMind project page on SourceForge, where you can read up on all the details and download a copy for free:

```
http://freemind.sourceforge.net/
```

Take FreeMind for a spin — you can very quickly build detailed maps of thoughts. Now, imagine mapping out your bookmarks in this way. You can accomplish this using DeliciousMind, a Java-based command line tool for converting del.icio.us bookmark exports in XML into FreeMind documents. This tool is available at the following address.

```
www.blainekendall.com/deliciousmind/
```

Just follow the directions at this page after downloading `deliciousmind.zip`, and you should end up with a fresh new FreeMind document of your most recent bookmarks. Check out Figure 3-14 for a peek at how this looks.

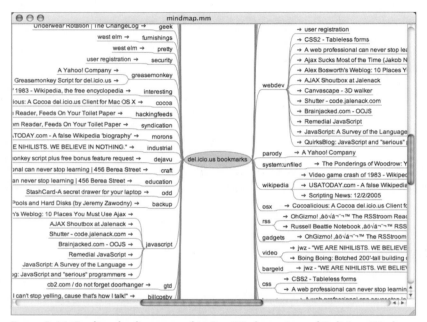

FIGURE 3-14: Bookmarks diagrammed in FreeMind, courtesy of DeliciousMind

Summary

The world of desktop applications using the del.icio.us API to manage your bookmarks is a pretty lean one at present. You'll have the most luck on Mac OS X with integrating your collection into your daily habits outside the browser. There are a few apps to be found for Windows and Linux, but the most powerful application on these platforms is the Web browser.

In the next chapter, you'll return to your browser — only this time, the remixes and mashups live out on the Web. You'll see alternative user interfaces for del.icio.us, add-on services that cooperate with del.icio.us, and new ways to tag and analyze your links.

Remixing del.icio.us

part

Exploring del.icio.us APIs and Data

Now that you've gotten an introduction to some of the technologies used in mashups, as well as a quick spin around del.icio.us itself, it's time to dig a bit deeper and get your hands dirty with some code and data.

In this chapter, you get to see del.icio.us from a programming perspective. Here, you explore many of the ways in which the service exposes your bookmarks and others' through Web service calls, XML data feeds, and JSON-encoded structures. You are also introduced to a few modules and packages available for various programming environments that can make working with del.icio.us APIs more convenient.

Making Calls to the del.icio.us API

Although there are some notable exceptions, most of the things you can do manually on del.icio.us via a Web browser can be done programmatically via third-party applications or scripts. This is thanks to the HTTP and XML Web API offered by del.icio.us, through which you can post and delete bookmarks, as well as query and filter existing bookmarks by dates and tags. In addition, you can perform tag management functions, renaming tags and bundling them together in groups.

Keep in mind, however, that this API is under development and prone to change. This machine interface to the service tends to lag slightly behind the feature set exposed to human users. At this writing, it leaves out a few things such as recommendations, account management, and inbox manipulations. Whether these features are planned for inclusion in the future, who knows? But in any case, the features that are exposed by the API are all quite handy.

 If you'd like to follow along in the official API documentation you can find it here:

```
http://del.icio.us/help/api/
```

You may find additional updates to available functionality, or at least see the original description of these services and compare them to the examples in this chapter.

Using cURL to Make del.icio.us API Calls

Before we get into any specific implementation languages, we're going to take a look at the "raw" API calls. One of the easiest ways to do this is from a shell using the command line tool cURL.

On the Web If you'd like to try these calls yourself and you're using Linux or OS X, you've likely already got this tool at your disposal. If you're using Windows, or would just like to read a bit more about this tool, pay a visit to the following URL to download cURL and check out its documentation:

```
http://curl.haxx.se/
```

In short, cURL is a kind of Web multi-tool. Using the del.icio.us API means making a lot of HTTP GET requests using Basic Authentication, something that cURL makes relatively painless. And, although later you'll likely pick a favorite language and library with which to access the API in your own tinkering, this is a good way to get acquainted with what's going on behind the scenes. The abstractions introduced by a language-specific wrapper can make things easier, but it's always good to keep in mind just what's been abstracted away.

If you plan to follow along in a command line terminal, there's one bit of setup you may want to get out of the way first, however. The shell-based examples in this chapter assume you've assigned a few shell variables to your del.icio.us user name and password, like this pair of commands in a BASH shell:

```
$ export DEL_USER=yourusername
$ export DEL_PASSWD=yourpassword
```

Substitute the appropriate values for your own user name and password when you set these variables for yourself. These, in turn, will be used with cURL's -u option to enable HTTP Basic Authentication, like so:

```
$ curl -u $DEL_USER:$DEL_PASSWD
http://del.icio.us/api/posts/update
<?xml version='1.0' standalone='yes'?>
<update time="2006-01-31T00:31:42Z" />
```

If you don't want to use variables like this, you're free to manually insert your user name and password whenever you like — but at least from here you'll know what $DEL_USER and $DEL_PASSWD stand for.

So, with that bit of toolkit preparation out of the way, it's time to take a look at the API itself.

Fetching Bookmarks

At present, the del.icio.us API can be divided into two feature sets: bookmark management and tag management. And, because you can't really have tags without bookmarks, let's check out that part of the API first.

When you get down to it, there's not much to managing bookmarks. Like any typical database, CRUD pretty much covers the range — that is, Create, Read, Update, and Delete. For del.icio.us, however, the Create and Update functions are the same thing: When posting details using the URL of an existing bookmark, you can choose to replace that bookmark. Because everything centers around URLs in del.icio.us, that helps simplify things a bit.

Fetching Your Recent Bookmarks

So to get down to business, assuming you've already gathered a few bookmarks, you can try out a few queries to fetch bookmarks and get some interesting results right away.

One of the first, most basic queries you can try is the following:

```
$ curl -u $DEL_USER:$DEL_PASSWD
http://del.icio.us/api/posts/recent?count=3
```

This command should get you something similar to Listing 4-1.

Listing 4-1: Bookmarks returned as XML from the API

```
<?xml version='1.0' standalone='yes'?>
<posts tag="" user="deusx">

  <post
href="http://developers.sun.com/techtopics/mobility/midp/
articles/osx/"
       description="Do-It-Yourself MIDP on Mac OS X"
       extended="&quot;Mac OS X ships with a wide assortment
of free developer tools, but these don't include everything you
need for J2ME development. &quot;"
       hash="1fef8ca178d01f8ec3c3f1f70b55fd48"
       tag="osx mobile wireless midp mac"
       time="2006-01-31T00:31:41Z" />

  <post href="http://mpowers.net/midp-osx/"
       description="MIDP for OS X"
       extended="&quot;This package is a Darwin/OSX port of
the Mobile Information Device Profile (MIDP) Reference
Implementation v1.0.3.&quot;"
       hash="067ad6afd926aa9da7d534fd2b7ff2de"
       tag="mobile osx mac wireless"
       time="2006-01-31T00:30:54Z" />

  <post href="http://www.dyadin.com/dyadin.php"
       description="Dyadin the Game"
       extended="I haven't played this yet, but the concept
reminds me just a tad of Zelda: Four Swords with the GameCube /
GBA integration and multiple planes of cooperative play"
       hash="dc6e1b23e8d2a8396b8cb738ac747398"
       tag="gaming nifty indiegames dyadin"
       time="2006-01-30T15:51:04Z" />

</posts>
```

The usage of cURL should be pretty self-explanatory: The command's -u option enables HTTP Basic Authentication, using the user name and password defined just a bit ago in shell variables. And the sole argument to the command is a URL for the del.icio.us API. This URL requests your latest bookmarks, with a query parameter specifying that only the latest three be returned. Note that I've reformatted the XML in Listing 4-1 a bit for clarity — what you see straight from the API will be just a bit less friendly to view directly.

The data format itself is pretty simple. An overall parent tag <posts> contains many <post> elements, each of which represents a bookmark posted to del.icio.us. Each <post> element offers the following attributes:

- href: The URL described by this bookmark.
- description: A brief title describing the bookmark link.
- extended: An optional, more lengthy set of notes about the bookmark.
- hash: An MD5 hash of the bookmark's URL, available as a unique identifier.
- tag: A space-separated list of the tags attached to the bookmark.
- time: The time at which the bookmark was posted.

This first query also accepts a tag parameter:

```
$ curl -u $DEL_USER:$DEL_PASSWD \
'http://del.icio.us/api/posts/recent?count=3&tag=hacks'
```

This command should be all on one line, but a backslash comes in handy to escape a carriage return when working on the shell (or formatting shell commands for a book). Also, notice that there are single quotes around the URL now: In my shell, and likely also in yours, the ampersand in the URL can be accidentally interpreted as an attempt to launch the cURL command as a background process on a UNIX system. This is a common mistake and can cause some strange behavior if you're not expecting it — the single quotes prevent the ampersand from being interpreted by the shell in this way.

At any rate, this new query should return some XML not unlike Listing 4-2.

Listing 4-2: Recent bookmarks tagged with "hacks"

```
<?xml version='1.0' standalone='yes'?>
<posts tag="hacks" user="deusx">
  <post
href="http://www.instructables.com/ex/i/6227EC9EE1DB1028ABAA001
143E 7E506/?ALLSTEPS" description="Burning visible images onto
CD-Rs with data (beta)" extended="&quot;By carefully choosing
the right 1s and 0s to burn to a CD, it is possible to burn
visible images on normal CD-Rs.&quot;  I always figured this
was possible, but never bothered to explore it."
hash="c60b031641cd27959643fd0bf1b5a9c2" tag="nifty hacks
hardware" time="2006-01-29T22:17:40Z" />
```

Listing 4-2 *continued*

```
   <post href="http://www.neatorama.com/2005/12/27/poor-mans-
air-conditioning/" description="Neatorama » Blog Archive »
Poor Man's Air Conditioning." extended="Window air conditioner
+ generator + beater car = hott"
hash="a1ebea6d28d47177e9c991fba4ee95bb" tag="hacks hardware
notwishlist" time="2006-01-27T20:53:43Z" />
   <post href="http://www.flickr.com/photos/andy_m/sets/
1791706/" description="radio babylon - a photoset on Flickr"
extended="&quot;&quot;" hash="b2290294b2456a171c0f8a5f034d4d6d"
tag="nifty hardware hacks audio wireless" time="2006-01-
22T06:00:10Z" />
</posts>
```

There's no reformatting this time for Listing 4-2. This is closer to what you'll really see resulting from a query to the del.icio.us API, depending on what line wrapping is introduced by this book or your terminal window. Beyond that, the main difference between Listing 4-1 and Listing 4-2 is that all the links in Listing 4-2 are tagged with `hacks`. Also, note that the tag with which this list was filtered has appeared in the `tag` attribute of the root `<posts>` tag along with your user name.

So, with the `posts/recent` query, you can use any combination of the `count` or `tag` parameters to access your most recent queries. If you omit the `count` parameter, it will default to 15 — and if you supply a `count`, it cannot exceed 100.

Also, you should get used to seeing this XML because this is the format in which you'll see all lists of bookmarks returned from the API. There's not much to it, and although API wrappers will make things easier for you, the raw data isn't that complex to handle if you find a need to do so.

Filtering Bookmarks by Date, Tag, and URL

Now that you've whetted your appetite on these first couple of API calls, you can delve a bit deeper into more advanced bookmark queries.

The `posts/get` query will allow you to request bookmark data by tag, date, or individual bookmark URL. These filters are applied, respectively, by using the `tag`, `dt`, and `url` parameters.

By default, today's date is used as the value for the `dt` parameter if it's left out of the query. So, for example, this query fetches all of your bookmarks for today:

```
$ curl -u $DEL_USER:$DEL_PASSWD 'http://del.icio.us/api/posts/get'
```

If you try this command, you will see XML returned that looks just like Listing 4-1 and Listing 4-2. The difference is that `posts/get` gives you no control over the count as `posts/recent` does, so this query just returns all posts for the current date — whereas `posts/recent` will span dates if the `count` exceeds today's postings.

If you want to supply a date, it needs to be in an ISO 8601 format like this:

```
$ curl -u $DEL_USER:$DEL_PASSWD \
    'http://del.icio.us/api/posts/get?dt=2005-01-30'
```

This query will, of course, request all bookmarks from January 30, 2005. You can introduce a tag filter into the mix with a query like this:

```
$ curl -u $DEL_USER:$DEL_PASSWD \
    'http://del.icio.us/api/posts/get?dt=2005-01-30&tag=apple'
```

With the additional parameter added, the day's bookmarks will be limited to those tagged with `apple`. Now, consider the following query:

```
$ curl -u $DEL_USER:$DEL_PASSWD \
    'http://del.icio.us/api/posts/get?tag=apple'
```

Just in case you expected that this would return your entire collection of bookmarks tagged with `apple`, remember that the default for the `dt` parameter is today's date. So, this query will be limited to just today's bookmarks.

Finally, the `url` parameter allows you to look up a single bookmark:

```
$ curl -u $DEL_USER:$DEL_PASSWD \
'http://del.icio.us/api/posts/get?url=http%3A//www.geekculture.com
/joyoftech/joyarchives/781.html'
```

```xml
<?xml version='1.0' standalone='yes'?>
<posts dt="2006-01-30" tag="" user="deusx">
  <post href="http://www.geekculture.com/joyoftech/joyarchives/
781.html" description="The Joy of Tech #781" extended="&quot;Hey
Bob, did you realize you're sharing your iPhoto library?&quot;"
hash="a931ebcaece99efdfe3be3c1b7e9fb65" others="3" tag="apple
iphoto mac photos" time="2006-01-30T12:27:21Z" />
</posts>
```

Why might this be useful? Well, with this parameter you can query all of the extended information for a bookmark — for example, title, notes, tags, and so on. So, if you're implementing an application wherein you can edit existing bookmarks, this is how you can fetch the bookmark's details before editing.

Navigating Bookmarks by Date

Using filters to fetch bookmarks is a useful way to navigate your collection, but the API offers a few more methods to help out. For example, say you wanted to build an interface for stepping back through the daily history of postings — this is where the `posts/dates` API request comes in handy:

```
$ curl -u $DEL_USER:$DEL_PASSWD \
    'http://del.icio.us/api/posts/dates'
```

The result of this query is a new XML format, shown in Listing 4-3.

Listing 4-3: Posting dates returned from the posts/dates request

```xml
<?xml version='1.0' standalone='yes'?>
<dates tag="" user="deusx">
  <date count="9" date="2006-01-31" />
  <date count="26" date="2006-01-30" />
  <date count="15" date="2006-01-29" />
  <date count="36" date="2006-01-28" />
  <date count="48" date="2006-01-27" />
  <date count="26" date="2006-01-26" />
  <date count="28" date="2006-01-25" />
  <date count="22" date="2006-01-24" />
  <date count="30" date="2006-01-23" />
  <date count="31" date="2006-01-22" />
  <date count="16" date="2006-01-21" />
  <date count="40" date="2006-01-20" />
  <date count="50" date="2006-01-19" />
  <date count="25" date="2006-01-18" />
  <date count="21" date="2006-01-17" />
  <date count="47" date="2006-01-16" />
  <date count="18" date="2006-01-15" />
  <date count="9" date="2006-01-14" />
  <date count="21" date="2006-01-13" />
  <date count="13" date="2006-01-12" />
  <date count="41" date="2006-01-11" />
  <date count="37" date="2006-01-10" />
  ...
</dates>
```

Note that Listing 4-3 is actually a truncated view of the results of this command, indicated by the ellipsis. As of this writing, my own collection contains posts for almost 800 dates, and they're all listed by this query. In your own application or script, you can use this query first before making any others in order to get an idea of posts available over time. You could use this information to populate a selection menu, or to power previous/next buttons. Using these dates in combination with the posts/get query and its dt parameter, you can step back and forth through the timeline of bookmark posts.

This query also accepts a tag parameter for use in filtering the dates and counts:

```
$ curl -u $DEL_USER:$DEL_PASSWD \
    'http://del.icio.us/api/posts/dates?tag=apple'
<dates tag="apple" user="deusx">
  <date count="1" date="2006-01-30" />
  <date count="1" date="2006-01-23" />
  <date count="1" date="2006-01-10" />
  <date count="1" date="2006-01-07" />
  <date count="2" date="2005-11-17" />
  ...
</dates>
```

Again, these results are truncated, but this resulting data will be limited to dates and counts where the tag `apple` was used.

So You Want to Grab All Your Bookmarks?

This final bookmark query, `posts/all`, should be considered a secret weapon and last resort. If you absolutely, positively must fetch all of your bookmarks, this how you do it:

```
$ curl -u $DEL_USER:$DEL_PASSWD 'http://del.icio.us/api/posts/all'
```

You can also supply a `tag` parameter to filter bookmarks fetched by this query:

```
$ curl -u $DEL_USER:$DEL_PASSWD \
    'http://del.icio.us/api/posts/all?tag=apple'
```

Note   Performing a `posts/all` query is a major event, and should be done very sparingly. It will return massive amounts of data if you've been posting bookmarks for a while, and will put a bit of a strain on the del.icio.us servers. You could use `posts/all` when first starting an application, to import and back up bookmarks. Otherwise, you should use `posts/get` and `posts/recent` for more "surgical" fetches. In fact, the API offers another query, `posts/update`, which will return the time of your account's last update:

```
$ curl -u $DEL_USER:$DEL_PASSWD \
    'http://del.icio.us/api/posts/update'
<?xml version='1.0' standalone='yes'?>
<update time="2006-01-31T00:31:42Z" />
```

This query, along with `posts/dates`, should help you work incrementally and avoid using `posts/all` — but the `posts/all` option is there, should you really need it.

Managing Bookmarks in Your Collection

Now you've seen the methods available for fetching and filtering bookmarks from your collection on del.icio.us. That covers the "R" in CRUD, but what about the rest? Well, as I mentioned earlier, del.icio.us uses URLs as primary keys in this database. So, adding a bookmark is the same as updating a bookmark when using the same URL. That leaves us with two more bookmark management methods: `posts/add` and `posts/delete`.

Adding New Bookmarks and Updating Existing Bookmarks

First up, then, is the `posts/add` method of the del.icio.us API. With this method, you can create new bookmarks from your own code, supplying all of the same information as you can when using a bookmarklet or a posting form on del.icio.us itself.

Like all the other methods shown so far, `posts/add` is accessed via HTTP GET with Basic Authentication. This is where the del.icio.us API departs from being a pure REST Web services API: One of the main characteristics of a REST API is that HTTP GET is used for idempotent (i.e., read-only) operations — whereas HTTP POST is reserved for operations intended to cause a change to data stored somewhere.

But, with del.icio.us, all it takes is a carefully constructed set of query string parameters:

```
$ curl -u $DEL_USER:$DEL_PASSWD \
'http://del.icio.us/api/posts/add?url=http%3A//decafbad.com&
description=0xDECAFBAD&extended=Friends%20don%27t%20let%20friends%
20drink%20decaf%21&tags=coffee%20blogs%20programming&dt=2005-01-
31T08%3A43%3A12Z&replace=yes'
```

Now, up until this point, I've been fairly careful in the example queries in this chapter not to use many characters in need of URL escaping. But, with this example, the gloves are off. So, let's take a few minutes to dissect this example. First, there's the base URL for the query, namely:

```
http://del.icio.us/api/posts/add
```

Next come all the query parameters — name/value pairs joined by ampersands and appended to the base URL after a question mark. The names of these query parameters and their purposes are:

- `url`: The URL of the bookmark.
- `description`: Short descriptive title for the bookmark.
- `extended`: Longer extended notes posted with the bookmark.
- `tags`: A space-separated list of tags for the bookmark.
- `dt`: A datestamp for the item in ISO 8601 format.
- `replace`: Whether to replace an existing bookmark's information with these details.

Other than a few differences in terminology, these parameter names all match up with the XML bookmark representation, as well as the form fields used for posting a new bookmark. And for this particular query, the parameters are given with the following raw values:

- `url`: `http://decafbad.com`
- `description`: `0xDECAFBAD`
- `extended`: `Friends don't let friends drink decaf.`
- `tags`: `coffee blogs programming`
- `dt`: `2005-01-31T08:43:12Z`
- `replace`: `yes`

Of course, here's where an API wrapper can start to come in handy: In order to supply all of these as query parameters, you're going to need to apply URL escaping to all of them. Passing a URL as a parameter to a URL can get a bit hairy, as can using the various forms of punctuation you're likely to run across in composing titles and notes for describing bookmarks. But doing this encoding by hand is a gigantic pain.

So, to make things a little easier, Listing 4-4 offers a quick one-off Perl script to help build the `posts/add` URL before performing the query with cURL. This script should be useful — because if you've got cURL, you've probably got Perl.

Listing 4-4: ch04_add_bookmark.pl

```perl
#!/usr/bin/perl
############################################################
# ch04_add_bookmark.pl - Add a bookmark to your account
############################################################
use strict;

# Establish the user name, password, and API base URL
my $DEL_USER   = 'yourusername';
my $DEL_PASSWD = 'yourpassword';
my $DEL_API    = 'http://del.icio.us/api/posts/add';

# Collect the details to be posted as a bookmark.
my %params = (
    url         => "http://decafbad.com",
    description => "0xDECAFBAD",
    extended    => "Friends don't let friends drink decaf.",
    tags        => "coffee blogs programming",
    replace     => "yes"
);

# Build the final API query by encoding all the details.
my $api_url = "$DEL_API?".
    join '&',
    map  { $_.'='.enc($params{$_}) }
    keys %params;

# Perform the API query via system()
system("curl -u $DEL_USER:$DEL_PASSWD '$api_url'");

# Subroutine to apply URL encoding to a given string.
sub enc {
    my $str = shift;
    $str =~ s/([^A-Za-z0-9])/sprintf("%%%02X", ord($1))/seg;
    return $str;
}
```

The Perl script in Listing 4-4 is a simple, no-frills way to get this bookmark posted. As you can likely guess, your account user name and password belong in the variables $DEL_USER and $DEL_PASSWORD. The hash %params is built with all the fields to be used in posting this bookmark.

A transform involving `join`, `map`, and `enc` builds the URL-encoded query string for `posts/add`, which is then supplied with your user name and password to an invocation of cURL via `system()`.

The only complex part of this script is in the definition of the subroutine `enc()`: There's a regex search-and-replace statement here, which translates any non-alphanumeric character into a hex code version of its character code. And this, in a nutshell, is URL encoding.

As you'll see shortly, more proper del.icio.us API wrappers do quite a bit more than simply provide URL encoding — but this is a good start for now.

A sample successful run of this program should appear like so:

```
$ perl ch04_add_bookmark.pl
<?xml version='1.0' standalone='yes'?>
<result code="done" />
```

And, if all goes well, you should see this bookmark added to your account — as shown in Figure 4-1. Note that, with the `replace` parameter value passed in as `yes`, this API call works as both a Create and Update operation. If you pass `no` as the value, the API will refrain from replacing, thus limiting this query to just Create operations on your bookmarks.

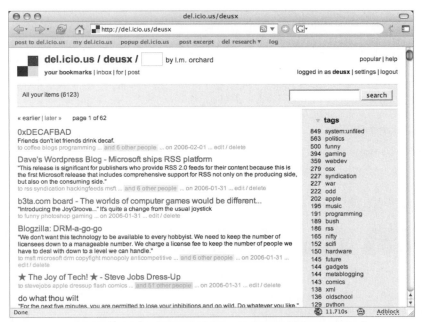

FIGURE 4-1: Bookmark successfully posted using ch04_add_bookmark.pl

Deleting a Bookmark

As opposed to the encoding gymnastics required to add a new bookmark, deleting a bookmark via `posts/delete` is simple. This method takes just one parameter, `url`. Thus, to delete the bookmark you just posted, try this command:

```
$ curl -u $DEL_USER:$DEL_PASSWD \
    'http://del.icio.us/api/posts/delete?url=http%3A%2F%2Fdecafbad%2Ecom'
<?xml version='1.0' standalone='yes'?>
<result code="done" />
```

Note that the parameter here — it being a URL passed into a URL — also needs to be escaped. You might want to try tweaking the program in Listing 4-4 just a bit to take care of the escaping for you in deleting this bookmark.

One interesting thing about this query is that you'll get this resulting XML whether or not the bookmark had already been posted before. The only time you'll get a different answer is when something's not gone quite right with the server.

Managing Tags and Tag Bundles

With bookmark management covered, its time to take a look at the other half of the API: tag management. This part of things is pretty basic, but it's an important aspect of del.icio.us to manage from the API.

Listing Your Tags

While it's important to get a list of all dates on which bookmarks were posted to your account, getting a list of all of your tags is just as important for use in filtering bookmark queries. This is where the `tags/get` API method comes in. With this, you can make a query for your tag collection. You can use this information to populate selection menus, or just perform a little analysis on your tagging habits.

This method is very simple to use, like so:

```
$ curl -u $DEL_USER:$DEL_PASSWD 'http://del.icio.us/api/tags/get'
```

When you run this query, you'll get XML data, as shown in Listing 4-5.

Listing 4-5: Tag list XML returned by a tags/get query

```
<?xml version='1.0' standalone='yes'?>
<tags>
  <tag count="1" tag="!mobiledesktop" />
  <tag count="1" tag="31337" />
  <tag count="4" tag="80s" />
  <tag count="7" tag="8bit" />
  <tag count="7" tag="MSFT" />
  <tag count="4" tag="achewood" />
  <tag count="2" tag="actionscript" />
  <tag count="1" tag="adbusters" />
```

Listing 4-5 *continued*

```
    <tag count="21" tag="advertising" />
    <tag count="13" tag="aggregators" />
    <tag count="68" tag="ajax" />
    ...
</tags>
```

The results of a `tags/get` query in Listing 4-5 look quite a lot like the data from Listing 4-3. Just swap `date` and `dates` for `tag` and `tags` — both of these data sets include a count of bookmarks under each grouping.

Renaming and Cleaning Up Your Tags

Because of the nature of tagging and tags themselves, there's really no such thing as and no need for methods to create or delete tags. You attach tags to bookmarks as you post them. If a particular tag didn't exist before you attached it to a bookmark, it's created at that point. If at some point a particular tag no longer appears on any of your bookmarks, it's effectively deleted. Or, rather, the tag just vanishes from existence — there's not really any independent existence for tags outside of the bookmarks to which they're attached.

That said, however, one of the most useful aspects to tags is that they can be treated as common intersections between the things they describe. As you go along posting bookmarks and attaching tags at a furious pace, you may find that your collection of tags begins to accumulate misspellings, synonyms, and just plain weird divergences. Eventually, you may want to prune your tags a bit, converge the synonyms on common terms (e.g., from `javascript` to `js`), and switch over to using a tag that's seeing more popular use at the moment (e.g., from `WebDevelopment2005` to `webdev`). All of these things help increase the value of your tags — both to you and others.

This is where the `tags/rename` API method comes in handy: Rather than needing to repost all of the affected bookmarks by hand or by machine with revised sets of tags, you can use `tags/rename` to selectively alter tags across your entire collection of bookmarks at once.

To make this long story short, here's an example usage of the `tags/rename` query:

```
$ curl -u $DEL_USER:$DEL_PASSWD \
    'http://del.icio.us/api/tags/rename?old=cellphone&new=mobile'
<?xml version='1.0' standalone='yes'?>
<result>done</result>
```

In this invocation, the tag `cellphone` is replaced with `mobile` wherever it appears in the collection of bookmarks. The parameters used in this query are:

- `old`: The existing tag subject to change.
- `new`: A new tag with which to replace the existing tag.

So, this API method is pretty self-explanatory once you understand what its uses are. Of course, all the usual requirements for URI-escaping the parameters apply — but for the most part, you should try to stick to simple words and alphabetic characters in tags anyway, so they'll tend to be safe as query string values.

What Are Tag Bundles?

With just a few special exceptions — e.g., `for:deusx` and `system:media:audio` — tags all live in a flat namespace with respect to how del.icio.us treats them. Some people attempt to denote hierarchy by using slashes or other delimiters, but these are really just personal conventions without any special meaning for del.icio.us or its API calls.

For example, you could get in the habit of using tags such as `webdev/flash`, `webdev/js`, and `webdev/css`. But, you'd never be able to directly do a filter on `webdev/*` to grab bookmarks with these tags. In your own code, you could simulate this functionality by calling `tags/get`, performing a wildcard match on the results, and making filtered queries with the matches. Although this might be a useful hack, it isn't officially supported.

What have gained official support recently, however, are tag bundles. These are lightweight clusters of tags you can manage from your account settings — at this writing, they're under the experimental features at this URL:

```
http://del.icio.us/settings/deusx/bundle
```

Remember to replace *deusx* with your own user name to access this page. Figure 4-2 shows you what creating a tag bundle looks like from a browser, and Figure 4-3 shows the end result.

FIGURE 4-2: Creating a tag bundle through the browser

FIGURE 4-3: Tags organized into bundles

At present, tag bundles are in a very early stage of development. Mostly, they just serve to help visually group tags on your account's bookmark listings. Tag bundles can't be used directly to filter bookmark searches, nor can they be shared among users. As this feature is further developed, however, the benefits of using tag bundles are likely to build upon these beginnings.

For your own applications, however, the del.icio.us API offers methods to create, delete, and list your tag bundles. While the service itself may not yet make much use of tag bundles, these methods enable you to build upon them. Rather than relying on personal tagging convention and funky delimited hierarchies with wildcards, tag bundles offer a directly supported way to manage at least one level of grouping in your tags.

One caveat in all of this, however: Tag bundles are among the experimental features on del.icio.us, so your mileage may vary when you try using this part of the API.

Listing Tag Bundles

After you've had a chance to manually create a few tag bundles via your browser, you'll have some material with which to try this first API method, `tags/bundles/all`:

```
$ curl -u $DEL_USER:$DEL_PASSWD \
    'http://del.icio.us/api/tags/bundles/all'
<?xml version='1.0' standalone='yes'?>
<bundles>
  <bundle name="hackingfeeds" tags="aggregation aggregator
aggregators atom feeddemon feedparser feeds newsriver rss
syndication" />
</bundles>
```

As with the other XML formats produced by the API, the result of this query is pretty simple: a root <bundles> tag containing many <bundle> elements, with each <bundle> element's attributes providing details defining a tag bundle.

At present, I have only a single hackingfeeds bundle defined, so you can see the single <bundle> element with the name of the bundle in the name attribute along with a space-delimited list of tags in the tags attribute.

Creating a Tag Bundle

Now, to create a tag bundle, you use the tags/bundles/set method of the API. This query expects two parameters:

- bundle: This is the name of the bundle to be created.
- tags: This parameter is the space-separated list of tags from which the bundle will be created.

And, here's an example usage of this method in creating a new bundle named politics:

```
$ curl -u $DEL_USER:$DEL_PASSWD \
'http://del.icio.us/api/tags/bundles/set?bundle=politics&tags=bush
+politics+war+iraq'
<?xml version='1.0' standalone='yes'?>
<result>ok</result>
```

The return data from this call is, as usual, pretty uninformative. If you'd like to verify the existence of the new bundle after making this query, try tags/bundles/all again:

```
$ curl -u $DEL_USER:$DEL_PASSWD \
    'http://del.icio.us/api/tags/bundles/all'
<?xml version='1.0' standalone='yes'?>
<bundles>
  <bundle name="politics" tags="bush iraq politics war" />
  <bundle name="hackingfeeds" tags="aggregation aggregator
aggregators atom feeddemon feedparser feeds newsriver rss
syndication" />
</bundles>
```

You should see the additional tag appearing in your list now.

Deleting a Tag Bundle

Finally, when you want to get rid of a tag bundle, the method tags/bundles/delete is made available via the API. It expects a single parameter, bundle, which should be the name of the bundle to delete. Here's an attempt to delete the bundle created in the previous part:

```
$ curl -u $DEL_USER:$DEL_PASSWD \
    'http://del.icio.us/api/tags/bundles/delete?bundle=politics'
<?xml version='1.0' standalone='yes'?>
<result>ok</result>
```

And, once more, you may want to try `tags/bundles/all` to verify the result of this call:

```
$ curl -u $DEL_USER:$DEL_PASSWD \
    'http://del.icio.us/api/tags/bundles/all'
<?xml version='1.0' standalone='yes'?>
<bundles>
  <bundle name="hackingfeeds" tags="aggregation aggregator
aggregators atom feeddemon feedparser feeds newsriver rss
syndication" />
</bundles>
```

Back down to one tag bundle again, now. So, the deletion was a success!

Abstracting Access to the del.icio.us API

As mentioned earlier, it's good to have a grasp on what's going on with the API itself before introducing abstractions to make things easier. Well, now that you've just finished a grand tour of the del.icio.us API, close to bare HTTP and XML metal, you can probably see where a few higher-level conveniences would start to come in handy. Take, for instance, dealing with things like URI-encoding for query string parameters — or how about a little XML parsing to actually *do* something with the data returned from the API calls?

Using pydelicious for a Pythonic API

One way you can make using the del.icio.us API more Pythonic is with pydelicious by Frank Timmermann, which you can download from the following site:

```
http://deliciouspython.python-hosting.com/
```

Once you've got it installed, pydelicious will provide fairly easy-to-use methods for calling on the del.icio.us API using standard Python syntax. These wrapper methods automatically parse the XML returned from the API into native Python data structures.

Listing 4-6 demonstrates a few of the features of pydelicious, just to give you a flavor.

Listing 4-6: ch04_pydelicious_example.py

```python
#!/usr/bin/env python
"""
ch04_pydelicious_example.py - An example using pydelicious
"""
DEL_USER   = 'yourusername'
DEL_PASSWD = 'yourpassword'

import pydelicious

api = pydelicious.apiNew(DEL_USER, DEL_PASSWD)
```

continued

Listing 4-6 *continued*

```python
print "Posting bookmark."
api.posts_add(
    url         = 'http://decafbad.com',
    description = '0xDECAFBAD',
    extended    = "Friends don't let friends drink decaf.",
    tags        = 'programming coffee caffeine'
)

print "Deleting bookmark."
api.posts_delete('http://decafbad.com')

print "Recent posts:"
for post in api.posts_recent():
    print "\t%(description)s" % post

print "Top 10 tags:"

def tag_order(a, b):
    return cmp( int(b['count']), int(a['count']) )

tags = api.tags_get()
tags.sort(tag_order)

for tag in tags[:10]:
    print "\t%(tag)s - %(count)s" % tag
```

Working with Net::Delicious in Perl

For Perl, you can take advantage of Aaron Straup Cope's module Net::Delicious. This module is installable via CPAN, and you can visit this address for more details:

```
http://search.cpan.org/dist/Net-Delicious/
```

This module serves the same purpose for Perl as pydelicious does for Python — that is, to provide a convenient, idiomatic wrapper around all of the operations of the del.icio.us API. Listing 4-7 provides an example very similar to that shown in Listing 4-6, as it takes Net::Delicious through a few of its paces.

Listing 4-7: ch04_net_delicious_example.pl

```perl
#!/usr/bin/perl
###############################################################
# ch04_net_delicious_example.pl
###############################################################
```

Listing 4-7 *continued*

```
our $DEL_USER   = 'yourusername';
our $DEL_PASSWD = 'yourpassword';

use Net::Delicious;
use Log::Dispatch::Screen;

my $api = Net::Delicious->new({user=>$DEL_USER,
                               pswd=>$DEL_PASSWD});

print "Posting bookmark.\n";
$api->add_post({
    url         => 'http://decafbad.com',
    description => '0xDECAFBAD',
    extended    => "Friends don't let friends drink decaf.",
    tags        => 'programming coffee caffeine'
});

print "Deleting bookmark.\n";
$api->delete_post({
    url => 'http://decafbad.com'
});

print "Recent posts:\n";
for my $post ($api->recent_posts()) {
    print "\t".$post->description()."\n";
}

print "Top 10 tags:\n";
my @tags = sort { $b->count <=> $a->count } $api->tags();
for my $tag (@tags[1..10]) {
    print "\t".$tag->tag." - ".$tag->count."\n";
}
```

Including PhpDelicious for PHP

There are a handful of del.icio.us API wrappers available for PHP. However, as of this writing, the most complete encapsulation I've found is PhpDelicious by Edward Eliot. You can find a description of this library and download it here:

```
www.ejeliot.com/pages/5
```

Again, because this is the same API for the same site, this wrapper looks much the same as wrappers for Python and Perl. Listing 4-8 offers one more transliteration of the demonstration you've already seen written in the other two languages.

Listing 4-8: ch04_php_delicious_example.php

```php
<html><body><pre>
<?php
    /**
        ch04_php_delicious_example.php
    */

    define('DEL_USER',   'yourusername');
    define('DEL_PASSWD', 'yourpassword');

    // http://www.ejeliot.com/pages/5
    require_once 'includes/php-delicious.inc.php';

    $api = new PhpDelicious(DEL_USER, DEL_PASSWD);

    echo "Posting bookmark.\n";
    $api->AddPost(
        'http://decafbad.com',
        '0xDECAFBAD',
        "Friends don't let friends drink decaf.",
        array('programming', 'coffee', 'caffeine')
    );

    echo "Deleting bookmark.\n";
    $api->DeletePost('http://decafbad.com');

    echo "Recent posts:\n";
    foreach ($api->GetRecentPosts() as $post) {
        echo "\t".$post['desc']."\n";
    }

    echo "Top 10 tags:\n";

    function tag_order($a, $b) {
        $a_cnt = $a['count'];
        $b_cnt = $b['count'];
        if ($b_cnt == $a_cnt) { return 0; }
        return ($b_cnt < $a_cnt) ? -1 : 1;
    }

    $tags = $api->GetAllTags();
    usort($tags, "tag_order");

    foreach (array_slice($tags, 0, 10) as $tag) {
        echo "\t".$tag['tag']." - ".$tag['count']."\n";
    }

?>
</pre></body></html>
```

Making the API Rubilicious

And finally, for the Ruby fans out there, here's one more variation on the theme. You can find the del.icio.us API wrapped up in a nice module available as a Gem here:

    www.pablotron.org/software/rubilicious/

Rubilicious covers the full range of operations made available by the API, as well as offering a few more features not directly offered — such as conversion to the XBEL bookmark format. You can check out Listing 4-9 for the final translation of the demonstration program.

Listing 4-9: ch04_rubilicious_example.rb

```ruby
#!/usr/bin/env ruby
###############################################################
# ch04_rubilicious_example.rb
###############################################################
DEL_USER   = 'deusx'
DEL_PASSWD = 'cascade'

require 'rubilicious'

api = Rubilicious.new(DEL_USER, DEL_PASSWD)

puts "Posting bookmark."
api.add(
    'http://decafbad.com',
    '0xDECAFBAD',
    "Friends don't let friends drink decaf.",
    'programming coffee caffeine'
)

puts "Deleting bookmark."
api.delete('http://decafbad.com')

puts "Recent posts:"
api.recent().each { |post|
    puts "\t#{post['description']}"
}

puts "Top 10 tags:"
api.tags().sort{ |a,b| b[1]<=>a[1] }.slice(0..10).each{ |tag|
    puts "\t#{tag[0]} - #{tag[1]}"
}
```

Tracking Bookmarks via RSS Feeds

As you've seen in this chapter, the del.icio.us API offers quite a lot of potential for use in managing your bookmarks and tags. However, it's worth noting that the API is focused on *your* bookmarks. That is, you can't access anyone else's bookmarks unless you also know their user name and password. Of course, that's a good thing when you're talking about posting and deleting bookmarks — but del.icio.us is all about *sharing* bookmarks, so where's the shared data?

Well, the best place to find this is in the set of RSS feeds del.icio.us offers. These were mentioned in Chapter 1, but it's worth taking a slightly more in-depth look at them. Whereas the API is limited to your own bookmarks for the operations it offers, the RSS feeds provide machine-readable access to a wide variety of timely del.icio.us data.

On the Web

It's a bit out of the scope of this chapter to give a complete rundown on the RSS format and associated technologies, so you may want to do a little research into the topic in case you aren't already up-to-speed. Chapter 1 offered a Wikipedia article to get you started, but here's a tutorial with a bit more meat to it:

        www.mnot.net/rss/tutorial/

And again, you can find some details on the RSS feeds at del.icio.us in the help section:

        http://del.icio.us/help/rss

If you're using an RSS-capable browser such as Firefox, you'll probably notice the orange "transmission waves" icon appearing for just about every page you visit on del.icio.us. This is because del.icio.us is just loaded with RSS feeds. What's really interesting is that unlike some sites, these aren't all the same feed. Just about every view of del.icio.us you can call up via browser has an associated machine-readable feed.

Drinking from the Fire Hose

One of the first feeds to start with is the main site feed, located here:

        http://del.icio.us/rss/

This feed is a bit like drinking from a fire hose because it spews a constant stream of the latest bookmarks. So, as opposed to using the single-user–focused API, this RSS feed gives you everything from everybody.

As with all the API calls, you can fetch this feed using cURL if you like — although you'll probably have better luck using a parser for your favorite language. Still, it might be instructive to take a peek directly at what del.icio.us includes in feeds. Check out Listing 4-10 for a slightly truncated sample.

Listing 4-10: Truncated sample del.icio.us RSS 1.0 feed

```
<?xml version="1.0" encoding="UTF-8"?>

<rdf:RDF
 xmlns:rdf="http://www.w3.org/1999/02/22-rdf-syntax-ns#"
 xmlns="http://purl.org/rss/1.0/"
 xmlns:cc="http://web.resource.org/cc/"
 xmlns:taxo="http://purl.org/rss/1.0/modules/taxonomy/"
 xmlns:dc="http://purl.org/dc/elements/1.1/"
 xmlns:syn="http://purl.org/rss/1.0/modules/syndication/"
 xmlns:admin="http://webns.net/mvcb/"
>

<channel rdf:about="http://del.icio.us/">
<title>del.icio.us</title>
<link>http://del.icio.us/</link>
<description></description>
<items>
 <rdf:Seq>
  <rdf:li rdf:resource="http://www.blogher.org/" />
  ...
 </rdf:Seq>
</items>
</channel>

<item rdf:about="http://www.blogher.org/">
<title>BlogHer [beta] | Where the women bloggers are</title>
<link>http://www.blogher.org/</link>
<description>A network dedicated to the creation of the
ultimate guide to blogs written by and/or about
women.</description>
<dc:creator>fleuree</dc:creator>
<dc:date>2006-02-02T02:23:45Z</dc:date>
<dc:subject>blogs conferences feminism guide women</dc:subject>
<taxo:topics>
  <rdf:Bag>
    <rdf:li resource="http://del.icio.us/tag/women" />
    <rdf:li resource="http://del.icio.us/tag/blogs" />
    <rdf:li resource="http://del.icio.us/tag/feminism" />
    <rdf:li resource="http://del.icio.us/tag/conferences" />
    <rdf:li resource="http://del.icio.us/tag/guide" />
  </rdf:Bag>
</taxo:topics>
</item>
...
</rdf:RDF>
```

The first noteworthy thing about Listing 4-10 is that del.icio.us serves up RSS 1.0 feeds, using RDF/XML to encode details about the latest bookmarks. Most of the elements used in this feed are fairly standard fare for RSS 1.0 feeds. This format maps well onto the fields of a bookmark posting. One interesting feature, however, is that tags attached to a bookmark are given both as a space-separated list in a `<dc:subject>` element, as well as a list of tag page URLs under a `<taxo:topics>` element.

Watching the Popularity Contest

Having peeked at the raw data, what might be a bit more interesting — or at least less bewildering — than the site's main feed is the popular links feed at this URL:

```
http://del.icio.us/rss/popular
```

This feed is more focused, containing only those links that have been posted by the greatest number of users. You can get a pretty good feel for the general state of the bookmarking world from items appearing here, although it's still a mixed bag by definition.

Checking Your Inbox

If you'd like to narrow things down even further still, check out your inbox feed:

```
http://del.icio.us/rss/inbox/deusx
```

As usual, replace the *deusx* with your own user name. If you've gathered a collection of users in your inbox, either before you picked up this book or since Chapter 1, this feed will present you with the combined bookmarks of everyone in that collection. This feed can have a lot of value, helping you keep up with your friends and acquaintances, who probably have a good chance of sending interesting things your way as a group.

Something interesting to point out here is that your inbox feed is neither private nor password protected like the API. Drop anyone's user name into this URL, and you'll see that person's aggregated bookmark inbox.

Being Picky (and Private) About Your Friends

Do you want to individually monitor a few users' collections? You can build a feed URL that singles out just one person:

```
http://del.icio.us/rss/deusx
```

With the preceding feed, you'll see everything posted to my own collection. Swap the *deusx* out for another user's name, and the focus will switch to that person's bookmarks. You can use these feeds to build up your own private inbox in a news aggregator, organizing the subscriptions into folders or however your software allows.

Letting Your Friends Be Picky (and Private) About You

As mentioned in Chapter 1, you can target links to individual users by using the `for:` tag prefix. Bookmarks targeted in this manner are somewhat private because only you can view the page aggregating such posts aimed at you. You can check this page out at:

```
http://del.icio.us/for/deusx
```

Something to notice on the page of bookmarks intended for you is that there's a link to a feed at the bottom, as shown in Figure 4-4.

What's special about this feed URL is that it's got a special private key attached in a query parameter, like so:

```
http://del.icio.us/rss/for/deusx?private=XXXXXXXXXX
```

You can see this page only when logged in, but this private key in the feed URL allows you to subscribe to the feed without a login from your aggregator. Although this private key won't really allow anyone access to your account in general, you should still keep this URL secret.

Note that these bookmarks tagged for your attention are just *partially* private — the bookmarks themselves are public, but the `for:` tag is hidden. This obscures the clue that a particular bookmark was meant for your eyes, but does not obscure the bookmark entirely.

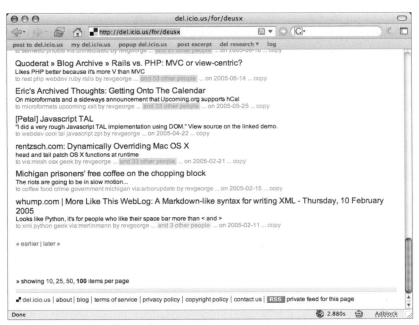

FIGURE 4-4: Link to private for: tag feed at the bottom of the page

Staying on Topic

Yet another way you can slice up the bookmarks on del.icio.us is by tags. Using this URL, you can get a decently topical feed on just about any subject in which you're interested:

```
http://del.icio.us/rss/tag/ajax
```

This URL will fetch you all the latest bookmarks tagged with `ajax`. For the most part, this will come up with all sorts of Web development resources with the occasional essay on cleaning tips. To change the topic, swap `ajax` for whatever other tag you'd like.

Mixing It Up

You can request a feed by using a combination of tags and a user name. For example, if you want to get a really focused feed on Ajax and buzzword-compliant Web technologies, try this URL:

```
http://del.icio.us/rss/tag/web20+ajax
```

Combining tags in this way will get you the intersection between them, feeding you bookmarks that have *all* of the specified tags.

These tag intersections can also be applied to individual users. So, say for instance you want to see links from me only when they've got something to do with Mac OS X. You can use this feed URL:

```
http://del.icio.us/rss/deusx/osx
```

Or, if you think I'm a real Ajax and Web 2.0 guru, you can narrow right down to my bookmarks on the subject:

```
http://del.icio.us/rss/deusx/web20+ajax
```

Tracking a Single Link

One more way you can slice things with feeds is down to the level of an individual URL. For example, here's a feed for a page popular as of this writing:

```
http://del.icio.us/rss/url?url=http://en.wikipedia.org/wiki/
List_of_algorithms
```

If you've got an MD5 encoder handy, you can swap out a query string parameter for a hash of the URL in question to get this feed:

```
http://del.icio.us/rss/url/0a5015b77a92c268938bb1e02222949b
```

Both of these feeds give you the same thing: a running list of everyone who's bookmarked the given URL. The usefulness of this may seem a bit dubious, but where it can really come in handy is if you'd like to gather details for your *own* Web pages. You could subscribe to feeds related to your own blog entries, for instance, and watch to see if they become overnight Internet meme successes.

You'll see this feed used later on, in Chapter 9.

Accessing Bookmarks with JSON

Just about every method for accessing data and performing queries presented in this chapter has been meant for use on the server side of things. The reason for this is that it's a bit difficult to access the API and RSS feeds offered by del.icio.us because of cross-domain security restrictions. Because you're probably not one of the few people in the world who can post content directly at del.icio.us, browsers visiting your page won't allow access to that domain.

To partially address this problem, del.icio.us has recently started offering bookmark feeds in JSON: that is, bookmark data encoded directly as a subset of JavaScript syntax. You can read all about it in the help section at this address:

```
http://del.icio.us/help/json
```

But, to jump right in and get a quick screenful of JSON, try fetching this URL:

```
http://del.icio.us/feeds/json/deusx
```

You can also supply an optional limit on the number of bookmarks returned by a JSON feed request with a count parameter:

```
http://del.icio.us/feeds/json/deusx?count=15
```

And you can supply combinations of tags to filter the results:

```
http://del.icio.us/feeds/json/deusx/json+web20
```

As you can see in Listing 4-11, this is a very compact stream of data, and not really meant for visual inspection. However, it's perfect for interpretation by JavaScript. You can directly include this feed on a Web page with a tag in the header like this:

```
<script type="text/javascript"
    src="http://del.icio.us/feeds/json/deusx"></script>
```

When your page loads, this dynamically generated JavaScript code will get requested and interpreted just like any other library you'd include on the page. When that happens, a new object is made available to other scripts on the page under the variable `Delicious.posts`.

There's a JavaScript code sample on the help page showing how to build a list of links, but Listing 4-12 offers another demonstration in a slightly different style. The help page uses strict DOM scripting, while `ch04_json_display.html` here uses a slightly simpler yet quick-and-dirty approach. You can see the results of this code in a browser in Figure 4-5.

Listing 4-11: Sample raw JSON feed from del.icio.us

```
if(typeof(Delicious) == 'undefined') Delicious = {};
Delicious.posts =
[{"u":"http://support.opml.org/2006/02/01#a671","n":"\"How to
install your own server\"","d":"OPML Editor support: OPML
Community Server Howto","t":["frontier","opml","webdev"]},
{"u":"http://www.kempa.com/blog/archives/001047.html","n":"\"Be
fore demolishing the building, the city couldn\'t be bothered
to remove these artifacts. All sorts of historically important
ephemera, knowingly demolished.\"  As if I didn\'t have enough
reasons to despise the Super Bowl and the Mayor","d":
"Kempa.com: Destroying History - Motown Building Razed for
Super Bowl Parking","t":["detroit","morons","motown"]},
{"u":"http://rentzsch.com/suck/stopStopStopHurtingTheInternet",
"n":"\"My God, they've made metal look good.\" ...and with a
bonus quote and link to my link to the IE7 demo.","d":
"rentzsch.com: Stop Stop Stop Hurting the Internet","t":
["msft","msie","vista","gui","safari","apple","webdev"]}]
```

Listing 4-12: ch04_json_display.html

```html
<html>
    <head>
        <title>del.icio.us via JSON</title>

        <script type="text/javascript"
            src="http://del.icio.us/feeds/json/deusx"></script>

        <script type="text/javascript">
            function init() {
                var out = '';

                out += '<ul>';
                for (var i=0; i<Delicious.posts.length; i++) {
                    var post = Delicious.posts[i];
                    out += '<li>';
                    out += '<a href="'+post.u+'">
'+post.d+'</a>';
                    if (post.n) out += '<p>'+post.n+'</p>';
                    out += '</li>';
                }
                out += '</ul>';
```

Listing 4-12 *continued*

```
                document.getElementById('links').innerHTML =
out;
            }
            window.onload = init;
        </script>

    </head>

    <body>
        <h1>del.icio.us links</h1>
        <div id="links">
            Loading links...
        </div>
    </body>

</html>
```

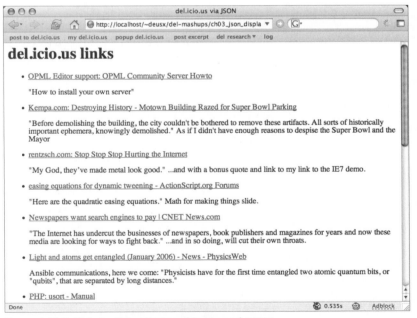

FIGURE 4-5: del.icio.us links displayed by way of JSON

Summary

This chapter provided a deeper look at the various Web API operations del.icio.us makes available to users, as well as a few of the data query services you can use to get at your own bookmarks and links posted by others. These are all just starting points, really, because you can take any one of these avenues for access and expand it into a rich mashup in your own code. You'll see these services come up in use repeatedly throughout the rest of the book.

In the next chapter, you take a bit of a step back from the server side of things and check out what opportunities for tinkering exist in the Web browser side of the mashup equation.

The What and How of Hacks

Because the rest of this book will present more elaborate hacks, it might be a good idea to spend some time exploring just what it means to make one. While this chapter won't give you a complete education, it will provide you with a brief taste of the various formats and technologies employed by hacks and mashups today. You'll see these appear throughout the rest of the book, so the pointers presented here should prepare you with a few leads to chase in digging deeper to understand what you see later on.

What Is a Hack?

So, what exactly is a hack — and what, in particular, makes a del.icio.us hack?

As you are probably already well aware, hacking del.icio.us — at least in the sense used in this book — does not entail cracking servers or login passwords. The hacks presented in this book are more in the spirit of tinkering and making mashups with data and APIs already made available by del.icio.us and other services.

Consider the term "mashup," originally used to describe a style of music in which parts of multiple, often disparate songs are tangled together into something new.

This musical remixing tends to happen regardless of the intentions of the original artists — and almost exclusively without their cooperation. Similarly, technological mashups on the Web began as unauthorized intertwinings of sites into new creations. But increasingly, the creators and owners of Web-based services are getting wise to the benefits of making their data and functionality easy to integrate into third-party constructions.

Remotely scriptable application interfaces and easy-to-parse data formats grease the skids for tinkerers. If you have a sufficiently compelling offering, this sort of openness can potentially increase usage and exposure for everyone involved. Where other sites and services attempt to build user lock-in and "stickiness" to retain people and attention, letting go and making room for experimentation is the way of the mashup.

On the Web Want to read more about musical and Web-based mashups? Wikipedia has an article on each available for your perusal here:

```
http://en.wikipedia.org/wiki/Mashup_(music)
http://en.wikipedia.org/wiki/Mashup_(web_application_hybrid)
```

Each of these should give you some good general starting points for further exploration in either of these topics.

For just a taste of more advanced del.icio.us hacks and mashups, take a look at the figures that follow.

Figure 5-1 shows a TouchGraph-powered graphical analysis of relationships between del.icio.us tags by Alf Eaton. You read more about this in Chapter 6, but for now, consider this a sneak peak at what can be done with alternate presentations of data available from del.icio.us.

In Figure 5-2, you can see Apple's iTunes downloading audio files as a podcast. The podcast itself is actually an RSS feed of MP3s with the `system:media:audio` tag applied. This trick will get more attention in Chapter 6 as well, as an example of how services provided by del.icio.us can be used as a connector or router between technologies.

Finally, Figure 5-3 presents a snapshot from diggdot.us, an aggregator of content from del.icio.us, digg.com, and slashdot.org. This is the most obvious of the three mashups pictured here because it literally smashes together the feeds of information from three sites. Chapter 7 provides a bit more information about this mashup.

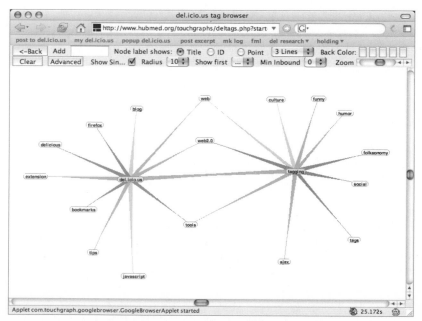

FIGURE 5-1: Using TouchGraph to chart relationships between del.icio.us tags

FIGURE 5-2: Downloading audio in iTunes as a podcast from a del.icio.us tag feed

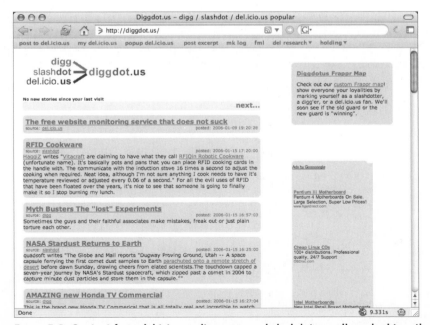

FIGURE 5-3: Content from del.icio.us, digg.com, and slashdot.org all mashed together

What Makes Hacks Possible?

So, before you can really get into making hacks and mashups, you'll need to know a bit about what makes them possible. Mainly, this means remixable APIs and data formats. These come in many forms, so it'll help to see the variety of ways in which these resources are made available — both officially and unofficially.

In terms of formats, those based on XML are some of the friendliest for the purposes of mashups. On the other hand, JSON is a relative newcomer on the scene that offers a bit less markup and a lot more simplicity. In terms of APIs, you'll find plenty of examples offered as XML-RPC, SOAP, and REST services. Each of these has its own style of doing things and tools for using it in your programs.

XML

While not itself a format, XML is a modern construction set for data formats. Short for Extensible Markup Language, XML lays down basic rules for establishing structure and encoding information. This makes it possible to build a lot of base machinery in a generic and reusable way, rather than starting from scratch every time. XML allows developers to provide rich data in a way that's relatively easy to parse and process in programs, yet still somewhat accessible to human eyes during hands-on tinkering.

Although you're very likely to have learned about or encountered XML on the Web already, it's useful to mention it here. By and large, XML is the most popular kind of data you'll encounter in exploring hacks. In particular, most of the API services offered by del.icio.us return data in XML. Check out Listing 5-1 for an example of what a query for recently posted bookmarks looks like.

Listing 5-1: Bookmark postings as XML from the del.icio.us API

```
<?xml version='1.0' standalone='yes'?>
<posts tag="" user="deusx">

    <post href="http://www.andymatuschak.org/pages/sparkle"
          description="Sparkle"
          extended="&quot;Sparkle is a module that developers
can stick in their Cocoa applications (five-step install!) to
get instant self-update functionality.&quot;"
          hash="482dfbc8f679933ce2e1abd57ac478f1"
          tag="osx mac dev programming rss syndication"
          time="2006-01-13T03:24:29Z" />

    <post
href="http://www.earthcode.com/ajax/2005/12/jslog.html"
          description="Earthcode.com: JSLog - Ajax logger"
          extended="&quot;This is a lightweight, self-contained
logging panel which takes the place of alert() boxes for your
AJAX and DHTML applications. It is unobtrusive, easy to use,
and can stay in your code through deployment. &quot;"
```

Listing 5-1 *continued*

```
                    hash="d1f1d040db1989c47e35e195172ee104"
                    tag="js javascript webdev"
                    time="2006-01-12T11:58:57Z" />

        <post href="http://www.physorg.com/news9794.html"
                description="'Doomsday vault' to house world's seeds"
                extended="&quot;Norway is to build a &quot;doomsday
vault&quot; in a mountain close to the North Pole that will
house a vast seed bank to ensure food supplies in the event of
catastrophic climate change, nuclear war or rising sea levels,
New Scientist says.&quot;"
                    hash="14f23cac723ab2c725abbb2b9cfdb8fc"
                    tag="norway globalwarming environment farming"
                    time="2006-01-12T11:55:59Z" />

    </posts>
```

The data in Listing 5-1 describes three bookmarks posted to del.icio.us, including details on the bookmark URLs, titles, descriptions, tags, and posting time, and provides a unique hash ID for each. This format gives you an easy way to grab and process bookmarks with just about any language or platform where XML itself is supported.

 XML is a technology built by the World Wide Web Consortium (or W3C). You can find some pretty high-level starting points at the XML home page:

    www.w3.org/XML/

But again, this page offers very high-level information. You can also get a lot of historical information and more avenues for information at this Wikipedia article:

    http://en.wikipedia.org/wiki/XML

JSON, or JavaScript Object Notation

JSON is a bit of an up-and-coming competitor for XML, at least with regards to Web services and especially when used with browser-based scripting. The name is an abbreviation of **J**ava**S**cript **O**bject **N**otation. And, as the name suggests, JSON is the representation of data using a subset of JavaScript syntax. So, while this format is by definition directly executable as JavaScript code, the limited syntax enables it to be parsed by other languages without completely reinventing the JavaScript wheel — all while remaining a very rich and expressive encoding scheme.

A few new feeds offered by del.icio.us come in JSON flavors, an example of which you can see in Listing 5-2. Compare this style of encoding things with the XML from Listing 5-1.

Listing 5-2: Bookmark postings as a JSON feed from del.icio.us

```
[
    {
        "u":"http://www.andymatuschak.org/pages/sparkle",
        "n":"\"Sparkle is a module that developers can stick in
their Cocoa applications (five-step install!) to get instant
self-update functionality.\"",
        "d":"Sparkle",

"t":["osx","mac","dev","programming","rss","syndication"]
    },
    {
        "u":"http://www.earthcode.com/ajax/2005/12/jslog.html",
        "n":"\"This is a lightweight, self-contained logging
panel which takes the place of alert() boxes for your AJAX and
DHTML applications. It is unobtrusive, easy to use, and can
stay in your code through deployment. \"",
        "d":"Earthcode.com: JSLog - a Lightweight Ajax logger",
        "t":["js","javascript","webdev"]
    },
    {
        "u":"http://www.physorg.com/news9794.html",
        "n":"\"Norway is to build a \"doomsday vault\" in a
mountain close to the North Pole that will house a vast seed
bank to ensure food supplies in the event of catastrophic
climate change, nuclear war or rising sea levels, New Scientist
says.\"",
        "d":"\'Doomsday vault\' to house world\'s seeds",
        "t":["norway","globalwarming","environment","farming"]
    }
]
```

Now, this JSON flavor of del.icio.us data is relatively new, and there are a few things included in the XML not present in Listing 5-2 — such as posting date and unique hash ID. But, this encoding style is much more concise than that of XML. And, for data whose structure is as simple as this, JSON parsers are much more lightweight and easy to use. In fact, in most cases, this data gets transliterated directly into the native array and hash structures of the language you're using to process it.

In many ways, JSON provides much less of an impedance mismatch with modern scripting languages than XML — at the expense of losing the toolset available for processing XML. However, some would say that this is a feature, not a bug.

On the Web

JSON is a data format first proposed and codified by Douglas Crockford. You can read his specification for JSON here:

    www.crockford.com/JSON/

Along with the specification, you can find links to JSON parser and encoders implemented in many popular programming languages, as well as other articles and tutorials.

There's also a Wikipedia article with some useful pointers, located at this URL:

    http://en.wikipedia.org/wiki/JSON

XML-RPC

XML-RPC uses HTTP and XML to perform procedure calls on code living at remote Web servers. Basically, this is the granddaddy of all Web services technologies. XML-RPC provides a specification for building distributed applications in a way that's simple and programming language–neutral. Just about any Web server capable of running CGI programs written in a decently capable scripting language will do. There are libraries and modules for just about every programming environment under the sun, but the technology itself is easy to implement from scratch, should the need arise.

Although you won't find any XML-RPC in the APIs from del.icio.us, one of the most popular uses of XML-RPC is in the Blogger and MetaWeblog APIs offered by most blogging packages.

For example, Listing 5-3 shows some simple Python code that can be used to post a new entry to a blog using the MetaWeblog API. Listing 5-4 shows the XML data generated by `xmlrpclib` in making the request to a WordPress blog installation to perform the procedure call. Listing 5-5 shows the XML sent back in response when a new blog post is successfully created.

Listing 5-3: Python code for posting an entry to a Weblog

```python
#!/usr/bin/env python
import xmlrpclib

URI    = "http://www.example.com/blog/xmlrpc.php"
USER   = "admin"
PASSWD = "your_passwd"
BLOGID = 1

srv = xmlrpclib.ServerProxy(URI, verbose=1)

post = {
    'title'            : 'Hello world!',
    'dateCreated'      : '2005-01-12T08:15:12Z',
    'description'      : 'This is the text of a post',
    'mt_convert_breaks' : False
}

srv.metaWeblog.newPost(BLOGID, USER, PASSWD, post, True)
```

Listing 5-4: XML-RPC request data for a new blog post

```xml
<?xml version='1.0'?>
<methodCall>
  <methodName>metaWeblog.newPost</methodName>
  <params>
    <param><value><int>1</int></value></param>
    <param><value><string>admin</string></value></param>
    <param><value><string>your_password</string></value></param>
    <param>
      <value>
        <struct>
          <member>
            <name>mt_convert_breaks</name>
            <value><boolean>0</boolean></value>
          </member>
          <member>
            <name>dateCreated</name>
            <value><string>2005-01-12T08:15:12Z</string></value>
          </member>
          <member>
            <name>description</name>
            <value><string>This is the text of a
                           post</string></value>
          </member>
          <member>
            <name>title</name>
            <value><string>Hello world!</string></value>
          </member>
        </struct>
      </value>
    </param>
    <param>
      <value><boolean>1</boolean></value>
    </param>
  </params>
</methodCall>
```

Listing 5-5: XML-RPC response data for a new blog post

```xml
<?xml version="1.0" encoding="UTF-8"?>
<methodResponse>
  <params>
    <param>
      <value>
        <boolean>1</boolean>
      </value>
    </param>
  </params>
</methodResponse>
```

The XML from Listing 5-4 is sent to an XML-RPC endpoint via HTTP POST, and the data in Listing 5-5 is sent back as the response body.

Although this XML is pretty verbose, it actually has a lot in common with JSON: It's an attempt to work with structures that closely match common programming environments. XML-RPC provides for data structures such as ordered arrays and hashtable-like structs with named members. You can see a bit of this concept demonstrated in the example code from Listing 5-3.

For the most part, you should never have to process or parse this XML yourself. Instead, the idea is to rely on a module or library to do all the work of encoding and decoding to and from structures in the local language idiom. It's helpful to know what's going on in the raw data for purposes of debugging, but the heavy lifting is usually taken care of for you.

The nice part of XML-RPC is that these remote Web services can be made to look just like local calls to procedures or subroutines in your favorite language — even if the remote service is built using an entirely different set of technologies.

On the Web XML-RPC is a technology first proposed back in the mid-nineties by Dave Winer while at UserLand Software. You can visit the official XML-RPC homepage here:

    www.xmlrpc.com/

You can also find a lot of useful overview and pointers in this Wikipedia article:

    http://en.wikipedia.org/wiki/XML-RPC

SOAP

SOAP stands for Simple Object Access Protocol. Like XML-RPC, it uses XML and HTTP to facilitate remote procedure calls. SOAP is generally the backbone of modern Web services specifications. As such, it packs a lot of documentation and support within development tools and IDEs — but at the cost of additional complexity and necessary infrastructure when compared with its predecessor, XML-RPC.

SOAP provides a highly abstracted and cross-platform approach for connecting distributed pieces of applications together across the Web. Where XML-RPC seeks to provide a rough correspondence between the data structures of various programming languages, SOAP strives for a much greater degree of definition. In XML-RPC, the request and response structures are rather ad hoc and application-dependent. However, in SOAP, facilities exist to nail down the exact data types and structures to be expected in all requests and responses.

This allows SOAP services and clients to be not only platform-independent, but even implementation-independent as well. Because SOAP service definitions can describe every available procedure call in great detail along with all the parameters going in and return structures coming out, these are basically specifications that leave little room for guessing.

Where XML-RPC plays things loose and flexible, SOAP seeks to nail things down and specify everything. Unfortunately, this translates into fairly verbose and human-hostile XML encodings and tool complexity for hands-on tinkering. (So, alas, no code samples here.) But, on the other hand, all this machine-readable description can provide a lot of automated assistance in using SOAP services in development and when using an IDE with auto-completion and drag-and-drop features.

On the Web

SOAP grew out of the original XML-RPC specification to become a complete technology on its own. You can check out the W3C's SOAP home page here:

```
www.w3.org/TR/soap/
```

Another Wikipedia article comes in handy here — check it out at this location:

```
http://en.wikipedia.org/wiki/SOAP
```

REST and Plain Old XML

REST is an acronym for Representational State Transfer. This is a fancy term to describe the construction of distributed Web-based services, in a way intended to build upon the native strengths of HTTP and the Web. This is in contrast to XML-RPC and SOAP, both of which basically treat the Web as a mere transport for remote procedure calls.

In a sense, REST flips remote procedure call–based Web services on their head by focusing on resources and data formats manipulated by a limited set of verbs — such as GET, PUT, POST, and DELETE. This is not entirely unlike the operations available when using SQL queries with relational database tables.

The big idea with REST, however, is that relationships between resources can span the entire Web. Furthermore, the constrained and well-defined set of verbs available allow for the construction of a lot of abstract and reusable architectural building blocks such as Web caches and content filters.

A related approach to REST is called "Plain Old XML," which uses HTTP to shuttle XML documents around in response to GET and POST requests. POX is simpler than XML-RPC and SOAP, and close in spirit to REST. However, this approach doesn't strictly follow the architectural principles of REST. For example, HTTP GET requests may be used to cause modifications or used as remote procedural calls — while in REST, GET requests should simply retrieve data and never directly modify anything.

The API exposed by del.icio.us is more properly identified as a POX-style API. Bookmark deletions and additions are done via HTTP GET requests using URLs with parameters in the query string. Also, most of the operations on the del.icio.us API more closely resemble procedure calls, rather than the REST vision of Web resources.

In any case, both REST- and POX-based Web services generally seek to offer a more tinkerer-friendly approach that uses the natural semantics of HTTP and XML rather than convoluted encodings of native programming language structures tunneled over the Web. On the other hand, REST- and POX-based services demand much more hands-on work and lack greatly in the area of powering the assisted-programming features of Integrated Development Environments.

On the Web The term REST originates in a doctoral dissertation by Roy Fielding, available here:

> www.ics.uci.edu/~fielding/pubs/dissertation/top.htm

This is pretty heady reading, so you might also appreciate this more practical overview of the concepts behind REST:

> www.xfront.com/REST-Web-Services.html

You can also find a lot of discussion surrounding the origins of the term "Plain Old XML" with this Technorati search:

> http://technorati.com/search/%22plain+old+xml%22

Again, here are a couple of Wikipedia articles from which you may get some useful pointers:

> http://en.wikipedia.org/wiki/Representational_State_Transfer
> http://en.wikipedia.org/wiki/Plain_Old_XML

Web Robots and Screen Scrapers

If all else fails, there's always *screen scraping*. Basically, if you can do it yourself in a browser, there's usually a way to automate it by building a Web robot. You can script the same sorts of Web-based interactions performed in a Web browser and scrape useful data out of formats generally intended for human consumption. This is the down-and-dirty approach, dragging the functionality of a site kicking and screaming into the form of a scriptable API.

Keep in mind, however, that when a Web site fails to offer an API, there's often a good reason. If you're lucky, it might simply be that the site owners haven't yet had the chance to implement a scriptable interface. But, it might also be that they purposefully don't *want* to allow auto-mated access: Where an API is offered, it's likely that allowances have been made to provide for the capacity necessary for automated access. Machines can be quite a bit more demanding than humans. So, more advanced functionality might be offered only to human visitors because it's just too resource-exhaustive to offer otherwise.

Thus, on some sites, you can get away with scraping first and asking forgiveness later. But, be aware that some sites are monitored for undesired spiders and scrapers. While routing around these perceived stumbling blocks is fully within the *spirit* of mashups and tinkering, this approach can quite often result in fragile code and accusations of abuse.

Screen Scrapers and del.icio.us

In fact, apropos of the subject of this book, the owners of del.icio.us have explicitly stated that screen scrapers are not welcome. For example, while the API offered by del.icio.us provides a wide range of functionality for querying and manipulating bookmarks, as of this writing much of the recommended functionality remains accessible only via the user interface intended for human consumption. While it's tempting to remedy this lack through scraping and spidering, you could soon be locked out of del.icio.us altogether and find your application broken or banned.

So, to heed the policy at del.icio.us, this book won't spend much time (if any) beyond just acknowledging the possibility and existence of robots and scrapers.

How Are Hacks Made?

On their own, these data formats and APIs don't remix themselves. What you need are some programming languages and environments to act as the glue that pulls everything together. Because we're talking about hacks involving services and sites on the Web, the places where hacks happen generally fall into two categories: client-side scripting in the browser and server-side programming on a Web server.

Hacks and mashups will often involve things that dance across this client/server boundary. But still, this distinction is where you'll need to make mental shifts between technologies and environment characteristics. There are things that are easy to do in one place, and hard or impossible to do in another. And sometimes, there are things that can't be done without the two sides working in tandem.

Browser-Side Scripting

For most makers of mashups, the Web browser is the closest tool at hand. And these days, it just so happens that the modern browser plays host to a surprisingly capable and rich programming environment.

This is in large part thanks to a confluence of browser features that have all started, surprisingly, to actually work together. You'll still find many of the cross-browser issues that have been the traditional bane of Web developers — but some of the technologies and techniques that have been percolating for years have finally reached a sufficient state of maturity and stability where they can be used for interesting things by a large enough segment of the Web browsing populace.

JavaScript

Since its inception in the early 1990s, JavaScript has gained a bad reputation thanks to its use in powering such annoyances as popup ads and status bar message crawls, and generally making your browser twitch. There was also the awkward birth of DHTML, which seemed to hold so much promise yet was so often stymied by its mutually incompatible implementations spawned during the browser wars.

In the intervening years, however, and as the browser wars died down, things have gotten better. DHTML and browser DOM scripting capabilities have improved; cross-browser quirks have been catalogued and workarounds have been built. Furthermore, many more "serious" developers have turned their eyes upon JavaScript itself — having found that despite being called a "toy language," JavaScript offers quite a few of the attractive benefits that have brought popularity to other so-called agile languages.

If you haven't looked into JavaScript lately, here are a few starting points for catching up with the state of the art in browser scripting:

A (Re-)Introduction: `http://simon.incutio.com/archive/2006/03/07/etech`

Douglas Crockford's JS resources: `www.crockford.com/javascript/`

Planet JavaScript: `http://planet.openjsan.org/`

DOM Scripting: The Blog: `http://domscripting.com/blog/`

DOM Scripting Task Force: `http://domscripting.webstandards.org/`

QuirksMode: `www.quirksmode.org/`

Bookmarklets

Bookmarklets are a way to embed active JavaScript code into bookmarks, enabling you to fire off scripts in the context of a page you're currently viewing without needing access to modify the original page source. These can be launched from the bookmarks menu, or a toolbar made available by most browsers — thus offering a way to sort of expand the abilities of your browser on the fly.

These bits of JavaScript code have become valuable in situations such as Web development, enabling you to tweak pieces of the page on the fly before altering the underlying HTML. And as you saw back in Chapter 2, bookmarklets play a key role in making del.icio.us easier to use as part of your daily habits.

You may have caught these the first time, back in Chapter 2. But for your reference in this chapter, check out the following sources on bookmarklets:

Wikipedia article on bookmarklets: `http://en.wikipedia.org/wiki/Bookmarklet`

Bookmarklets home page: `www.bookmarklets.com/`

Tantek's favelets: `http://tantek.com/favelets/`

Web development bookmarklets: `www.squarefree.com/bookmarklets/`

Greasemonkey

The Greasemonkey extension for Mozilla Firefox takes the power of a bookmarklet to a whole new level. Greasemonkey allows the execution of "user scripts" written in JavaScript that can do all the things bookmarklets can, and more.

This extension makes functionality available to user scripts not ordinarily available to bookmarklets — such as cross-domain HTTP requests and local data storage. Also, user scripts execute automatically when pre-determined URL patterns are matched, rather than requiring you to click a button to run the code. This allows you to build up a set of regular customizations to sites you visit, without requiring that you remember to activate them.

 Want to start playing with Greasemonkey and user scripts? You can install the extension from its home page:

        http://greasemonkey.mozdev.org/

And, once you've got the extension installed, you can start exploring available user scripts here:

        http://userscripts.org/

Ajax and XMLHttpRequest

Ajax stands for **A**synchronous **J**avaScript **A**nd **X**ML and is a buzzword that's gained some prominence in the past few years. The primary hype-worthy advance to Web development gained from Ajax is the ability to fetch new data from a Web server via JavaScript.

Before Ajax, once a blob of HTML was delivered to the browser, it was all the developer had to work with from the outside world until a new page could be fetched and entirely reloaded from the Web server. But with Ajax, the transfer of information becomes much more atomic and lightweight, allowing the framework of code and page structure to remain in place while discrete updates are requested and delivered from the Web server.

Combine this with fresh JavaScript and DHTML techniques that have reached a certain tipping point of maturity, and you've got the ability to build responsive Web applications wherein the browser and server connect in a more cooperative relationship than ever before.

The heart of Ajax is the XMLHttpRequest object, first implemented by Microsoft in Internet Explorer 5 for Windows and first used to support the WebDAV-based Outlook Web Access. Later on, the developers of browsers such as Mozilla Firefox and Apple's Safari followed suit by implementing this proprietary object interface themselves. You're not likely to find RFCs or W3C specifications about XMLHttpRequest anytime soon, but this cloning of Microsoft's interface has created an *ad hoc* cross-browser standard for firing HTTP requests from JavaScript.

Taken individually, the components of Ajax are nothing new and have been around in various forms since the early days of Web browsers. However, what's caused the rise of Ajax as a buzzword is the fact that these technologies appear to have all reached a tipping point in compatibility, usage, and availability that has sparked renewed attention.

Jesse James Garrett coined Ajax in early 2005. You can catch his essay posted here:

> www.adaptivepath.com/publications/essays/archives/000385.php

You might also like to visit these Ajax-centric blogs for the latest developments in the world of highly dynamic Web applications:

Ajaxian: www.ajaxian.com/

Ajax Blog: http://ajaxblog.com/

Transforming XML with XSLT

Along with REST and Ajax, XML and XSLT as a pair have seen improvements in terms of browser-side support. As mentioned earlier, XML is the basis of many of the data formats ripe for remixing in hacks and mashups. And when you're dealing with XML, XSLT is one of the most powerful technologies available for processing it.

XSLT stands for **E**xtensible **S**tylesheet **L**anguage **T**ransformations. Expressed as XML itself, XSLT is somewhat like a scripting language that gives you a wide range of tools to navigate the structure of XML documents, extract data, and declare rules to transform from one XML format to another — even converting to text-based formats outside of XML.

Support for XSLT directly in browsers offers a lot of power: Syndication feeds can benefit from XSLT processing instructions obeyed by browsers, allowing the conversion of raw RSS and Atom feeds into human-friendly XHTML on the fly. You could use in-browser XSLT to transform raw Web services output into complete Ajax and XHTML alternative user interfaces based on that data.

 Like XML, XSLT is a technology created by the W3C. You can visit the XSLT home page here:

> www.w3.org/TR/xslt

And as a bonus, take a look here for a quick rundown on styling RSS with XSLT, as mentioned previously:

> http://interglacial.com/~sburke/stuff/pretty_rss.html

Server-Side Scripting

Thanks to maturing JavaScript and HTTP capabilities in browsers, there's a lot of hacking to be done on the client side. But, the Web browser is a sandbox, and eventually you'll run into its boundaries. This is thanks in part to cross-domain access restrictions — an annoyance for the sake of greater PC security — as well as the difficulty or impossibility in using local storage or databases. This is where you'll need to leave the confines of the Web browser and start working on the server side of the equation.

On a Web server, you've got much less restricted access to the full power of the machine. Granted, if you're working on a shared server, you may still have some limits placed upon you. But nonetheless, a server can be a much larger playground than a browser. In addition, desktop PCs are nowadays powerful enough to be used as servers. Or, where fully dedicated network access is unavailable — such as behind a firewall or home router — your desktop PC can at least play host to automated and scheduled tasks involved in your mashups.

One of the easiest ways to get down to work making hacks is with one of the flexible scripting languages available — such as Perl, Python, PHP, and Ruby. Each of these languages is perfectly capable of doing whatever you'd like with all of the API and data formats mentioned earlier in this chapter.

Perl

Perl could be considered the granddaddy of all mashups because it was created as a way to combine the features of venerable UNIX shell tools such as awk, sed, and grep. From the first days when CGI scripts were possible on the Web, Perl was used to write them. So, in the years since, it's only natural that Perl would have amassed quite a bit of support for the sorts of things you'll need to do in building del.icio.us hacks.

In the Comprehensive Perl Archive Network (or CPAN) you'll find plenty of reusable modules available for fetching resources from the Web; parsing HTML and XML; and supporting services made available with XML-RPC, SOAP, and REST interfaces. And once you've gotten your hands on some data within a Perl script, you'll have plenty of power available for transforming that data into something interesting.

 You can find a pretty extensive collection of resources for Perl available here:

```
www.perl.com/
```

In addition, the CPAN is an invaluable resource to Perl programmers. You'll want to check it out at this address:

```
www.cpan.org/
```

PHP

PHP itself actually began as a set of Perl scripts. A few years later, however, it had graduated into a full-blown system of its own, implemented in C. Since then, it has grown, acting as the glue between one library API after another — gaining functions to access databases, networking libraries, XML parsers, and a slew of other modules. For many developers today, PHP has quite handily taken over from Perl as the king of open source Web development. Although Perl is available as a module for installation on Web servers, PHP in this role offers a bit more simplicity in its care and feeding and so has reached a much greater degree of ubiquity.

At the PHP home page, you can find downloads to install the language on your own server, as well as documentation on the language itself. Check it out at this URL:

```
www.php.net/
```

And, like Perl, PHP has a community-maintained code archive available as well. It's called the PHP Extension and Application Repository — or PEAR. You can find lots of useful and reusable code in this archive:

```
http://pear.php.net/
```

Python

Whereas Perl and PHP each bear the marks of incremental improvements from somewhat messy beginnings, Python was intended from the beginning as a language emphasizing clarity and clean extensibility. A bit of a departure from the C-like syntax of other languages, Python code often very closely resembles the pseudo-code provided in textbook examples with its enforced indentation-as-syntax and minimal use of strange punctuation characters. Python also presents a well-developed object-oriented system, with lots of support for dynamic dispatch and reflection.

In terms of Web development, however, Python does not enjoy the same widespread availability and use as PHP and Perl. Instead, with more complex application frameworks like Zope, the Python community seems to have historically aimed for higher architectural goals. This seems to be changing a bit lately, but Python certainly has a long way to go before it catches up with the rest of the Web development pack.

Nonetheless, Python has an extremely rich library of modules available for making mashups. And unlike the installations via CPAN often required with Perl or the rebuilds sometimes demanded by PHP, a surprising number of these modules accompany Python right out of the box. In this regard, Python enthusiasts often say that their favorite language comes with "batteries included."

Python also has a home page, where you can locate installation packages and language documentation:

```
www.python.org/
```

Also, check out the latest developments on Zope, the open source application server and content management server written in Python:

```
www.zope.org/
```

You may also be interested in these up-and-coming Python Web technologies aimed at more lightweight development:

```
http://pythonpaste.org/
http://turbogears.org/
```

Ruby

Ruby was created with succession in mind because the ruby is the birthstone of the month following that of the pearl. Accordingly, Ruby starts by using much of Perl's syntax as a base. But, where Perl's motto is "There's More Than One Way to Do It," the goal of Ruby is to follow the Principle of Least Surprise where a simpler and consistent environment is preferred.

Like Python, Ruby also seeks to provide a much cleaner syntax than other languages. In addition, Ruby is a devotedly object-oriented language, taking after many of the traits of Smalltalk. And finally, Ruby offers a lot of easy facilities for functional programming — such as closures, continuations, and anonymous functions.

Where Ruby has really caught fire, however, is with the meteoric rise in popularity of the Ruby on Rails Web development framework.

One of the main features of Ruby on Rails is the ability to run just a few commands to get up and running with a full-fledged Web application in seconds, complete with database integration and page templates. From there, it's extremely easy for developers to gradually tweak and add code to tailor a generated scaffold into the shape and functionality desired. This sort of "immediate gratification" in Web development, combined with the elegant syntax and agile capabilities of Ruby, has served to greatly extend its presence in Web hosting packages.

 On the Web Ruby was created in Japan, but you can find a home page for English readers here:

```
www.ruby-lang.org/en/
```

Because Ruby on Rails is pretty much the main reason for Ruby's recent explosive growth, here's the location of that project's home:

```
www.rubyonrails.org/
```

Summary

Hacks and mashups on the Web, and involving del.icio.us in particular, all depend on the existence of open data formats and APIs as well as agile and flexible programming languages. Services that offer data exchange in formats based on XML and JSON via XML-RPC, SOAP, REST, and Plain Old XML interfaces can be remixed and turned into new and interesting applications. Rich scripting environments exist both on the client and server sides of the Web, offering lots of possibilities through the use of "glue" languages such as JavaScript, XSLT, Perl, PHP, Python, and Ruby.

This chapter breezed quickly through all the above, which you'll see represented in future chapters and in various combinations. In the next chapter, however, you get to see how del.icio.us itself works, in preparation for exploring hacks.

Tagging Hacks

Tagging is one of the things for which del.icio.us has gained quite a bit of fame. On the surface, it seems like such a simple feature. But, there's enough subtlety in the idea that it has succeeded in coaxing metadata out of people where other approaches in the past have generally failed or yielded lackluster results at best.

For such an unassuming concept, you can find a surprising number of articles and academic papers exploring the benefits of tagging versus other classification methods, as well as proposing conventions by which tagging can be made more descriptive for powerful hacks. This chapter offers a few ways in which you can make tagging more useful, as well as how your tags can be used in hacks with other services and software.

What's the Big Deal About Tagging?

You've already seen references to tagging and tags at various points throughout this book. And, if you've used del.icio.us for any length of time, you've already been exposed to tags and examples of their use. But, up to this point in the book, this feature has largely been treated without much fanfare. On the surface it seems like such a trivial thing: Tagging is free-form classification in a flat namespace using simple word-based descriptors. But this is a subtle idea, and there's so much more to it.

Tags Are Categories That Help Plan Themselves

Tags are kind of like categories in that they're used to group things. But categories tend to be a premeditated sort of thing — that is, one tends to come up with categories ahead of time before amassing a collection. Or, sometimes, a set of categories is invented after the fact, with a careful study and rearrangement of an existing collection into folders or buckets. In either case, there's some intentional planning given to categories.

With tags, however, planning is actually a bit of a hindrance. One of the best ways to tag items is almost akin to word association: Come up with descriptive terms at the time the item is discovered, and throw as many of them at the item as you can think of. After a collection of tagged items accumulates, patterns should emerge from the tags you've used. Certain tags will appear attached to similar items because you likely tend to associate similar words with them, thus forming an ad hoc grouping.

So, instead of carefully constructing the buckets into which items go ahead of time, you attach descriptors to items from which groupings can be inferred in the future. In other words, with tags, the categories help plan themselves. For an example of a developed tag collection, take a look at Figure 6-1.

FIGURE 6-1: Building a personal tagroll on del.icio.us

Tags Can Be Gardened Later

Now, of course, in coming up with the set of tags to attach to any newly discovered item, you probably have a bit of a classification scheme in mind already. Web development bookmarks get `WebDevelopment`, recipes may get `cooking`, and things you want for Christmas may get `alliwantforchristmas`. After awhile, you'll probably remember to reuse these tags for similar items.

Then again, you may later decide `wishlist` is better than `alliwantforchristmas`. The point is that your set of tags is meant to be a fluid, ad hoc, and constantly evolving classification scheme. The set of tools provided by del.icio.us facilitates this fluidity, even giving the ability to rename tags you've used in the past to bring things into line with your changing ideas about how to describe things (as shown in Figure 6-2).

In this way, your tags can be groomed and trimmed like a garden. You should think of your tags as a living and evolving set of descriptors. When deciding on tags to use, you don't need to steadfastly commit to anything up front because you can always tweak things later.

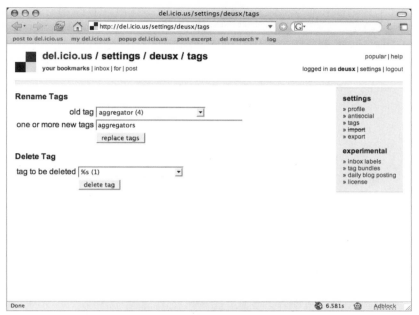

FIGURE 6-2: Renaming and deleting tags on del.icio.us

Tagging Is a Multiplayer Game

Where things get interesting for tagging, however, is when it becomes a multiplayer game. This is, in a nutshell, what the term *folksonomy* is all about.

 You can read more about the coined term "folksonomy" here on the Wikipedia:

    http://en.wikipedia.org/wiki/Folksonomy

In order to share bookmarks, it's very useful to come to agreement on what tags to use for a particular sort of item. Among other motivations, people like to see their bookmarks show up in popular places and queries — so there's a little bit of incentive for using the same tags as everyone else. There's personal value in it, too, because when you start catching on to the popular tagging conventions, you'll also know where to find further interesting things.

Thus, while you may have started using WebDevelopment as a tag, you may later see that the more popular tag is webdev for the sorts of things you're finding. And so you may shift your habits accordingly in the future, and maybe even go so far as to fix your tags from the past. This sort of natural convergence of tags driven by social sharing is what can help imbue tagging with even more value: Rather than relying solely on your own word association in a vacuum, social tagging can help nudge you and everyone toward common terms (as shown in Figure 6-3).

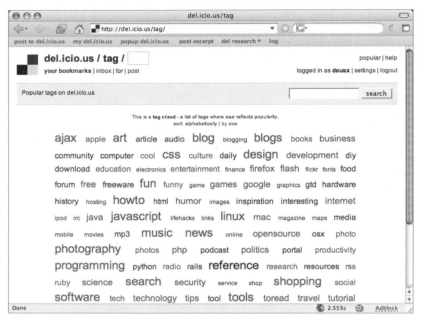

FIGURE 6-3: A cloud of all popular tags used on del.icio.us

Tags Can Be Organized by Analysis

When used as raw data, tags and the items to which they've been attached can be analyzed to discover relationships and patterns inherent in their usage. By working out which tags tend to appear alongside which others, and what tags were used with items posted by many people, you can come up with graphs and maps of the tagging universe.

While not the same thing as parent/child relationships between nested category folders or buckets, analysis can offer some structure to tagging. And, when you're in the act of applying tags to an item, tag analysis can offer suggestions as to which tags may be appropriate to use (see Figure 6-4). Furthermore, while you're browsing around the collection of items, tags found on the items you're currently viewing can be used to suggest further avenues for search (see Figure 6-5).

Although machine intelligence can't completely replace well-trained human librarians, tag analysis can go a long way toward relieving human beings of some of the burden of careful organization and wrangling over taxonomy.

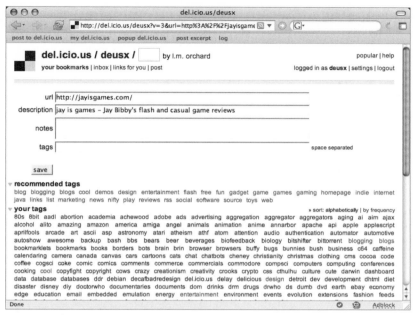

FIGURE 6-4: Tag suggestions offered while posting a bookmark

FIGURE 6-5: Further tags offered while browsing bookmarks by tag

Tagging Has Room for Expansion by Convention

As metadata, tags can convey more information than simple grouping. On del.icio.us, tags can't contain spaces or question marks, but otherwise you can use just about any other combination of letters and numbers and other symbols. Traditionally, sticking with words is your best bet, although some people like to try to form hierarchies by using slashes and other delimiters. This is kind of going against the nature of tagging, but it's allowed nonetheless.

There are also ways of overloading tags with meaning beyond grouping. For instance, there are a few overloaded tag conventions that are officially supported by del.icio.us, such as the `for:deusx` pattern and `system:media:audio`. The first, using a `for:` prefix, allows you to target bookmarks for individual users. The second, automatically applied by the system on bookmarks with URLs ending in `.mp3`, causes RSS feeds filtered on this tag to include `<enclosure>` elements to facilitate podcasting.

Outside of those officially overloaded tags, users have started establishing their own conventions, such as:

- `toread` or `toblog` for facilitating reading or blogging workflow
- The `via:deusx` pattern to indicate from whom a bookmark was first discovered
- `geo:lat` and `geo:long` for use in indicating an associated geographic location

There are limits to what can be done through overloading the grouping semantics of tags, but this can be a very useful way to expand the descriptive capabilities of tagging.

Tagging Is an Imperfect Yet Useful System

Of course, tagging is not a perfect system, and the universe of tags on a system like del.icio.us will always be fuzzy and somewhat weird. Thoughtful taxonomists could, in time, construct a much better and more precise arrangement of things. One person's tags may not directly map onto another's, and depending on the community makeup one conception of a tag may collide with another — take, for example, the rock band named Europe versus the geographical region of Europe. And, of course, the whole multiplayer aspect of the system depends entirely on how willing everyone is to participate, providing good tags for their items and watching what's emergent in the popular tag cloud.

But the point is that even with the imperfection, there's value to tagging. That is, tags actually get used, and they actually help in finding things. If there's some risk of introducing noise with the signal, the benefit is that at least there's some signal. Classification systems in the past have suffered from starvation because of the up-front effort required to use them when balanced with the end-result reward or sense of immediate gratification. They may have produced clean data in the end, but there might be little of it. Social tagging, on the other hand, combines just the right elements of ease-of-use and natural tendencies toward consensus to both be used *and* provide useful and fresh metadata.

So, with no further ado, let's dig into some of the above-mentioned facets of tagging.

Making Tags Useful

Tags are already useful for the purposes of organizing material from the Web, but their organizational function can be augmented by convention and personal practice. Because you can use tags to filter bookmark queries, you can consider tags as a sort of routing system.

Flagging Interesting Pages for Later Reading

If you're an avid infovore, you're likely to accumulate a lot of backlogged reading. This can especially be true if you use a feed reader or news aggregator and if you keep track of some active tag feeds on del.icio.us. One method that del.icio.us users have begun using to cope with this backlog is to build a sort of reading queue by posting bookmarks tagged with `toread` or `read_later`.

When you use the `read_later` tag, you can later visit your collection at this URL:

```
http://del.icio.us/deusx/read_later
```

Remember to swap your user name for *deusx*, and you've got an instant buffer for catching up when you have time. And, if your time is really short, you could use a special-purpose bookmarklet to quickly and automatically post the current page with a `read_later` tag.

Check out this blog post by Cédric Beust discussing just such a bookmarklet.

```
http://beust.com/weblog/archives/000254.html
```

So, with this bookmarklet, you can click on links and stories, maybe skim just enough to know you're interested, and then post it to your reading queue and close the page until later. Once you've had a chance to read pages you've flagged for later, you can then use the normal bookmarklet to post and edit to remove the `read_later` tag — and maybe replace it with some more appropriate tags you can think up after having actually had a chance to read the page.

Marking Links for Later Consideration During Blogging

Another variation to complement the `toread` or `read_later` notion is the `toblog` tag.

You could think of this as a sort of workflow: First, news articles and such go into your reading queue via the `read_later` tag. When later finally arrives, you'll have time to read the bookmarks and revise your tags by reposting. You might decide a few things are worth writing about on your blog, but maybe you haven't got the time or inspiration to do it yet — so just attach a `toblog` tag and continue catching up with the rest of your reading. Then, once you're ready to write some stellar entries for your blog, the `toblog` queue will be waiting for you.

Integrating Routed Bookmarks into Your Browser via Feeds

If you use a browser that has feed-powered bookmark folders as Firefox has with its Live Bookmarks feature, you can pull feeds of your bookmarks tagged as `read_later`, `toread`, or `toblog` right into your bookmark toolbar alongside the other bookmark buttons you probably already use to post bookmarks to del.icio.us. Check out Figure 6-6 for an example of this in action.

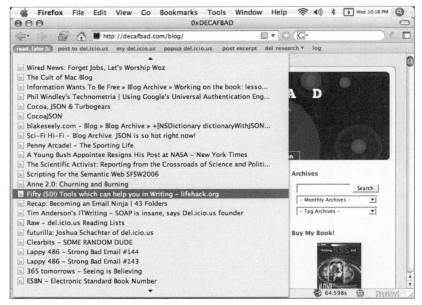

FIGURE 6-6: A tag-filtered feed powering a Live Bookmarks folder in Firefox

In Firefox, you can activate this feature by simply clicking the orange "transmission waves" icon, which appears whenever you're on a page that has an associated feed — and that includes just about every page available on del.icio.us.

Better Social Networking Through Tagging

Tagging is, implicitly, a socially driven system. When it works well, the influence of people upon each other's tagging practices helps form consensual groupings and conventions. However, the operation of these forces is really quite impersonal, forming more of an emergent and non-intentional form of social networking wherein the participants never quite need to communicate directly for the system to work. And, in fact, in many ways this system works well *because* its users don't need to interact personally.

However, as opposed to abstract agents in a system, people are explicitly social creatures in the end. They enjoy direct communication and information exchange, among other pleasantries. So, toward this end, a few conventions have developed to facilitate more intentional social connections. While these tagging conventions don't really serve to turn del.icio.us into a social rendezvous as such, they do allow for a measure of hat tipping and messaging between people.

Giving Credit with the via: and cite: Tag Prefixes

People often tag their links with a user name prefixed by `via:` (e.g., `via:deusx`) to credit from whose collection the bookmark was originally found. Similarly, some prefer to use the `cite:` tag prefix in providing credit to people and sites.

These tags are more of a courtesy or a tip of the hat because there are no official del.icio.us features (as of this writing) that do anything extraordinary with them. As usual, you can filter bookmarks on a `via:` tag, as shown in Figure 6-7, with a URL like the following:

```
http://del.icio.us/tag/via:deusx
```

And, you can get an RSS feed of these bookmarks filtered like so:

```
http://del.icio.us/rss/tag/via:deusx
```

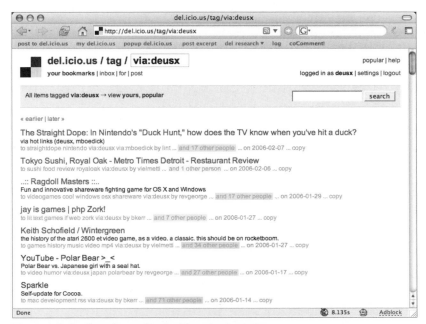

FIGURE 6-7: Bookmarks credited with a via:deusx tag

But, beyond these queries, no support is available to, for example, search for all of the `via:-` prefixed tags in existence in order to do some social network analysis. And because there's no immediate intention to turn del.icio.us into a dating site, such features aren't likely to appear any time soon.

You see, on one hand, if some particular user emerges as a frequent source of the sorts of links you find interesting, it would be interesting to know how to find more. And it can be a nice gesture to give a nod toward the person from whom you first found something new. On the other hand, some might say that introducing an ego-enabling system of credit-gifting is neither helpful nor desirable for the workings of del.icio.us and tagging in general.

In any case, as an unofficial convention, the `via:` tag prefix can prove useful to the extent that everyone's friendly, personal politics are left out of the system, and everyone gets pointed down the scent trails toward more interesting things.

Using the for: tag Prefix for Interpersonal Messaging

You've seen the `for:` tag prefix mentioned before in Chapters 1 and 4, but it's worth checking out one more time in the context of this chapter. In short, when you tag any bookmark with a user name prefixed by `for:` (e.g., `for:deusx`), that bookmark will be targeted for the user's attention. This is a tagging convention whose overloaded meaning has special support from del.icio.us. The tags themselves are hidden from public view, made available by way of a private page and RSS feed that list bookmarks tagged in this way.

The link for this private tag query is available in the page header navigation when you're logged into your account on del.icio.us. You can also find it at a URL like this:

```
http://del.icio.us/for/deusx
```

Just replace *deusx* with your own user name, and you're there. Check out Figure 6-8 for an example of this page.

As you can see, this page doesn't depart much from most other bookmark listings, but each of the links in Figure 6-8 has a hidden `for:deusx` tag attached. The page also has an associated RSS feed — but unlike the feeds made available on many other pages, this one has an authentication key included. This is meant to make it easier to subscribe to your private feed in an aggregator without needing a login. Although it doesn't automatically allow someone access to your del.icio.us account in general, you should keep this URL and its key under wraps.

Analyzing Tag Relationships

One of the benefits of the relative simplicity of tags as data is that they're fairly easy to analyze. Tags can be observed, measured, charted out over time, and indexed in ways that can provide a lot of useful or interesting intelligence. While del.icio.us itself is developing further tagging capabilities, third-party sites can offer additional functionality by way of using the API and data feeds.

FIGURE 6-8: Personally tagged bookmarks on display

Visualize Relationships Between Tags with TouchGraph

When posting a new bookmark or when browsing around through bookmark listings, del.icio.us offers constant suggestions as to what tags are possibly related to what you're posting or viewing. These tags are presented in simple flat lists, however, so you may not be able to get a sense of the structure of tag relationships.

Using the open source graphing package TouchGraph, Alf Eaton offers a Java applet that can graphically map the relationships between tags on del.icio.us. Take a look at it here:

```
http://hublog.hubmed.org/archives/001049.html
```

To use this applet, first supply a tag in the form and submit (e.g., coffee). Very shortly, the applet should load up and initialize, providing you with a spidery spread of tag connections. This applet is dynamic and interactive, so you can click and drag tag nodes around. You can also double-click them to further chase relationships into that tag. As shown in Figure 6-9, you can expand this view into one or more tag clusters to trace deeper connections.

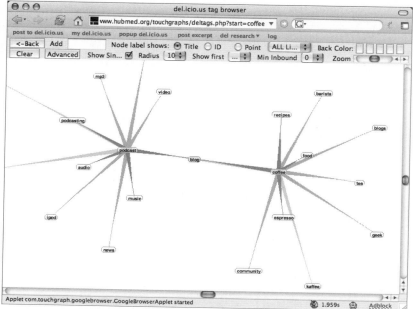

FIGURE 6-9: Graphing the tag relationships that branch out from "coffee" with TouchGraph

Perform Power Searches on Your Tagged Bookmarks

While del.icio.us does allow some facilities for searching and filtering through your bookmarks, there's a lot to be desired from what works at present. There are no easy ways to perform more advanced searches using Boolean logic, or perform union filters with multiple tags, among other things offered by other search engines and databases.

Well, the "del.icio.us illogical interface" offered by Victor Engmark can help fill in some of these gaps. Check it out here:

```
www.10b0.net/delicious/
```

This site asks for your del.icio.us user name and password, which it uses to access the API in order to download and cache a copy of all of your bookmarks in XML. Then, you can perform lots of complex queries on your bookmark collection, as described here:

```
www.10b0.net/delicious/doc.php
```

Figure 6-10 presents the search interface offered by this site, with the results of a search shown in Figure 6-11. If you don't trust your user name and password to this site, however, it looks like all the PHP and XSL source code to run your own copy of this search tool is made available for download. Either way, this interface can provide a lot of power for digging through your collection of bookmarks.

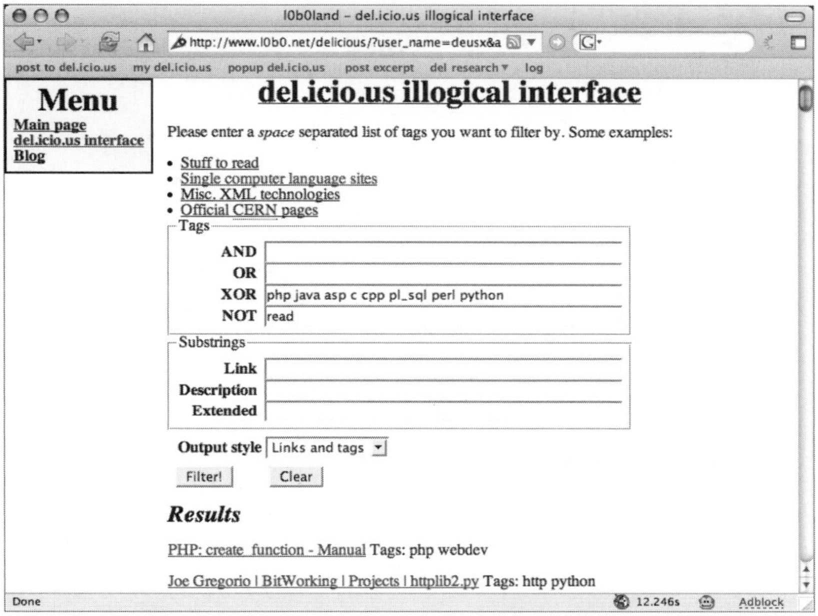

FIGURE 6-10: Preparing to search on a set of programming languages as tags

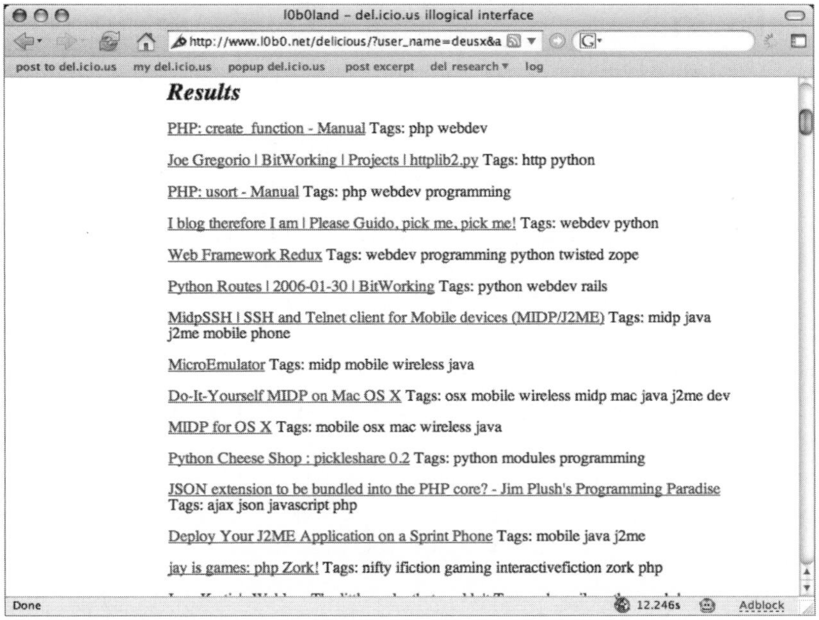

FIGURE 6-11: Results of a combined search for programming tags

Mashup Tags from Many Services

If it's tag-based mashups you're after, here's one involving tags from a few different services arranged right alongside filtered results from del.icio.us:

```
http://tagbert.com/
```

After submitting a tag search on Tagbert, you'll be able to see an aggregated page of results centered on this tag from del.icio.us and a handful of other tag-enabled sites (see Figure 6-12). This sort of service can be useful as more and more services enable tagging services and users share tag meanings across sites.

FIGURE 6-12: Searching for "coffee" with Tagbert

Exploring Tagged Media Files in Bookmarks

These are early days in del.icio.us history with respect to officially enhanced tags. But you've already seen one example with the support of tags using the `for:` prefix. As it turns out, there are a few more such tag patterns — namely the `system:media` and `system:filetype` tag prefixes. To get the straight scoop on this support, check out the help page here:

```
http://del.icio.us/help/mediafiletypes
```

The notion behind media and file type tags is this: When a new bookmark is posted to del.icio.us, the URL is checked against a set of known file extensions. If one of these is found at the end of the URL, the corresponding file type tag is automatically applied. Then, the media tag associated with that file type tag is also applied. Check out Table 6-1 for a quick reference to these mappings.

Table 6-1   File Extensions Mapped to File Type and Media Tags

File Extension	File Type Tag	Media Tag
.mp3	system:filetype:mp3	system:media:audio
.wav	system:filetype:wav	system:media:audio
.mpg	system:filetype:mpg	system:media:video
.mpeg	system:filetype:mpeg	system:media:video
.avi	system:filetype:avi	system:media:video
.wmv	system:filetype:wmv	system:media:video
.mov	system:filetype:mov	system:media:video
.tiff	system:filetype:jpg	system:media:image
.jpeg	system:filetype:jpeg	system:media:image
.gif	system:filetype:gif	system:media:image
.tiff	system:filetype:png	system:media:image
.doc	system:filetype:doc	system:media:document
.pdf	system:filetype:pdf	system:media:document

So, for example, consider this URL posted as a bookmark:

```
http://example.com/music/jingle.mp3
```

The system would automatically attach the tags system:filetype:mp3 and system:media:audio to this bookmark for you. As another example, think about the following link as a bookmark:

```
http://example.com/writing/mybook.doc
```

This bookmark would appear posted with both the tags system:filetype:doc and system:filetype:document attached.

Now, as with any other tags, you can use these as filters in queries to del.icio.us. So, say for example you wanted to find all of the documents posted recently. Try this URL on for size:

```
http://del.icio.us/tag/system:media:document
```

You could also subscribe to this filter as an RSS feed like so:

```
http://del.icio.us/rss/tag/system:media:document
```

Build an Image Gallery from Bookmarked Images

One of the main benefits gained from the automatic application of media and file type tags is the ability to filter for bookmarks of a certain file format. Because there's no way to perform a wildcard search on URLs for file extensions, these tags give you a supported way to do it. So, if you filter on `system:media:image`, you can fairly reasonably assume that the results will all be images of one sort or another — PNGs, GIFs, and JPEGs to be precise.

If you combine a JSON feed filtered on `system:media:image` with a little in-browser JavaScript, you can construct a photo gallery managed through bookmarks on del.icio.us. Check out Listing 6-1 for some basic HTML to kick off building just such a gallery. (You can download all the source code for this chapter from the book's Web site at `www.wiley.com/go/extremetech`.)

Listing 6-1: ch06_bookmark_lightbox.html

```
<html>
    <head>
        <title>Bookmark Lightbox</title>
        <link href="ch06_bookmark_lightbox.css"
              type="text/css" rel="stylesheet" />

        <script src="http://del.icio.us/feeds/json/deusx/system:media:image"
                type="text/javascript"></script>

        <script src="ch06_bookmark_lightbox.js"
                type="text/javascript"></script>
    </head>
    <body>
        <h1>Bookmark Lightbox</h1>
        <ul id="thumbs"></ul>
    </body>
</html>
```

Listing 6-1 offers `ch06_bookmark_lightbox.html`, a shell of an HTML page meant to host the CSS and JavaScript that will build the photo gallery.

A JSON feed from del.icio.us, filtered on `system:media:image`, is included in the page head along with this project's CSS and JS code. As usual, replace `deusx` with your own user name in the JSON URL to access your own bookmarks. In the page body, you'll find an empty `<ul>`

element with an ID of thumbs. This empty list will be dynamically populated with images once the page is loaded.

Next, in Listing 6-2, CSS styles are defined in ch06_bookmark_lightbox.css.

Listing 6-2: ch06_bookmark_lightbox.css

```
body, div, td, li {
    font: 12px arial;
}
#thumbs {
    list-style: none;
    margin: 0;
    padding: 0;
}
#thumbs li {
    float: left;
    width: 23%;
    height: auto;
    padding: 0;
    margin: 0.5ex;
}
img.thumb {
    width: 100%;
    height: auto;
}
```

The styles defined in Listing 6-2 for ch06_bookmark_lightbox.css are entirely up to you for customization, but the intent here is to style the list of thumbnails as a rough grid of floating images. This is quick and dirty, however, because it scales the images down in width and allows the height to vary in order to retain the image's shape and aspect ratio. You may want to improve upon this in your own tinkering, perhaps performing server-side image scaling and working on a better layout.

Finally, in Listing 6-3 you can find the source code for ch06_bookmark_lightbox.js, the main JavaScript code that turns del.icio.us bookmarks into thumbnails on the page.

Listing 6-3: ch06_bookmark_lightbox.js

```
/**
    ch06_bookmark_lightbox.js

    Display bookmarked images in a "lightbox" of thumbnails.
*/
function init() {
```

continued

Listing 6-3 *continued*

```
    // Grab a reference to the container for image thumbnails
    var lbox = document.getElementById('thumbs');

    // Iterate through the list of bookmarks loaded via JSON.
    for (var i=0, post; post=Delicious.posts[i]; i++) {

        // Create a new list element for the thumbnail
        var li = document.createElement('li');

        // Build a link to wrap around the image
        var a = document.createElement('a');
        a.setAttribute('href',  post.u);
        a.setAttribute('title', post.n);

        // Build the actual image from bookmark data
        var img = document.createElement('img');
        img.setAttribute('class', 'thumb');
        img.setAttribute('src',   post.u);
        img.setAttribute('title', post.d);
        img.setAttribute('alt',   post.n);

        // Nest the image in the link.
        a.appendChild(img)

        // Nest the link in the list item.
        li.appendChild(a);

        // Add the list item to the list of thumb.
        lbox.appendChild(li);
    }
}

// Set the main function to run at page load.
window.onload = init;
```

There's not much to the code in Listing 6-3 for `ch06_bookmark_lightbox.js`. It iterates through the bookmarks loaded up via JSON and, for each bookmark found, builds a list item containing an image wrapped in a link. These list items are each added to the initially empty list in the HTML page hosting this JavaScript. The source for the image in each item is taken from the bookmark's URL, as is the target for the link.

When you load this page up in your browser, you'll see a rough grid of scaled down images, as shown in Figure 6-13. Clicking on any of the images will lead to the original full-sized version. Try adding more images as bookmarks, and watch them appear here when you reload the page.

While this isn't a very richly featured photo gallery, it should give you a small taste of how you can use del.icio.us and tagging to facilitate the collection and management of resources beyond plain links to Web pages.

FIGURE 6-13: Viewing bookmarked images as thumbnails

Listen to Streaming Audio Bookmarks with Play Tagger

There's a bit more to the story with these file types beyond simple filtering, and this is particularly true when it comes to system:filetype:mp3. Try visiting this tag filter page, also shown in Figure 6-14:

```
http://del.icio.us/tag/system:filetype:mp3
```

Notice that on this page each of these links has a small, square "play" button next to it. If you click one of these buttons and all is well, the audio link itself will start to stream from the server and play in your browser. This feature is called Play Tagger, and you can read more about it here:

```
http://del.icio.us/help/playtagger
```

What this feature does, in short, is dynamically insert embedded streaming player buttons in front of all links on a page whose URLs end with .mp3. You'll find these players appearing on all del.icio.us pages where MP3s are bookmarked.

As a very cool bonus feature, the JavaScript code that powers Play Tagger is not restricted for use on just the pages at del.icio.us. If you'd like to enable these MP3 buttons on your own site, just drop the following JavaScript include into your HTML:

```
<script type="text/javascript" src="http://del.icio.us/js/
playtagger"></script>
```

This included JavaScript code will unobtrusively register itself to be run at page load, wiring up every MP3 link on the page with play buttons. In addition, if you check out the help page, you can get a browser bookmarklet that will inject Play Tagger audio players into any page on the Web.

FIGURE 6-14: Bookmarks tagged with system:filetype:mp3 featuring Play Tagger buttons

Podcasting Audio and Video Via Bookmarks

But wait, there's still more to this media thing on del.icio.us — check out the following tag-filtered RSS feed:

```
http://del.icio.us/rss/tag/system:media:audio
```

If you check out the raw data of this feed, you'll see an RSS 2.0 feed something like what's shown in Listing 6-4. But wait a minute — didn't Chapter 4 show that del.icio.us served up RSS 1.0 feeds?

Well, that's true in the general case, but look more closely at this feed: Not only has it changed feed formats when serving up the `system:media:audio` tag filter, it's also gained `<enclosure>` elements pointing at the audio file URLs. You'll find that this same feature applies to the `system:media:video` tag as well. This means that media bookmarks filtered on `system:media:audio` and `system:media:video` are available as podcast feeds.

In a nutshell, podcasting is a way to use RSS feeds to subscribe to scheduled downloads of audio and video media, which revolves around the `<enclosure>` tag. You might view textual stories in a news aggregator fed by RSS feeds, but podcasting uses new items found in RSS feeds to trigger the acquisition of media files. Special-purpose feed aggregators that do this tend to be referred to as "podcatchers" or "podcast tuners."

 Want to learn more about podcasting and podcast feeds in general? Consult the Wikipedia:

```
http://en.wikipedia.org/wiki/Podcasting
```

Listing 6-4: Example RSS 2.0 feed with enclosures from del.icio.us

```xml
<?xml version="1.0" encoding="UTF-8"?>

<rss version="2.0"
xmlns:blogChannel="http://backend.userland.com/blogChannelModule">

<channel>
<title>del.icio.us/tag/system:media:audio</title>
<link>http://del.icio.us/tag/system:media:audio</link>
<description></description>

<item>
<title>MacTips #5 - SMS Messaging</title>
<link>http://www.think-mac.net/blog/tips/MacTips%20%235%20-
%20SMS%20Messaging.mp3</link>
<enclosure url="http://www.think-mac.net/blog/tips/MacTips%20%235%20-
%20SMS%20Messaging.mp3" type="audio/mpeg" />
</item>

<item>
<title>War of the Worlds - Orson Welles Radio Broadcast (1938)</title>
<link>http://radio.indymedia.org/uploads/waroftheworlds_1938-10-
30.mp3</link>
<enclosure
url="http://radio.indymedia.org/uploads/waroftheworlds_1938-10-30.mp3"
type="audio/mpeg" />
</item>

<item>
<title>EP037_Craphound.mp3 (audio/mpeg Object)</title>
<link>http://escapepod.podlot.net/EP037_Craphound.mp3</link>
<enclosure url="http://escapepod.podlot.net/EP037_Craphound.mp3"
type="audio/mpeg" />
</item>

</channel>
</rss>
```

Subscribe to del.icio.us Podcast Feeds with the Juice Receiver

One of the earliest cross-platform podcast receivers is nowadays called Juice. This is an open source project, available for download here:

```
http://juicereceiver.sourceforge.net/index.php
```

You can use Juice to subscribe to the podcast feeds available through del.icio.us; it allows you to automatically receive new media files posted as bookmarks. Grab a copy of this program and install it — although you'll probably want to read up on the details at the project site, there's not much to it. Once the program's installed, try adding a podcast subscription by clicking the big green "+" button. You should see a popup dialog box like the one shown in Figure 6-15. The subscription will appear in the main window (see Figure 6-16) and podcast attachments should shortly begin downloading (see Figure 6-17).

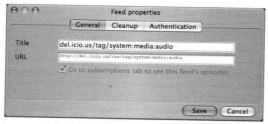

FIGURE 6-15: Adding a new podcast feed subscription in Juice

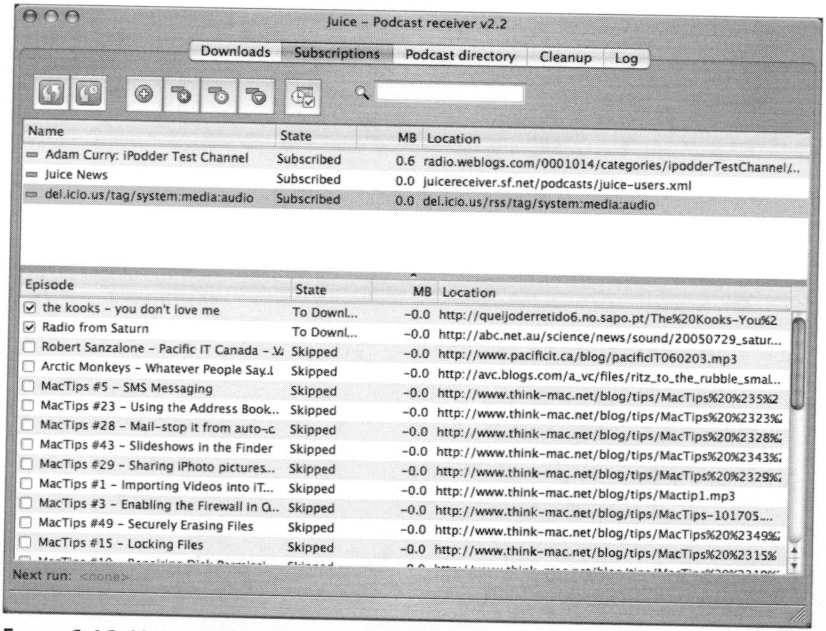

FIGURE 6-16: Main window listing subscriptions in Juice

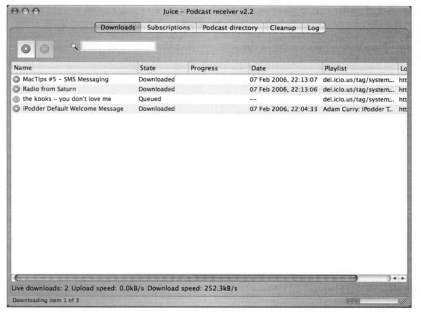

FIGURE 6-17: Downloading new podcast enclosures in Juice

For subscriptions, here are a few useful feed suggestions:

- For a firehose of all the latest audio, try this feed:

  ```
  http://del.icio.us/rss/tag/system:media:audio
  ```

- Want to hear musical mashups? Try this feed:

  ```
  http://del.icio.us/rss/tag/system:media:audio+mashup
  ```

- Check out some of the latest popular video bookmarks with this feed:

  ```
  http://del.icio.us/rss/popular/system:media:video
  ```

- Here's a feed that often delivers a lot of movie trailers:

  ```
  http://del.icio.us/tag/system:media:video+trailer
  ```

Try checking out different combinations of media tags and more mundane tags to refine your feed selection. The results here can be pretty random and sometimes even obscene — so be forewarned. But, with the right application of tag filters, or restricting your media subscription to certain users, you can keep yourself supplied with some pretty entertaining material.

Subscribe to del.icio.us Podcast Feeds in iTunes

If you're a fan of Apple's iTunes and maybe even own an iPod, you've got another option for podcatching at your fingertips. And the nice thing about using iTunes and an iPod for subscribing to podcasts is that it's an integrated solution — media downloaded from podcast feeds in iTunes can be automatically synched up to your iPod without much effort. This can be done with Juice and a different portable media device, but the process may not be quite as smooth.

On the Web   You can find out more about the podcasting features built into iTunes here:

```
www.apple.com/itunes/podcasts/
```

To subscribe to a podcast with iTunes, you'll first need version 4.9 or later — as of this writing, the latest version is 6.0.1, so this shouldn't be a problem. Once you're sure you have the right version, look for "Subscribe to Podcast" under the Advanced menu. Once you select this menu item, you'll see a dialog box like the one shown in Figure 6-18. Enter the URL to a del.icio.us media feed here, and you should shortly see the subscription and download progress appear, as in Figure 6-19.

FIGURE **6-18: Adding a new podcast feed subscription in iTunes**

FIGURE **6-19: Main window listing subscriptions and downloading podcasts in iTunes**

If you have an iPod attached, you can open up your preferences and, as shown in Figure 6-20, you should find a podcasts tab in the iPod settings. Here you can control the synching of podcasts downloaded by iTunes, whether you'd like everything to make it to the iPod or whether you'd like to be more selective. You can also control preferences here as to how long downloaded podcasts should stick around — these tend to be large files, so you may want to allow iTunes to toss them out after a while if you haven't had a chance to listen to or view them.

FIGURE 6-20: iPod preferences for podcast management in iTunes

Bookmarking the Real World with Geotagging

Geotagging is an example of the use of tags imbued with additional meaning, although these are not formally supported by del.icio.us itself. Instead, where del.icio.us users follow geotagging conventions, third-party programs and scripts have the opportunity to harvest useful geographical information from tags.

 To read more about geotagging and further geographical metadata adventures, check out the geobloggers here:

```
http://geobloggers.blogspot.com/
```

So in short, applying the geotagging convention involves three tags:

- `geotagged` — This tag indicates that this item has had geotagging applied.

- `geo:lat=###` — This tag specifies a latitude of a geographical location, where `###` is replaced by the actual value.

- `geo:long=###` — This tag specifies a longitude of a geographical location, where `###` is replaced by the actual value.

The first tag of the set, geotagged, allows for easy filtering on all items on which geotagging has been applied because there's no way to perform partial-tag searches at present to dig items associated with the other two tag prefixes, `geo:lat` and `geo:long`.

Composing Geotagged Bookmarks

Say, for example, that you wanted to collect some bookmarks of good places to eat. One of our favorite places for quick and tasty take-out is Zumba Mexican Grille in Royal Oak, Michigan. It so happens that they have a Web page, including a street address, which you can check out here and in Figure 6-21:

```
www.zumbagrille.com/contact.html
```

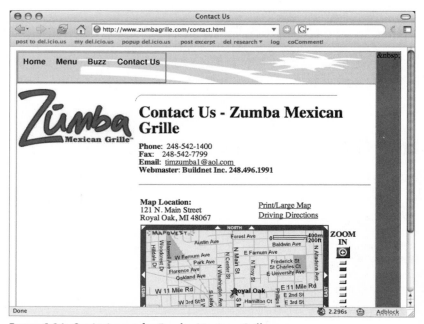

FIGURE 6-21: Contact page for Zumba Mexican Grille

So now you have both a Web and a real-world location for Zumba Mexican Grille. However, you need to convert this address into latitude and longitude coordinates. For this, you'll need a service that can do geocoding for you. Check out this free service available for use with addresses in the United States:

```
http://geocoder.us/
```

Using `geocoder.us`, you can enter just about any address information to get geographical coordinates in return (see Figure 6-22). Now, with both a Web address and proper geographical coordinates, you're ready to post a geotagged bookmark. In this example, the tags to be used are the following:

- `geotagged`
- `geo:lat=42.490049`
- `geo:long=-83.144301`

You can attach these three tags along any other combination of tags you like — with the exception of repeated geotags because that's likely not to make much sense. Check out Figure 6-23 for a geotagged bookmark posting in action.

Try this a few times, digging up the addresses and home pages for more businesses in your area. Find your house too, if you like — although that might be a geotagged bookmark you want to keep to yourself. In the end, you should have a number of locations in your collection, available for filtering on `geotagged` (see Figure 6-24).

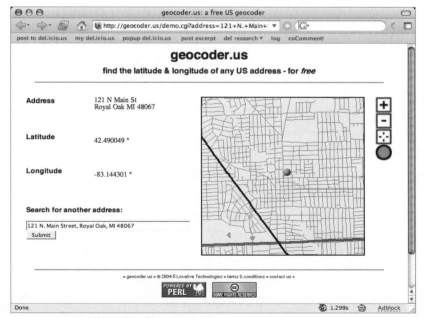

FIGURE 6-22: Converting an address to latitude and longitude

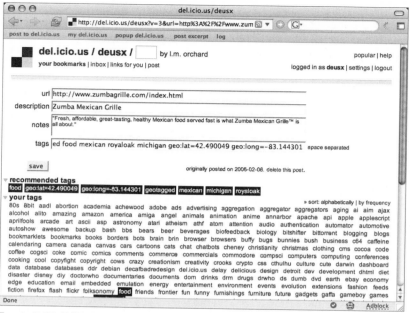

FIGURE 6-23: Editing a geotagged bookmark

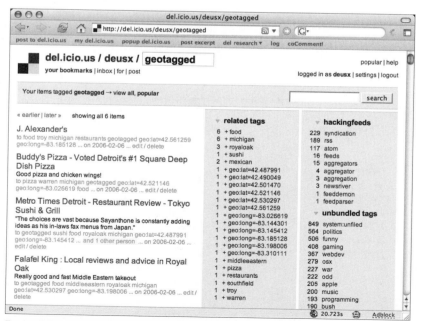

FIGURE 6-24: Viewing a collection of geotagged bookmarks

Visualize Geotagged Bookmarks Using Google Maps

Having geographical information attached to your bookmarks may seem interesting from an abstract perspective, but there might not seem to be much use to this data unless you can see it visualized on a map. Well, one way to do this is via the JavaScript API offered by Google Maps. Using this API in conjunction with a del.icio.us JSON feed, you can cobble together glue code capable of bringing visual life to your geotagged bookmarks as icon markers placed on a real-world map.

JSON feeds offered by del.icio.us were explained back in Chapter 4. However, unless you're already well acquainted with the Google Maps API, you might want to check out the documentation here:

```
www.google.com/apis/maps/
```

As you'll soon discover from the documentation, you're required to sign up for a Google Maps API key here:

```
www.google.com/apis/maps/signup.html
```

This key is assigned by account and URL, so you'll need both to have signed up for a Google Account and know the address where you can host an HTML page. The key is good for all pages below a certain directory, so you can include your whole site under the key if you like.

Once acquired, this key will be included in a URL similar to this:

```
http://maps.google.com/maps?file=api&v=1&key=ABGJDISAAAj8s98...
```

This URL is intended as a JavaScript include for use on an HTML page. With that in mind, check out Listing 6-5 for the source of ch06_gmaps_geotags.html.

Listing 6-5: ch06_gmaps_geotags.html

```html
<html>
    <head>
        <title>Bookmarks of Good Eats!</title>

        <script src="http://maps.google.com/maps?file=api&v=1&key=XXXXX"
                type="text/javascript"></script>

        <script src="http://del.icio.us/feeds/json/deusx/geotagged"
                type="text/javascript"></script>

        <link href="ch06_gmaps_geotags.css"
              type="text/css" rel="stylesheet" />
```

continued

Listing 6-5 *continued*

```
            <script src="ch06_gmaps_geotags.js"
                    type="text/javascript"></script>

    </head>
    <body>
        <h1>Bookmarks of Good Eats!</h1>
        <div id="map"></div>
        <ul id="legend"></ul>
    </body>
</html>
```

In Listing 6-5 is a barebones HTML page that will serve as the launch pad for mapping geo-tagged del.icio.us bookmarks. Notice that one of the first things appearing in the <head> of this page is a JavaScript include using the Google Maps API key address. You'll want to supply your own here, or else you'll receive a few JavaScript alerts when you try to load up this page.

Next in the page is a reference to a JSON feed of my bookmarks filtered by geotagged. This will pull in all of the bookmarks I've posted that include geographical metadata. Swap *deusx* for your own user name to base this on your own collection. The next two elements in the page header make reference to CSS and JS code, which you'll see defined very shortly.

Finally, the <body> of this page simply includes a title, a <div> with an ID of map, and an unordered list with an ID of "legend." The latter two elements are empty for now, but they will soon be filled with content on-the-fly via JavaScript.

Listing 6-6 offers the CSS included for this page as a reference to ch06_gmaps_geotags.css.

Listing 6-6: ch06_gmaps_geotags.css

```
body, div, td, li {
    font: 12px arial;
}
#map {
    width: 500px;
    height: 200px;
    border: 2px solid #000;
}
.note {
    width: 25ex;
}
ul#legend {
    list-style: none;
}
```

Listing 6-6 *continued*

```css
ul#legend li {
    clear: both;
}
ul#legend li img {
    float: left;
    padding-right: 2ex;
}
```

Listing 6-6 provides a simple set of styles in CSS for use in customizing this page — feel free to tweak them if you like. The onscreen size of the Google Map is determined by the `#map` rule, and the `.note` rule will influence the size of info bubbles displayed within the map. The rest of the styles help in formatting a legend of locations that will be built along with the map.

Now, let's get into the meat of this project with the start of `ch06_gmaps_geotags.js` in Listing 6-7.

Listing 6-7: ch06_gmaps_geotags.js (Part 1 of 8)

```javascript
/**
    ch06_gmaps_geotags.js

    Build map markers from geotagged bookmarks.
*/

// http://geocoder.us/
var HOME = {
    title: "Home Sweet Home!",
    url:   "http://decafbad.com",
    lat:    42.528458,
    long:  -83.152184,
    zoom:   6
};

var BASE_ICON, ICON_CNT;
```

The JavaScript in Listing 6-7 begins with a descriptive comment and constructs a constant with some geographic data. This record will be used to center the map, so this may be a good spot to supply details about your home address. Or, you might want to pick a spot somewhere near the center of other bookmarked locations you've collected. The properties of this object will be used as a pattern throughout the rest of this code to define markers, and they are as follows:

- `title`: The title of the marker

- `url`: A browsable URL associated with the location

- `lat`: Latitude of the location

- `long`: Longitude of the location

- `zoom`: A zoom level preferred for viewing this location, really used only with the home location.

The other two constants defined are `BASE_ICON` and `ICON_CNT`, both of which will come in handy when building markers and legend entries shortly. Next, let's get into the initialization section in Listing 6-8.

Listing 6-8: ch06_gmaps_geotags.js (Part 2 of 8)

```
/**
    Initialize the map, icon assets, and add the markers.
*/
function init() {
    var map     = initMap();
    BASE_ICON = initBaseIcon();
    ICON_CNT  = 0;
    addMarker(map, HOME);
    addPostPoints(map, Delicious.posts);
}
window.onload = init;
```

The `init()` function is defined in Listing 6-8, along with its registration as the page's `onload` event handler. This function will thus be called once the page has finished loading. The actions performed here are pretty straightforward:

- The Google Map is initialized on the page using `initMap()`.

- A template marker icon is initialized via `initBaseIcon()`.

- The count of marker icons used so far is set to zero.

- A marker for the home location is added to the map with `addMarker()`.

- Markers for bookmarks in the JSON feed are added with `addPostPoints()`.

Moving forward to Listing 6-9, you can find the implementation of `initMap()`.

Listing 6-9: ch06_gmaps_geotags.js (Part 3 of 8)

```
/**
    Initialize the Google Map instance, add appropriate
    controls.
*/
```

Listing 6-9 *continued*

```
function initMap() {
    var map   = new GMap(document.getElementById("map"));

    map.addControl(new GSmallZoomControl());
    map.addControl(new GMapTypeControl());

    var point = new GPoint(HOME.long, HOME.lat);
    map.centerAndZoom(point, HOME.zoom);
    return map;
}
```

The function initMap() is defined in Listing 6-9. It first creates a new GMap object instance anchored on the <div> element identified as map, after which map user interface controls are added. Finally, the map is zoomed and centered on the location defined as HOME and the map object is returned.

Listing 6-10 presents the implementation of the initBaseIcon() function.

Listing 6-10: ch06_gmaps_geotags.js (Part 4 of 8)

```
/**
    Prepare a base icon on which all other markers' icons
    will be based.
*/
function initBaseIcon() {
    icon = new GIcon();
    icon.shadow = "http://www.google.com/mapfiles/shadow50.tiff";
    icon.iconSize        = new GSize(20, 34);
    icon.shadowSize      = new GSize(37, 34);
    icon.iconAnchor      = new GPoint(9, 34);
    icon.infoWindowAnchor = new GPoint(9, 2);
    icon.infoShadowAnchor = new GPoint(18, 25);
    return icon;
}
```

In Listing 6-10, the initBaseIcon() function is pretty basic and mostly lifted straight from the Google Maps API documentation: It defines a set of basic properties for a map marker icon useful for customization later on.

Now, next up in Listing 6-11, we get to the geotagging meat of this project with the implementation of addPostPoints().

Listing 6-11: ch06_gmaps_geotags.js (Part 5 of 8)

```
/**
    Walk through del.icio.us bookmark posts made available
    via JSON.  Find geotagged bookmarks and attempt to
    extract the details to build a map marker from the tags.
*/
function addPostPoints(map, posts) {

    // Iterate through all the available bookmark posts.
    for (var i=0, post; post=posts[i]; i++) {

        // Prepare an empty data record.
        var data = {};

        // Extract the bookmark title and URL.
        data.title = post.d;
        data.url   = post.u;

        // Start off with the assumption that this is not
        // a geotagged bookmark.
        var is_geotagged = false;

        // Iterate through all the tags attached to this post.
        for (var j=0, tag; tag=post.t[j]; j++) {

            // If this bookmark is geotagged, flip the flag.
            if (tag == 'geotagged') is_geotagged = true;

            // Look for property value delimiter, otherwise
            // skip property tag handling.
            var eq_pos = tag.indexOf('=');
            if (eq_pos == -1) continue;

            // Look for geo:lat=XXX property
            if (tag.indexOf('geo:lat') == 0)
                data.lat = tag.substring(eq_pos+1);

            // Look for geo:long=XXX property
            if (tag.indexOf('geo:long') == 0)
                data.long = tag.substring(eq_pos+1);
        }

        // If this bookmark was geotagged, add a new marker.
        if (is_geotagged) addMarker(map, data);
    }
}
```

The code for addPostPoints() in Listing 6-11 iterates through all of the given bookmark posts supplied via JSON. For each of these, the title and URL are extracted into a data structure similar to the one seen in Listing 6-7 in the definition of HOME.

Next, it's time to process the bookmark's tags. Only those posts with geotagged attached are interesting to this program, so that's the first thing to be checked. If this tag is found, a flag is set. After that, an attempt is made to locate both the geo:lat and geo:long tags and to extract their values into the location data structure under construction for this bookmark.

If, after processing all the tags, it turns out that this was indeed a geotagged bookmark, the location data collected is used to add a new marker to the map using addMarker().

Speaking of addMarker(), Listing 6-12 offers its implementation.

Listing 6-12: ch06_gmaps_geotags.js (Part 6 of 8)

```
/**
    Given a map and a data record, construct a new marker
    for placement on the map.  In addition, add it to the
    map's legend.
*/
function addMarker(map, data) {

    // Create a new icon using the next lettered image.
    var idx    = (ICON_CNT++);
    var letter = String.fromCharCode("A".charCodeAt(0) + idx);
    var icon   = new GIcon(BASE_ICON);
    icon.image = "http://www.google.com/mapfiles/marker" +
        letter + ".tiff";

    // Add this icon and bookmark to the legend.
    addToLegend(data, icon);

    // Construct the location point and marker object.
    var point  = new GPoint(data.long, data.lat);
    var marker = new GMarker(point, icon);

    // If there is a title for this marker, hook up an
    // on-click info bubble for it.
    if (data.title) {
        var ele = createBubbleContents(data);
        GEvent.addListener(marker, 'click', function () {
            marker.openInfoWindow(ele);
        });
    }

    // Add the marker to the map and return.
    map.addOverlay(marker);
    return marker;
}
```

The first thing done in Listing 6-12's definition of addMarker() is to come up with a unique icon to use for this new marker. A counter in the global variable ICON_CNT is used to derive an image URL from a set of icons lettered A to Z, provided by Google. Because ICON_CNT is incremented with each call to this function, every marker added to the map will receive a new letter icon in sequence. Notice that the new icon is built using the BASE_ICON initialized earlier via initBaseIcon().

With an icon built, a new entry is added to the map legend with addToLegend(). After this, a GPoint object is constructed using the location data, which in turn is used to build a new GMarker object. Then, if the location data includes a title, a special on-click event handler is wired up to the marker that will cause an info bubble containing the marker's title to appear. The HTML for this info bubble is built using createBubbleContents(). Then, once everything is in place, this marker is added to the map using the addOverlay() method.

The next missing blank to be filled is the definition of addToLegend() in Listing 6-13.

Listing 6-13: ch06_gmaps_geotags.js (Part 7 of 8)

```
/**
    Construct and insert the elements necessary to add a marker
    to the map legend.
*/
function addToLegend(data, icon) {
    var img = document.createElement('img');
    img.setAttribute('src', icon.image);

    var text = document.createTextNode(' '+data.title);

    var link = document.createElement('a');
    link.setAttribute('href', data.url);
    link.appendChild(text);

    var item = document.createElement('li');
    item.appendChild(img);
    item.appendChild(link);

    var legend = document.getElementById('legend');
    legend.appendChild(item);
}
```

In Listing 6-13, the addToLegend() function serves to build the nested DOM elements required for an icon image and bookmark link contained within a list item element. This list item is added to the unordered list on the page with an ID of legend. This will help maintain a straightforward legend of markers as they're added to the map.

Finally, there's one last function to be defined — namely, `createBubbleContents()` in Listing 6-14.

Listing 6-14: ch06_gmaps_geotags.js (Part 8 of 8)

```
/**
    Construct and return the DOM elements necessary to
    populate a marker's pop-up info bubble.
*/
function createBubbleContents(data) {
    var div = document.createElement('div');
    div.setAttribute('class', 'note');

    var link = document.createElement('a');
    link.setAttribute('href', data.url);

    var text = document.createTextNode(data.title);
    link.appendChild(text);

    div.appendChild(link);
    return div;
}
```

Similar to `addToLegend()`, the definition of `createBubbleContents()` in Listing 6-14 uses DOM methods to construct the elements needed to present a bookmark link within a Google Maps popup info bubble.

With this last piece in place, it's time to fire up your browser and try things out. Again, make sure you've got your Google Maps API key pasted into the HTML and that the HTML itself is in the appropriate location as used when you acquired the key.

If everything goes well, you should see a map similar to Figure 6-25. Here, you can see a few of our favorite area restaurants and recommendations for tasty take-out food. Below the map, you should see a legend of icons mirroring the map. And, if you click on any of the markers within the map, you should see an info window pop up.

Once you've got this working, try adding more geotagged bookmarks to your account. Upon reloading the map, you should see them appear with new markers as long as your zoom level and map size include them in the viewing area. Also, try tweaking the JSON include URL with further tags on which to filter — you can subdivide your bookmarked locations into even more focused groups.

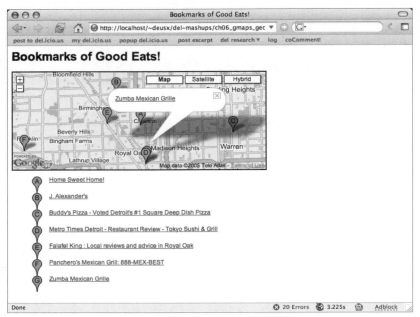

FIGURE 6-25: Bookmarks of good places to eat presented with a Google Map

Summary

In this chapter, you've been given a look at the ways in which tags can be used to organize, annotate, enrich, and filter bookmarks on del.icio.us. The tips and examples here have really just scratched the surface of all that's possible from tagging, so I hope this has given you some food for thought in future tinkering and play.

Coming up in the next chapter, you're going to take a look at how del.icio.us can be mashed up with other sites to intermingle data and augment the services of those sites.

Mashups and Enhancements

Although del.icio.us has a lot to offer, there's still room for improvement. However, thanks to the API methods and XML feeds provided by del.icio.us, you need not wait for the team managing the service to get around to implementing your favorite feature. And, as you'll find in this chapter, a lot of tinkerers are taking advantage of this openness to develop their own extensions to the service — including new ways to visualize bookmarks and tag data, and new ways to use or integrate del.icio.us into other sites or services.

This chapter presents a few of the mashups and enhancements that have been built around del.icio.us and social bookmarking. And, in the latter half of the chapter, you'll see how to build your own.

Tweaking the User Interface

The user interface provided by del.icio.us is very clean and simple, but some tinkerers have their own ideas for how this could be improved. This section of the chapter presents a few of the ways in which others have recast del.icio.us in terms of presentation and general functionality.

Keep Track of Your Favorite Bookmarks with Delancey

Rather than providing a complete replacement for del.icio.us, Delancey offers an alternative user interface for viewing and searching your collected bookmarks. This interface offers a highly responsive tag search field, as well as a few enhancements to make actually using your bookmarks more convenient. Check out Delancey at this address:

```
http://delancey.unto.net
```

You can see a few of the features of Delancey in Figure 7-1. This includes a tag search field with auto-completion drawn from your own collection of tags, as well as the multi-column layout of bookmark links. The idea here is to help make your del.icio.us bookmarks more personally useful and accessible on a daily basis.

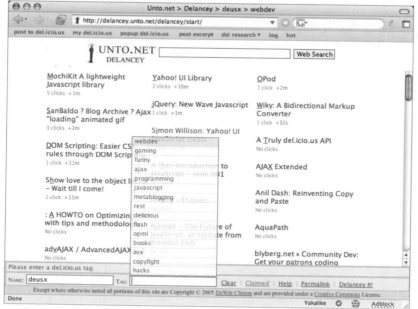

FIGURE 7-1: Viewing bookmarks in Delancey

Through a "claim" feature, you can tie Delancey to your own del.icio.us account. This is done in an interesting way that doesn't require you to share your del.icio.us password: By allowing Delancey to walk you through posting a special bookmark — which can be later deleted — the service can verify that you are indeed the owner of a given account. Delancey will notice that you've posted the bookmark and then allow you to assign a password for this user name — ideally one that's different than what you use on del.icio.us.

For a claimed collection, Delancey tracks your bookmark usage history. You'll be able to see how long it has been since last you visited a bookmark, as well as how many times you've clicked it. The collection is sorted in order of most used, thus naturally arranging itself according to your habits. The interesting thing to note is that Delancey keeps a regularly updated cache of your del.icio.us bookmarks, on top of which it overlays the usage history from its own database. Claiming your collection allows this database overlay to occur, but be aware that this data is stored in Delancey, not at del.icio.us.

In addition to the usage history tracking, you can preload Delancey with a particular tag and bookmark that view — and there's a Permalink navigation item in the page footer with a URL that changes appropriately every time you choose a new tag. This can come in handy when you attach a common tag to all of the bookmarks you want within quick reach — say, startpage or delancey. This, along with a Google search box at the top of the page, can make Delancey a very useful browser start page — you could use the permalink feature to grab the view of that tag and use that in your browser preferences.

Revising the User Interface with del.icio.us direc.tor

Like Delancey, del.icio.us direc.tor is another alternative user interface for your bookmark collection on del.icio.us. However, where Delancey focuses on usage tracking, del.icio.us direc.tor focuses on using a highly dynamic and responsive tag browser. You can try this tool out at the following URL:

```
http://johnvey.com/features/deliciousdirector/
```

As shown in Figure 7-2, del.icio.us direc.tor consists of a user interface sliced into two main areas — a series of tag-browsing columns at the top, and bookmark search results at the bottom. Using the columns of tags populated from your collection, you can narrow down the list of results by tags. Each column specifies an additional tag keyword in the field at the top of the page, in which you can also supply a keyword prefixed with d: to perform search filtering on the description field in bookmarks.

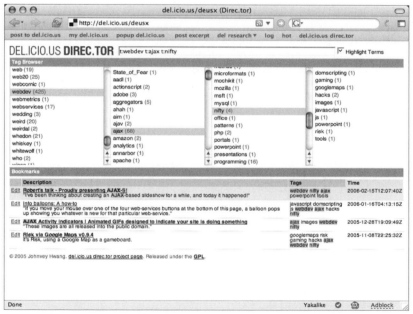

FIGURE 7-2: Viewing bookmarks in del.icio.us direc.tor

Using the Ajax-based interface offered by del.icio.us direc.tor, you can very quickly drill down through chains of tags and search terms to find bookmarks in your collection. Because this in-browser application makes smart usage of del.icio.us API calls and caches data in-memory with data structures tailored for the column-based searching, it can be very responsive to clicks and perusing.

One of the most interesting things about del.icio.us direc.tor is the way in which it was implemented. As you can read on the project's page, the user interface is launched by way of a bookmark activated while visiting any page at del.icio.us. This injects a `<script>` tag into the page, which in turn bootstraps the whole thing — that is, all of the JavaScript and XSLT code necessary to run del.icio.us direc.tor is loaded up into your browser upon activation of the bookmarklet. From that point on, it's self-contained and operates within the security domain of del.icio.us itself — thus allowing Ajax calls to any of the methods available from the del.icio.us API.

This makes del.icio.us direc.tor a technology demo as well as a useful bookmark browsing tool, but either way it's a very interesting del.icio.us add-on.

Previewing Bookmarks Visually with Thumblicio.us

Sometimes, it's nice to see what you're getting into before you click a link at del.icio.us. If this sounds like a familiar situation, then you may want to pay a visit to Thumblicio.us at this address:

```
http://thumblicio.us/
```

Thumblicio.us presents thumbnail screenshots of the latest popular bookmarks found at del.icio.us, as a mashup with a service called Thumbshots (`http://thumbshots.com`) that offers visual previews of Web sites as a paid commercial service. Beyond just visually browsing the popular links, however, you can also perform tag searches and peruse your own bookmarks in thumbnail form. There's also a pretty nice DHTML effect when rolling over thumbnails, which displays the title of the page under the mouse in an overlay frame. You can see a sample screenshot of Thumblicio.us in Figure 7-3.

FIGURE 7-3: Viewing preview thumbnails of popular del.icio.us bookmarks

Presenting Popular Links with Screenshots on Hot Links

Where Thumblicio.us offers quick visual peeks at popular bookmarks, Hot Links offers thumbnails, tags, descriptions, and more. Take a look here:

```
http://dev.upian.com/hotlinks/
```

Hot Links offers a handful of improvements on just plain thumbnails of sites. Page titles are visible, as are the ages of the links, and the full descriptions supplied by the people who book-marked the sites — these are all clustered together along with the thumbnail images. You can filter the page by keyword and tag searches, as well as limiting the view to a single user posting bookmarks.

Another interesting filter option is the ability to specify a threshold for the number of users posting a bookmark, so you can call up only those links that have reached a certain level of popularity — the screenshot in Figure 7-4 depicts this filter set at a popularity of 3 and above. RSS feeds of each level are also made available by Hot Links.

This site is not a generalized service, however — the list of users whose bookmarks appear on the site is fixed and managed by the site owner. So, although del.icio.us is indeed used as a source for bookmarks featured on the site, the bookmarks are drawn from a preselected pool of users. You can grab a copy of this list in OPML format, but you cannot add your own favorites to the site.

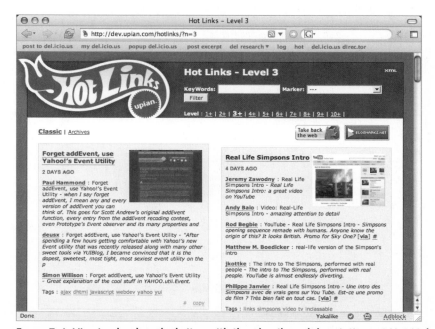

FIGURE 7-4: Viewing bookmarked sites with thumbnails and descriptions at Hot Links

Enhancing Bookmarking with Utility Services

The functionality offered by del.icio.us gets right to the point and lets you manage and search bookmarks with ease. However, this section offers a few ways to improve and enhance your use of del.icio.us.

Bookmarking Your Clipboard with Pasta

Pasta is a simple service, but it's a useful one — it gives you the ability to offload chunks of text from your clipboard and share it on the Web. Take a look at Pasta here:

```
http://pasta.cantbedone.org/
```

There's not much to see in the screenshot offered in Figure 7-5: You'll find a title field and a big text area awaiting your input. You can preview your text before submitting the final product — which is where things get interesting. After submission, your text is saved and you're forwarded to a del.icio.us bookmark posting form (see Figure 7-6). This form is pre-populated with your chosen title and a randomly generated unique URL at which Pasta has stored your submitted content (see Figure 7-7). From here, you can supply an extended description and tags if you like, and add the bookmark to your collection.

FIGURE 7-5: Composing some text on Pasta

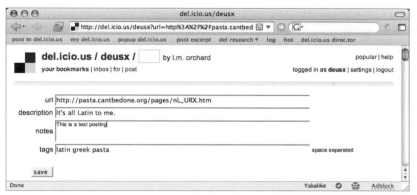

FIGURE 7-6: Automatically redirected to bookmark the text snippet from Pasta

FIGURE 7-7: Text posted on Pasta

Pasta doesn't need anything else to be useful — there's no Ajax and there are no colorful icons. Sometimes you just need to share some text, and the workflow enabled by automatically routing you to del.icio.us is just enough to make it worth checking out. You'll even find a handy bookmarklet to help keep Pasta always close at hand. Keep in mind, however, that even though Pasta doesn't offer any public listings of text postings, nothing is private — if someone can find your unique URL, he or she can find your content.

Simplifying Your Tags with Stemming

As you accumulate a collection of bookmarks, it's pretty likely that you'll build up a wide vocabulary of tags. And, more often than not, you'll have scatterings of tags that you'd find all mean basically the same thing, if you had time to spend studying them. Good del.icio.us citizens may spend a chunk of time pruning their tag garden — but of course, the very nature of off-the-cuff tagging discourages this sort of study. So, inevitably you end up with lots of redundancies and synonyms lurking in your tag set. What might ease tag gardening — thereby making its occurrence more likely — is a tool to help sniff out similarities between tags.

One such tool, the Amazing del.icio.us Stemmer, can be found at this URL:

```
http://activecellmedia.com/stemmer/
```

The implementation of this utility has passed through a few sets of authors, as you'll read at the above page, but the idea is this: Through the use of a stemming algorithm, words can be distilled down to a base root by discarding plurals and other modifiers. Once so distilled, these bases can be compared in order to group together words that are very likely all forms of the same word. Treating tags as words, the stemming algorithm can highlight which of your tags are candidates for gardening, trimming, and merging.

 On the Web Want to read more about stemming algorithms in general? Visit the Wikipedia here:

```
http://en.wikipedia.org/wiki/Stemming
```

You can look into the specific algorithm used by this service at the "official" Porter Stemming Algorithm home page:

```
www.tartarus.org/~martin/PorterStemmer/
```

Figure 7-8 provides an example of the del.icio.us stemmer in action. For instance, you could have attached the tags *aggregation*, *aggregator*, and *aggregators* to bookmarks at various points. These are all very similar words, and the stemming algorithm has caught that. You may wish to merge all of these tags together into one, in order to better consolidate and organize your collection. As mentioned before, del.icio.us offers a tool for tag gardening, available at this URL (after swapping *deusx* for your own user name):

```
http://del.icio.us/settings/deusx/tags
```

At this page you can choose to delete and rename individual tags, thereby revising tags attached to many bookmarks all in one action.

Analyzing and Visualizing Bookmarks

You can search for bookmarks on del.icio.us and browse recommendations, but there isn't a lot of support for statistics junkies. This section of the chapter presents a few of the services tinkerers have built to analyze and visualize trends and other data available for processing from del.icio.us.

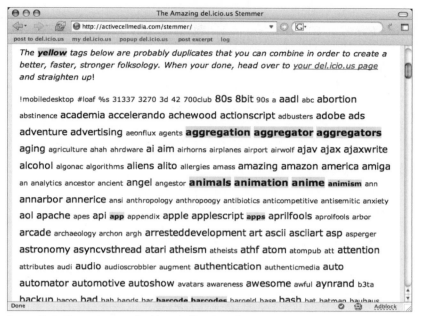

FIGURE 7-8: Stemming applied to a collection of tags

Watching Popularity Over Time with Populicio.us

One of the views you can access from the del.icio.us home page is a list of the latest popular bookmarks posted to the site. However, this page tracks popularity only over the past day or so. This is where Populicio.us comes in: Tracking popular bookmarks over greater time periods is the specialty of this service — check it out here:

```
http://populicio.us/
```

As you can see in Figure 7-9, Populicio.us offers popularity tracking windows for spans ranging from two days up to a full month. These links are displayed in ranking-ordered lists, along with totals of the bookmarks posted for each. You can also find RSS feeds associated with each of these views, keeping you updated on the most popular links.

These popularity scoreboards, built over larger windows of time, can help you find which sites and articles have higher staying power and potentially greater interest. Of course, as with any rankings list, Populicio.us has the potential to sponsor a popularity contest that can be gamed. This is not very likely, but this is a likely reason you won't see this feature integrated into del.icio.us anytime soon. Nonetheless, this service can be a very useful enhancement to del.icio.us to help you graze for interesting items.

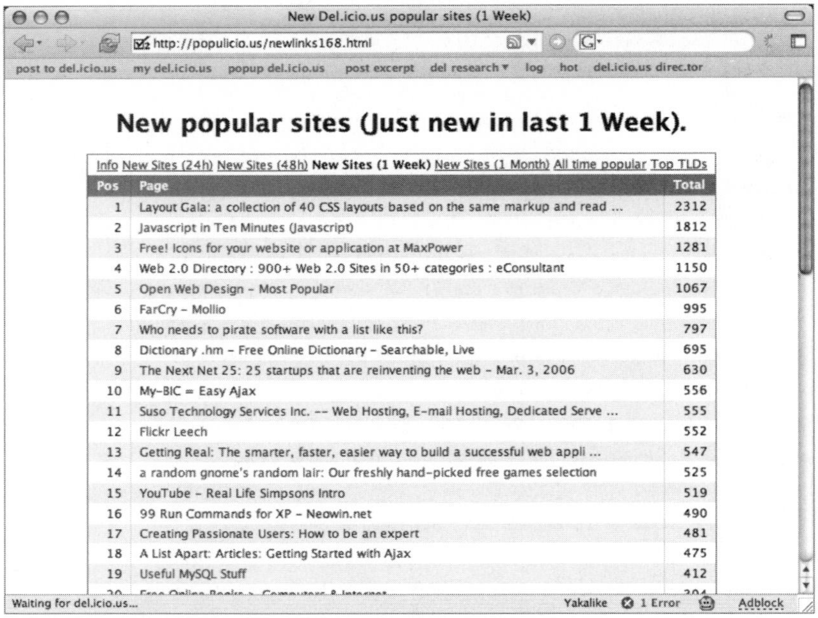

FIGURE 7-9: Popular sites for the past week on Populicio.us

Catching the Buzz with trendalicious

While Populicio.us is about tracking popularity over wider windows of time, trendalicious is about catching hot trends in the short term as they happen. Take a look at the service over at this URL:

```
http://glozer.net/trendalicious.html
```

The screenshot of trendalicious in Figure 7-10 depicts the simple link ranking offered by the service. It's straight and to the point, listing the total number of people who've posted a link, as well as how many have posted it within the last hour. The key metric is the recent postings, indicating spikes in activity in the short term.

The idea is that, by measuring these spikes in posting frequency and ranking them, you can catch a glimpse of popular memes as they're discovered and rise through the collective consciousness of del.icio.us users. Granted, this data can reflect the whims of attention-deficit disorder sufferers — but it can turn up some pretty interesting results for info junkies in very short order.

FIGURE 7-10: Viewing ranked bookmarking trends with trendalicious

Visualizing Trends with Vox Delicii

If the simple rankings of trendalicious are a bit *too* simple for you, you might better appreciate the trend data visualization available at Vox Delicii:

```
http://news.stamen.com/vox/
```

Vox Delicii is a Flash-based data visualization application aimed at presenting a multi-dimensional analysis of link popularity at del.icio.us through indicators of shape, position, color, and size. Interaction with rollovers and mouse clicks allows you to further explore trend data and compare time periods.

Popular bookmarks are arranged as chips in horizontal strips according to the day, in order of first appearance on del.icio.us. The size of each individual chip represents the relative number of bookmarks posted for the link on that day, and the color indicates the link's relative growth in bookmark adoption in comparison to the previous day.

Rolling over the chips will reveal the title of the links, as well as highlight the previous day's chip position if available. Clicking a chip will bring up detail on the bookmark, as well as align it with the previous day for comparison.

This is all very much better seen than explained, and the screenshot in Figure 7-11 depicts only a static portion of what is a very dynamic interface.

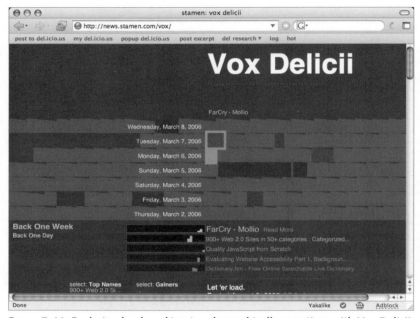

FIGURE **7-11**: Exploring bookmarking trends graphically over time with Vox Delicii

Watching Bookmarks Scroll by with LiveMarks

Is the one-hour window offered by trendalicious too slow for you? Then, you might want to try watching bookmarks stream by in real time with LiveMarks, located here:

```
http://sandbox.sourcelabs.com/livemarks/
```

As soon as you land on the page at LiveLinks, bookmarks begin fading in and scrolling down the page, updated live from an Ajax-enabled data source. You can see a screenshot of this site in Figure 7-12, but that static capture doesn't depict the steady drip of links injected into the page over time. It's like a conveyor belt of tasty sushi made from fresh bookmarks floating on by.

There's a trick to LiveMarks, however: It's not actually live. This Ajax application is more properly described as a what-if technology demo, driven by data fetched and cached from del.icio.us on a scheduled basis. You can read all about it at this wiki page:

```
http://swik.net/LiveMarks/How+LiveMarks+Works
```

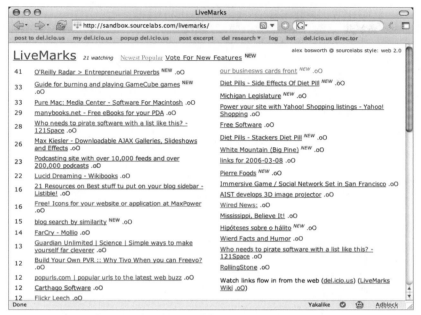

FIGURE 7-12: Watching bookmarks scroll by on LiveMarks

Smoke and mirrors aside, this is a pretty interesting demonstration of live updating and dynamic data display in a browser application — and the only thing keeping it from being truly live is a suitable data feed.

Tracking the Scoop with del.icio.us Pioneers

For every link that rises in bookmarking popularity, there's always someone who bookmarked it first. And, for whatever reasons, there's often a group of the same people in various fields of interest who find the good stuff first. The del.icio.us pioneers experiment is an attempt to identify these people, located here:

```
www.del.mailliw.com/
```

Because this site calls people out by name, this really and truly is an automated popularity contest. As shown in Figure 7-13, the del.icio.us pioneers experiment ranks users in order of how many popular bookmarks he or she was the first to post. You can click a disclosure triangle next to each name to reveal the list of popular links he or she was responsible for introducing.

This information can be useful if you'd like to track the bookmark collections of people who tend to dig up a lot of interesting stuff. Being the first to find what eventually becomes a hot topic can be an indicator that that person has good sources, and so is worth watching.

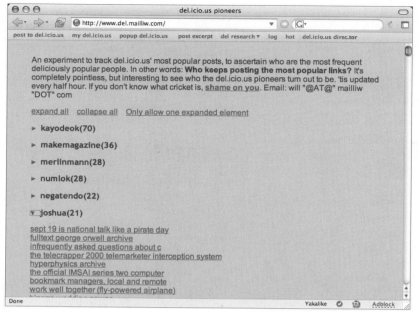

FIGURE 7-13: Tracking the popular link-finders with del.icio.us pioneers

Combining Other Sites and Services

One of the things that open APIs and data feeds from del.icio.us encourage is combination with the APIs and data offered by other sites and services. This part of the chapter presents a few of the mashups and remixes made available by third-party sites for del.icio.us users.

Combining News and Bookmarks with diggdot.us

Are you a fan of Slashdot, digg, and del.icio.us? Tired of bouncing back and forth between these sites throughout the day to keep up with the latest? Then, this mashup might be for you:

```
http://diggdot.us/
```

The special-purpose news aggregation service offered by diggdot.us is very simple and straight-forward: The latest items from Slashdot and digg, and popular links on del.icio.us, are fetched on a regular basis. These are then remixed and presented in a single stream for your viewing pleasure. There's also an RSS feed of the sites' combined output available for subscription, or even further remix if you should desire to do so. Figure 7-14 offers a peek at the features available at diggdot.us.

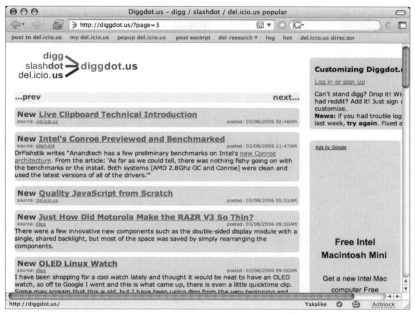

FIGURE 7-14: Bookmarks and news stories mashed up at diggdot.us

Although this site is quite useful in and of itself, it's also a bit of a showcase for the TurboGears Web application framework for Python. You can find links to this and the team responsible for the service — named FrozenBear — in an About box, further down the page.

Visiting a Modern News Portal at Popurls

If you're interested in, well, just about any of the many popular news sites on the Web — including the latest links from del.icio.us — then you should check out this one-stop portal site for almost a dozen news sources:

```
http://popurls.com/
```

Popurls.com, as shown in Figure 7-15, offers a nicely uncluttered presentation of links and headlines from del.icio.us and a slew of other news sources online, alongside photos from Flickr and videos from YouTube — all with a light sprinkling of advanced JavaScript and DHTML to help control the amount of information shown. Popurls.com is far from the only modernized portal site to be found on the Web — but it's one of the most recent, simply designed, and least encumbered with extraneous advertising.

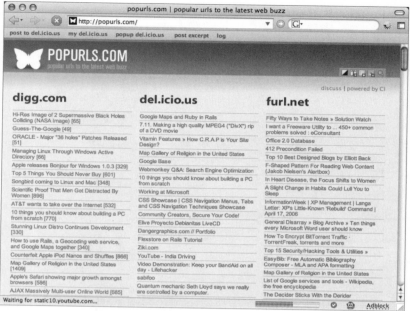

FIGURE 7-15: News headlines at Popurls.com

Subscribing to Bookmarks as Torrents with Prodigem

As you may have read in the previous chapter, del.icio.us automatically tags bookmarks linked to many types of multimedia resources. And, if you subscribe to the RSS feeds of file and media type tags on del.icio.us, the resulting feed will contain `<enclosure>` elements compatible with podcast and video cast tuner software. However, many of these media files are quite large and sometimes requests overwhelm the hosting sites. Wouldn't it be nice if there was a way to get these media resources by way of BitTorrent to share the load of transferring the files?

Well, it just so happens that Prodigem, a BitTorrent-based content hosting service, offers an automated service that acts as a gateway for direct downloads from del.icio.us bookmarks. Check it out here:

```
www.prodigem.com/torrents/user_pep_delicious.html
```

This service monitors the popular media RSS feeds from del.icio.us and automatically seeds torrents of the enclosed media files found as bookmarks. You can take a peek at a screenshot of a recent list of available torrents in Figure 7-16. Although potentially very handy, this is actually just a technology demo of the more broadly capable hosting API made available to users of the Prodigem hosting solution. This REST-based API exposes a full set of methods for uploading content for release, starting and stopping torrent seeding, and managing content licenses.

FIGURE 7-16: Prodigem Torrents made recently available from downloads bookmarked at del.icio.us

Building Your Own Mashup

Have these del.icio.us-related mashups gotten you in a mood to build one of your own? Thanks to the Web APIs exposed by services such as Technorati, Flickr, and del.icio.us, building your own TechnoFlickrDeli isn't far from reach. In fact, that's what we're going to do in the final part of this chapter.

Planning for a Mashup

As you already know, del.icio.us offers API methods and XML data feeds to access the book-marks and tags in your collection, as well as from the collections of others. Similarly, Flickr offers a set of API methods that give access to the photos in users' collections, as well as per-forming searches on keywords and tags. You can read all about the Flickr API here:

```
www.flickr.com/services/
```

Technorati, in turn, offers HTTP- and XML-based methods to perform a number of searches on the blogs crawled by the service — including general keyword searches for blogs and entries, analyses of links into and out of blogs, and queries for blog entries by tag. You can catch up on what Technorati has to offer at their Developer Center located at this address:

```
www.technorati.com/developers/
```

If you consider these three Web services — del.icio.us, Flickr, and Technorati — how might they be tied together in a single mashup? What's a common denominator among the three that might be used as a point where they can be joined together? For the purposes of this project, the answer is found in tagging. All three of these support tagging, whether by allowing users to tag their own content or offering the ability to search for items indexed by tags.

Bookmarks, photos, and blog entries — all three of these forms of content can be annotated with tags. So, by using tag-based API search methods, you can pull together an all-in-one aggregate view of content centered around a particular tag. And, to keep things interesting, you can use your personal tag collection from del.icio.us as the source from which to draw these tags on which to make search queries. Odds are if you've used a tag, you'll be interested in things for which others have used that tag.

Implementing TechnoFlickrDeli

This, then, is the idea behind TechnoFlickrDeli: This mashup will pull the set of tags you've used in your del.icio.us collection to help find things that you might like to see. This content will consist of blog entries, photos, and bookmarks related to your tags. The search methods offered by the APIs of Technorati, Flickr, and del.icio.us will be used to find this content and assemble it all into a single page for your viewing pleasure.

One of the most convenient environments for implementing this mashup is in PHP. You can find pre-built libraries to ease the use of all three services' APIs, and building the HTML for a mashup like this is pretty straightforward. So, to get started, take a look at the opening lines of ch07_technoflickrdeli.php in Listing 7-1. (You can download all the source code for this chapter from the book's Web site at www.wiley.com/go/extremetech.)

Listing 7-1: ch07_technoflickrdeli.php (Part 1 of 10)

```php
<?php
    /**
        ch07_technoflickrdeli.php

        Build a tag-based mashup of Technorati, Flickr,
        and del.icio.us
    */

    // Add the local PHP includes dir to path.
    ini_set("include_path",
        ini_get("include_path").":includes");

    // See: http://www.phpflickr.com
```

Listing 7-1 *continued*

```
require_once "phpFlickr.php";

// See: http://www.kailashnadh.name/ducksoup/
require_once "duckSoup.php";

// See: http://www.ejeliot.com/pages/5
require_once 'php-delicious.inc.php';

// See: http://magpierss.sourceforge.net/
require_once "magpierss/rss_fetch.inc";
```

The first lines of Listing 7-1 consist of a comment describing the program and its purpose. After this comes a call to the PHP function ini_set() to tweak the module include path. A local includes directory is added to the path — this allows you to create an includes subdirectory into which you can drop files from downloaded modules.

And, speaking of downloaded modules, the rest of Listing 7-1 contains require_once statements, each a reference to a module you'll need to fetch and install.

The first of these modules is named phpFlickr.php. And, as the comment suggests, you can find it available for download at this address:

    www.phpflickr.com

Installation of phpFlickr is simple: Just download the archive package, unpack it, and copy the contents into the includes directory. This will consist of a handful of PHP files, including phpFlickr.php, and a subdirectory named PEAR. You can leave out files like README.txt and such, but make sure all of the PHP code ends up in your includes directory.

The next statement requires a module named duckSoup.php, a simple PHP wrapper around the Technorati API. You can download this module at the URL indicated in the code comment:

    www.kailashnadh.name/ducksoup/

This module may also be installed into the includes subdirectory, by downloading the package archive and copying the file duckSoup.php into the subdirectory.

The next module required is PhpDelicious, first mentioned back in Chapter 3. If you haven't already installed it, pay a visit to the home page for a download:

    www.ejeliot.com/pages/5

Again, this module is a fairly comprehensive wrapper around the authenticated API provided by del.icio.us for personal bookmarks. This module will be used to fetch a list of tags from your account.

At the end of Listing 7-1, the final module required is MagpieRSS, a flexible RSS parsing module for PHP. You can find a download for this module at this page:

```
http://magpierss.sourceforge.net/
```

While PhpDelicious will allow you to get a list of tags from your account, MagpieRSS will serve to extract bookmarks from the RSS feed for an individual tag on del.icio.us.

Download each of these modules, and ensure they're all installed in the PHP module search path — either in an `includes` subdirectory alongside `ch07_technoflickrdeli.php` or in some other location more suitable to your Web server environment.

Coming up next, in Listing 7-2, is a set of configuration constants you'll need to tweak.

Listing 7-2: ch07_technoflickrdeli.php (Part 2 of 10)

```php
// del.icio.us API configuration
define("DEL_USER",      "deusx");
define("DEL_PASSWD",    "lodefizzle");
define("DEL_TAG_MAX",   20);
define("DEL_TAG_FEED",  "http://del.icio.us/rss/tag/");

// API keys for Technorati
define("TECHNORATI_API_KEY",
    "46333ab61e7345c2573024a47e67e8aa");

// API key for Flickr
define("FLICKR_API_KEY",
    "0ed040a7c16b0b24b5ae2288c4c4306c");

// Settings for data caching.
define("CACHE_DIR",         "./data/tfd-cache");
define("CACHE_AGE",         5 * 60 * 60);
define("MAGPIE_CACHE_DIR",  CACHE_DIR);
define("MAGPIE_CACHE_AGE",  CACHE_AGE);

// Figure out what tag to display from params
$the_tag = isset($_GET['tag']) ? $_GET['tag'] : 'funny';
```

Listing 7-2 is pretty much all configuration constant definitions. The first block of these, all prefixed with DEL_, are del.icio.us-related settings. For the most part, you can leave these alone — but you will need to fill in your own user name and password at del.icio.us. These will be used to authenticate to the API in order to fetch the list of tags used in your collection. Also, as I explain in a little bit, the DEL_TAG_MAX constant will determine how many of your tags to display as choices on the page when it gets built.

The next two constants — TECHNORATI_API_KEY and FLICKR_API_KEY — are API keys supplied by and required for use of the Technorati and Flickr Web services, respectively. If you've used a Web API like one of these before, this should be a familiar concept: In order to use one of these Web services, you need to register yourself or your application with the service in order to get an API key. API keys allow the services to track usage of their API methods for measurement and optimization purposes.

If you haven't already, you can find out how to acquire a Technorati API key at the following URL:

```
www.technorati.com/developers/apikey.html
```

And, as for Flickr, you can apply for an API key over on this page:

```
www.flickr.com/services/api/key.gne
```

The API keys shown in Listing 7-2 aren't real, usable keys, so you will need to acquire your own. However, as you can see, both of these are simple and short strings that you'll be able to paste into their respective configuration definitions once you've gotten hold of them. Again, you *will* need these for this mashup to function.

Following the API key definitions are a few settings to define the location of a cache directory where this script will store data fetched from the Web services for a period of time. Caching will prevent this script from continually hitting API methods, which will both speed up the script and spare the servers from overuse. This is especially important with del.icio.us, where servers have measures in place to automatically throttle or block heavy usage that looks like abuse. So, caching is just a good idea overall.

The CACHE_DIR value should be given a path that points to a directory on your Web server to which PHP scripts like this one may read and write files — preferably a subdirectory to which only this script will be expected to write. The data won't be very sensitive in security terms, per se, but this script won't be very organized in its file structure beyond the directory given. In other words, it'll make a bit of a mess, but only in a single folder.

The CACHE_AGE setting expects a value in seconds that will determine for how long cache entries should be considered fresh. You can tailor this however you like, although the value in Listing 7-2 is set to 5 hours. For personal use, you may want to tweak this to a lower time span — but if you offer up this script or some derivative of it as a public page, you should definitely consider raising this value.

The MAGPIE_CACHE_DIR and MAGPIE_CACHE_AGE constants serve the same purpose as the CACHE_DIR and CACHE_AGE constants — just specifically for use by the Magpie RSS library, which you'll see in use a bit further on in the code.

The last line of this listing attempts to determine which tag has been chosen for use in aggregating content for the mashup display. This is drawn from a tag query parameter supplied to the PHP script. This will come into play further on, in links constructed to display different tag searches.

Continue on to Listing 7-3, where you'll see the first Web service come into play.

Listing 7-3: ch07_technoflickrdeli.php (Part 3 of 10)

```
/**
    Fetch photo data from Flickr for a given tag.
*/
function fetchFlickrTag($tag) {
    $fapi = new phpFlickr(FLICKR_API_KEY);
    $fapi->enableCache("fs", CACHE_DIR);
    $results = $fapi->photos_search(
        array("tags"=>$tag)
    );

    $photos = array();
    foreach ($results['photo'] as $result) {
        $photo = $result;
        $photo['sizes'] =
            $fapi->photos_getSizes($result['id']);
        array_push($photos, $photo);
    }
    return $photos;
}
```

The function defined in Listing 7-3, fetchFlickrTag(), uses phpFlickr to make a call to the Flickr API to search for photos by the given tag. Notice that the first thing it does is create an instance of the phpFlickr class, using FLICKR_API_KEY as a parameter to the constructor. Once constructed, the enableCache() method on the instance is called, using the CACHE_DIR constant earlier defined — this will cause phpFlickr to cache data from all calls to the API and thus minimize the number of times it actually needs to make a call to the Web service.

Next, the photos_search() method of the phpFlickr instance is called with an associative array as a parameter. This array forms the set of search terms, specifically the tag supplied to the function as a string. This method returns a data structure containing the results of the API call.

This data structure is an associative array, where one of its keys is photo. Via this key, a list may be found that contains photo search results — these are processed in a loop intended to fill a second array with photo records. For each photo, a subsequent call to the phpFlickr method photos_getSizes() is made, using the photo's ID as a parameter. The data returned by this method contains the image URLs of the photo in question, at various sizes — you'll be able to use these to construct image tags to display in the page. So, this data structure is added to the photo record for use later.

The augmented list of photos is returned at the end of the function. You'll see this function in action when it comes time to build the HTML page.

Next up, in Listing 7-4, the Technorati API makes its debut in the script.

Listing 7-4: ch07_technoflickrdeli.php (Part 4 of 10)

```
/**
    Fetch blog entry data from Technorati for
    a given tag.
*/
function fetchTechnoratiTag($tag) {
    $tapi         = new duckSoup;
    $tapi->api_key = TECHNORATI_API_KEY;
    $tapi->type    = 'taginfo';
    $tapi->params  = array('tag' => $tag);
    $results = $tapi->get_content();
    return $results['item'];
}
```

In Listing 7-4, the function `fetchTechnoratiTag()` is defined. It accepts a tag and returns a list of blog entry records found matching that tag as a result. To do so, it first creates an instance of the `duckSoup` class, and then sets the `api_key` property to the value defined as `TECHNORATI_API_KEY` earlier in the script. The Technorati method to be called (`taginfo`) is set as the `type` property in the API instance, and an associative array containing the tag is supplied as the `params` property. Finally, the Technorati API call is performed by calling the `get_content()` method on the `duckSoup` instance, and the list of blog entries found for the tag is returned.

Now, it's time to define methods to handle accessing data at del.icio.us. Take a look at Listing 7-5 for the definition of the function `fetchDeliciousTag()`.

Listing 7-5: ch07_technoflickrdeli.php (Part 5 of 10)

```
/**
    Fetch bookmark feed data from del.icio.us
    for a given tag.
*/
function fetchDeliciousTag($tag) {
    $url = DEL_TAG_FEED . $tag;
    $data = fetch_rss($url);
    return $data->items;
}
```

Thanks to MagpieRSS, the implementation of `fetchDeliciousTag()` in Listing 7-5 is very simple. The URL to a tag's RSS feed is constructed by concatenating the value of `DEL_TAG_FEED` — defined at the top of the script — with the desired tag. This is fetched via the `fetch_rss()` function supplied by MagpieRSS. The structure returned by this function contains data parsed from the RSS feed, among which is a list of items. These items each describe a bookmark from del.icio.us, so this list is returned from this function.

One more function left — fetchAllDeliciousTags() — defined next in Listing 7-6.

Listing 7-6: ch07_technoflickrdeli.php (Part 6 of 10)

```
/**
    Fetch all del.icio.us tags, with caching.
*/
function fetchAllDeliciousTags() {
    $dapi = new PhpDelicious(DEL_USER, DEL_PASSWD);
    $tags = $dapi->GetAllTags();
    usort($tags, "cmpTags");
    return array_slice($tags, 0, DEL_TAG_MAX);
}

/**
    Compare tags for sorting in order of most used.
*/
function cmpTags($a, $b) {
    $a_cnt = $a['count'];
    $b_cnt = $b['count'];
    if ($b_cnt == $a_cnt) { return 0; }
    return ($b_cnt < $a_cnt) ? -1 : 1;
}

?>
```

Actually, there are two functions defined in Listing 7-6: fetchAllDeliciousTags() and cmpTags(). The first function uses PhpDelicious to grab all of your tags — and it, in turn, uses cmpTags() in the course of sorting the list of tags. This code should look very similar to what was presented back in Chapter 3, where PhpDelicious was first introduced.

To fetch your tags, fetchAllDeliciousTags() creates an instance of PhpDelicious, using your settings for DEL_USER and DEL_PASSWD. The GetAllTags() method is then used to grab the list from an API call to del.icio.us. The PHP function usort() is used along with cmpTags() to sort your tags, in order of most used. Finally, the top DEL_TAG_MAX tags are sliced off the top and returned.

This is the end of all the convenience functions that help you use the three Web APIs; now it's time to tackle producing the HTML output. This begins with Listing 7-7.

Listing 7-7 offers the start of the HTML page proper. In the head of the page, a CSS stylesheet named ch07_technoflickrdeli.css is linked, which provides the style and formatting for this page.

Listing 7-7: ch07_technoflickrdeli.php (Part 7 of 10)

```
<html>
    <head>

        <title>TechnoFlickrDeli</title>

        <meta http-equiv="content-type"
              content="text/html;charset=utf8" />

        <link href="ch07_technoflickrdeli.css"
              type="text/css" rel="stylesheet" />

    </head>
    <body>

        <h1>TechnoFlickrDeli: <?php echo $the_tag ?></h1>

        <div id="tags">
            <ul>
            <?php
            foreach (fetchAllDeliciousTags() as $tag) {
                if ($tag['tag'] == 'system:unfiled') continue;
                ?>
                <li>
                    <a href="?tag=<?php echo $tag['tag'] ?>">
                        <?php echo $tag['tag'] ?>
                    </a>
                    <span>(<?php echo $tag['count'] ?>)</span>
                </li>
                <?php
            }
            ?>
            </ul>
        </div>
```

Next, first thing in the body of the page, comes a header that presents the title of the application along with the tag chosen for the mashup. After this is a <div> with an ID of tags. Inside this <div> is an HTML list populated by a loop processing the results of a call to fetchAllDeliciousTags().

Each of the records in the list returned by fetchAllDeliciousTags() is an associative array, containing the keys tag and count. These are used to create HTML list elements, each with a hyperlink back to this script given the tag as a parameter. The text of these links offers the name of the tag and a usage count for each.

This HTML code provides a set of navigational links at the top of the page, enabling you to browse mashed up search results from each of your del.icio.us tags.

The next part, offered in Listing 7-8, presents a listing of blog entries found via a tag search at Technorati.

Listing 7-8: ch07_technoflickrdeli.php (Part 8 of 10)

```php
<div id="blogs">
    <h2>Blogs</h2>
    <ul>
    <?php
    foreach (fetchTechnoratiTag($the_tag) as $blog) {
        $blog_url   = $blog['weblog']['url'];
        $blog_name  = $blog['weblog']['name'];
        $permalink  = $blog['permalink'];
        $title      = $blog['title'];
        $excerpt    = $blog['excerpt'];
    ?>
        <li>
            <a href="<?php echo $blog_url ?>">
                <?php echo $blog_name ?>
            </a>
            ::
            <a href="<?php echo $permalink ?>">
                <?php echo $title ?>
            </a>
            <blockquote>
                <?php echo $excerpt ?>
            </blockquote>
        </li>
    <?php
    }
    ?>
    </ul>
</div>
```

In Listing 7-8, an HTML `<div>` with an ID of `blogs` is built. This `<div>` is populated via a loop processing the results of a call to `fetchTechnoratiTag()` with `$the_tag` as a parameter. Again, this variable contains the tag selected for the mashup, as found back in Listing 7-2. Each of the API calls on this page will be called with the value of this variable.

So, within this loop, a series of HTML blog entry summaries are constructed from the data structures returned from Technorati. These summaries consist of a link to the blog, a link to the entry, and a `<blockquote>` containing an excerpt of the blog entry.

Following this part of the template comes HTML to build a list of photos from Flickr, in Listing 7-9.

Listing 7-9: ch07_technoflickrdeli.php (Part 9 of 10)

```
<div id="photos">
    <h2>Photos</h2>
    <ul>
    <?php
    foreach (fetchFlickrTag($the_tag) as $photo) {
        $title = $photo['title'];
        $link  = $photo['sizes']['Square']['url'];
        $img   = $photo['sizes']['Square']['source'];
        ?>
        <li>
            <a href="<?php echo $link ?>"
                title="<?php echo $title ?>">
                <img src="<?php echo $img ?>" />
            </a>
        </li>
        <?php
    }
    ?>
    </ul>
</div>
```

The HTML provided in Listing 7-9 starts with a `<div>` with an ID of photos. It contains an HTML list, composed of photo records returned from a call to `fetchFlickrTag()`. Each of these items contains quite a number of details about the Flickr photos, but the only ones you're going to use here are a link to the photo image, a link to the photo detail page, and the photo title. Note that using the "Square" version of photos will allow this list of photos to be turned into a set of regular-sized thumbnails when it comes time to bring the CSS into the picture.

Finally, it's time to wrap up this page template with a list of bookmarks from del.icio.us. Listing 7-10 provides the finale.

Listing 7-10: ch07_technoflickrdeli.php (Part 10 of 10)

```
<div id="bookmarks">
    <h2>Bookmarks</h2>
    <ul>
    <?php
    foreach (fetchDeliciousTag($the_tag) as $bookmark) {
        $link  = $bookmark['link'];
        $title = $bookmark['title'];
        $desc  = $bookmark['description'];
        ?>
        <li>
```

continued

Listing 7-10 *continued*

```php
                <a href="<?php echo $link ?>">
                    <?php echo $title ?>
                </a>
                <blockquote>
                    <?php echo $desc ?>
                </blockquote>
            </li>
            <?php
        }
        ?>
        </ul>
    </div>

    </body>
</html>
```

In Listing 7-10, a call to `fetchDeliciousTag()` supplies a loop with bookmarks as RSS items. These are transformed into links with `<blockquote>`s containing the extended bookmark notes. All of these are contained within an HTML list in a `<div>` with an ID of bookmarks. This forms a plain list of links to bookmarks, not unlike the blog entry listing.

Adding Some Visual Style to TechnoFlickrDeli

As you may have noticed, all of the HTML from the listings so far is very simple. Well, that's because all of the visual style comes in from CSS, offered next in Listing 7-11 as the file `ch07_technoflickrdeli.css`.

Listing 7-11: ch07_technoflickrdeli.css

```css
/**
    ch07_technoflickrdeli.css

    CSS styles for ch07_technoflickrdeli.php
*/
body, li, p, td {
    font: 12px arial;
}
#tags ul {
    list-style: none;
    margin: 0;
    padding: 0;
}
#tags ul li {
```

Listing 7-11 *continued*

```
        display: inline;
        padding: 0.25em;
        margin: 0;
}
#photos, #blogs, #bookmarks {
        float: left;
        overflow: hidden;
}
#photos ul {
        list-style: none;
        margin: 0;
        padding: 0;
        width: 250px;
}
#photos ul li {
        display: inline;
        margin: 0;
        padding: 0;
        width: 75px;
}
#blogs {
        width: 250px;
}
#bookmarks {
        width: 250px;
}
blockquote {
        margin-left: 0.5em;
        font-size: 0.9em;
}
```

Listing 7-11 offers some CSS as `ch07_technoflickrdeli.css` to provide some visual styles to the HTML produced by this mashup. Although each of the major areas of the page — tags, blog entries, photos, and bookmarks — are all constructed as HTML lists, the CSS will cause each of these to be presented differently.

First, the list of tag links under the `<div>` with ID tags gets formatted as a rough "cloud" of links. The list elements are pulled out of their usual bulleted context and simply formatted as an inline series of links in a strip across the top of the page.

Next, the blog entries are left in a bulleted list form, but constrained to a narrow column floating toward the left of the page. As for the photos, these are constrained to a narrow column — but rather than a bulleted list, these are styled to appear as a regular grid, three thumbnails wide. Finally, bookmarks are displayed in much the same way as blog entries, in a column on the right side of the page.

You can see how all of this looks in Figure 7-17. You should see the tag links across the top of the page — these are drawn from your most commonly used tags and, when clicked, will take you to a mashup based on that tag. Try exploring these tags to see what interesting photos and items from around the Web strike your fancy.

FIGURE 7-17: Viewing content related to "javascript" in the TechnoFlickrDeli

Summary

In this chapter, you were given a sampling of the third-party tweaks, enhancements, and mashups involving del.icio.us and made available on the Web. With the construction of the TechnoFlickrDeli, you may have gotten some ideas for mashups of your own. These are the sorts of sites and services that are encouraged by providing open APIs and data feeds; each builds upon the success of del.icio.us and helps del.icio.us itself succeed.

In the next chapter, you see demonstrations of another aspect of del.icio.us APIs and data in ways to own your own bookmarks data, grab backups, and reuse your links however you like.

Getting Your Links Out of del.icio.us

One of the main goals of del.icio.us is sharing bookmarks: Every user account comes with a publicly accessible URL providing access to that user's posted links. You could use this as your bookmarking home page if you like, sending friends and acquaintances to this address to stay in the loop on all the interesting things you find around the Web.

And, in fact, that's just what a lot of people do. But, this isn't for everyone: Some people would rather send visitors to their own blog, or to a page hosted on their own servers. Whether it's because they feel a bit proprietary toward their own content and links — or feel a general distrust of leaving things completely in the hands of a third party — some del.icio.us users seek to replicate their bookmarks within environments under their own control.

If this sounds like you, then this might be the chapter you've been waiting for. Here, you'll see various solutions for integrating your del.icio.us bookmarks into your own Web pages and blogs. There are approaches that connect up with most popular blogging packages, as well as some techniques that work on just about any Web page. You can opt to simply display a copy of your freshest links cached from del.icio.us, or even go so far as to download and mirror your bookmarks completely apart from the bookmarking service.

Linkrolls via JavaScript Include from del.icio.us

One of the easiest ways to include del.icio.us bookmarks on a Web page is to use a linkroll powered by a del.icio.us JavaScript include feed. While this doesn't take you completely "off the grid" with respect to relying on del.icio.us services, it does accomplish the goal of presenting your bookmarks within your own site framework. To get started, pay a visit to this page:

```
http://del.icio.us/help/linkrolls
```

in this chapter

☑ Linkrolls via JavaScript include from del.icio.us

☑ Splicing links, photos, and blogs using FeedBurner

☑ Signing up for a daily blog posting from del.icio.us

☑ Feeding TypePad sidebar lists with del.icio.us RSS

☑ Building a yummy bookmark sidebar in Movable Type

☑ Creating new posts in WordPress from bookmarks

☑ Backing up and mirroring your bookmarks with Python

☑ Browsing your bookmarks with Ajax

☑ Building a caching API proxy using PHP

As presented in Figure 8-1, you'll see that this page is more than just a simple static help page. In fact, it's practically an application itself. Toward the top of the page, you're given a JavaScript include as a short snippet of HTML code. You can copy and paste directly into one of your Web pages to quickly display a sampler of your latest bookmarks that will get updated every time you refresh the page.

FIGURE 8-1: del.icio.us linkrolls help page

Scroll down a bit more, and you'll find a set of display options. You can use these to tweak what will be displayed in this JavaScript include, with live updates to the preview on the page as you play. In Figure 8-2, you can see a more customized version of my own links: I've changed the title, added in tags, and extended descriptions. The list of links has also been narrowed down by tag to just display those links tagged with `caffeine`. Notice that as you change options, the code snippet at the top of the page is also updated. So, once you've settled on the right arrangement of settings, the include code is all ready to go.

If you happen to manage the pages and content on your site by hand, then you're already well acquainted with pasting these sorts of snippets into your code. On the other hand, you may use some sort of content management system to build new pages. In Figure 8-3, you can see me creating a new page on `decafbad.com`, which includes the customized code snippet.

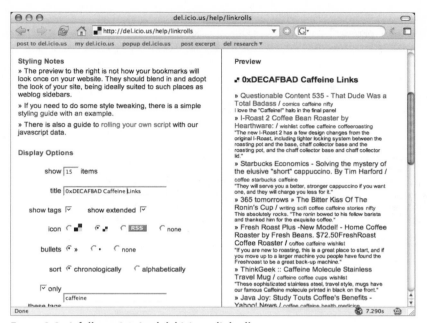

FIGURE 8-2: A fully customized del.icio.us linkroll

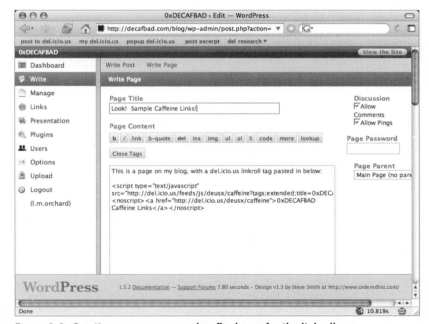

FIGURE 8-3: Creating a new page on decafbad.com for the linkroll

Once saved and published, Figure 8-4 demonstrates what this looks like once the page is finished. It's useful to note that these links follow your own site's style — they're not limited to the standard look and feel of del.icio.us. So, while you're still depending on the servers at del.icio.us, you're free to present your bookmarks with a treatment not dictated by their default link colors and fonts.

FIGURE 8-4: Linkroll code pasted into a page on decafbad.com

Splicing Links, Photos, and Blogs Using FeedBurner

Using a del.icio.us linkroll is a quick way to get your bookmarks into something like a sidebar on a Web page without much fuss. But, if you'd like to include a bit more in your linkroll, you might want to check out FeedBurner.

With FeedBurner, you can produce an enhanced version of any RSS or Atom feed, such as the main feed published from your blog. Feed enhancements include things such as an improved stylesheet for direct viewing in a modern browser, an easy-to-use "Universal Subscription Mechanism," and automatic format tweaking depending on the user agent of an aggregator or reader attempting to fetch your feed.

However, where FeedBurner gets interesting — for the purposes of this chapter, anyway — is in the feed *splicing* features. Although, at present, you can't really just splice in any old feed, you *can* mix in photos from a Flickr account and links posted to a del.icio.us account. So, you can use FeedBurner to try to round up your blog posts, photos, and bookmarks all into one master feed.

But wait, there's more: If having a merged feed of all your stuff posted online wasn't enough, you also request a JavaScript include of this feed's content rendered as HTML — not unlike a del.icio.us linkroll.

To get started, pay a visit to FeedBurner at this URL:

```
www.feedburner.com/
```

You'll need to sign up for an account there, which is a fairly straightforward procedure. After getting yourself logged in, Figure 8-5 shows you what "burning" a new feed looks like. You can supply a direct feed URL or a blog address from which FeedBurner will attempt to autodetect your feed location. This creates a new proxy feed at FeedBurner through which your original content will be filtered.

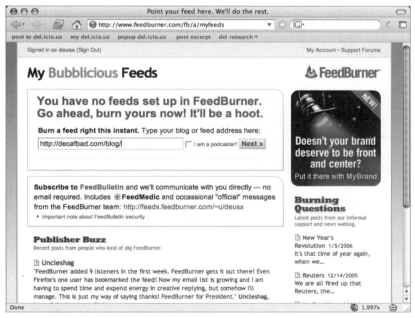

FIGURE 8-5: Burning a new feed at FeedBurner

After you create a version of your feed at FeedBurner, a new set of feed management options opens up. The first one to check out is shown in Figure 8-6 — under the Optimize tab, called Link Splicer. Here, you can choose del.icio.us from a list of other bookmarking services, as well as supply your account user name and a preference of link splicing granularity: You can opt to have every link you post included as a separate entry, or periodically batch the entire day's worth of bookmarks as one entry. For a sidebar-style linkroll, you probably want each book-mark as a separate entry, however.

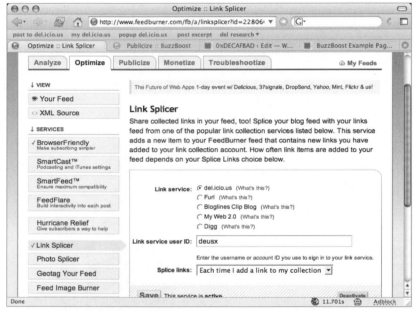

FIGURE 8-6: Splicing del.icio.us links into your FeedBurner feed

As shown in Figure 8-7, check out the Publicize tab in the feed options and click the BuzzBoost service. This is where you can configure options for a JavaScript include, a bit like you did for the del.icio.us linkroll. You can choose the number of items to display at once, whether links should open in the current or a new window, how much content to show for each item, as well as a few other tweaks.

Once you've gotten the BuzzBoost options arranged to your liking, it's time to paste the HTML snippet into a page of your own. In Figure 8-8, you can see me creating a new page through my WordPress management screen. And again, as with the del.icio.us linkroll, a feed rendered by a BuzzBoost is also subject to your site's CSS styles. In fact, if you look closely at Figure 8-8, you might see some extra CSS styles I've thrown in to further customize this FeedBurner display.

FIGURE 8-7: Producing an HTML version with BuzzBoost

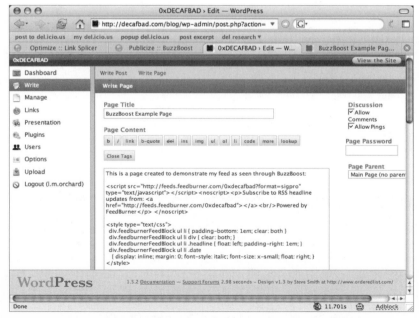

FIGURE 8-8: Creating a new Web page with the BuzzBoost HTML snippet

Finally, in Figure 8-9, you can see the end product: Recent blog posts and del.icio.us links all mashed together on one page. Notice that they follow all of the styles already present on my site, with the addition of the styles included when making the new page.

FIGURE 8-9: Completed Web page with working BuzzBoost include

Of course, although you get some more flexibility from using FeedBurner in conjunction with del.icio.us, some would say that now you've got *two* problems: Rather than just depending on the servers at del.icio.us, you're now also depending on FeedBurner to stay running in order to keep your site supplied with links. Of course, it's in the best interests of both del.icio.us and FeedBurner to continue operating — and the people at FeedBurner have some caching tricks up their sleeves to help soften the blow if the origin feed becomes unavailable.

Signing Up for a Daily Blog Posting from del.icio.us

If you're using a blogging package with an XML-RPC interface for posting entries via the Blogger API or MetaWeblog API — and most of them do, nowadays — del.icio.us offers a relatively new feature to publish a daily summary of your links to your blog. So, rather than leaning on del.icio.us to serve up a linkroll include for every hit to your site, you can have the links delivered to your blog and take it from there. This also has the nice side effect of getting scheduled backups of your bookmarks sent to your site — so if del.icio.us ever went away, you'd still have all of those daily summaries archived in your blog database.

At this writing, however, this feature is still experimental. The downsides to this feature are that you need to slog through a somewhat cryptic interface and trust del.icio.us with the password to your blog. Also, being meant for early adopters, it's likely to change, fail, or disappear at any moment. But, it could be useful to you if and while it works.

Discouraged yet? No? Good. You can get started by logging into del.icio.us and visiting this URL — replacing *YOUR_USERNAME* with, of course, your user name:

```
http://del.icio.us/settings/YOUR_USERNAME/daily
```

This page should appear as an empty list, if this is your first time seeing it. To schedule a daily posting to your blog, click on "add a new thingy." This should result in the form in Figure 8-10.

FIGURE 8-10: Configuring a new "thingy" to schedule daily delicious link postings

Now, be warned: You should have some decent knowledge of your blog's configuration to complete this form. It helps if you already use an XML-RPC–enabled blog editor because you'll have already encountered some of these settings there.

The job_name field can be given any arbitrary name you like, for example "daily_links_for_me."

The fields `out_name` and `out_pass` are intended for your login details for posting to your blog.

The `out_url` field expects the URL for your blog's XML-RPC endpoint. For example, it could look like one of these URLs:

```
http://example.com/wordpress/xmlrpc.php
http://example.com/movabletype/mt-xmlrpc.cgi
```

Next, there's a field for `out_time`. This is the hour, in Greenwich Mean Time, at which del.icio.us should attempt to post to your blog. So, for instance, I'm in the EST time zone right now, or GMT-5. So, when it's midnight here, it'll be 5:00 A.M. GMT. Thus, if I enter 5 for `out_time`, the schedule will fire at midnight, EST.

Finally, there are two fields left: `out_blog_id` and `out_cat_id`. The proper settings for these depend entirely upon your blogging software.

Movable Type supports multiple blogs and authors, and so `out_blog_id` will need to be supplied with the appropriate database ID for your chosen blog.

On the other hand, WordPress ignores this value because it's a single-blog application at present.

As for `out_cat_id`, you'll need to figure out an appropriate category into which these posts should go, and the database ID corresponding to that category. If you're lucky, you can find both of these settings in the preferences of a desktop blog editing application you've already configured. If not, you might have a little digging to do. For my blog at decafbad.com, it turns out that my links category has an ID of 15, a fact I discovered while poking around in the admin interface after creating the category.

Once submitted, you should see the new job listed, as in Figure 8-11. If all goes well, new entries summarizing your bookmarks should start appearing on a regular basis on your blog, as in Figure 8-12. You can also visit the job management page at del.icio.us to see the status of the last attempt to post to your blog, as well as cancel the scheduled job.

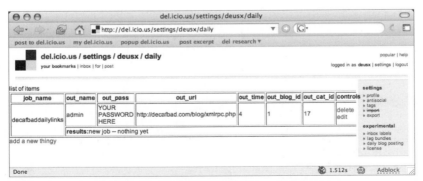

FIGURE 8-11: List of items representing your posting schedule

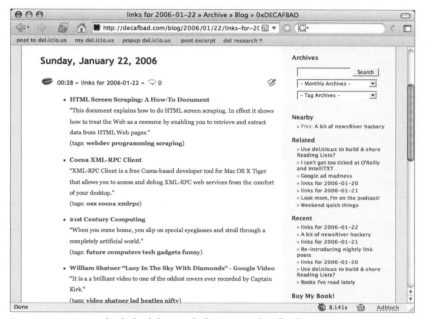

FIGURE 8-12: Example daily delicious link post on decafbad.com

Feeding TypePad Sidebar Lists with del.icio.us RSS

Do you host your blog with TypePad? If so, then you're probably familiar with many of the settings and options this service offers for publishing content, managing photos and lists, and tweaking your blog's layout and design. However, there's a lot of depth to this service, so you may not have explored everything squirreled away amongst the many tabs and panels and selections.

For instance, if you wanted to add a list of your recent bookmarks from del.icio.us to your blog sidebar on TypePad, you might expect to do so through the TypeLists management tab. However, as of this writing, you won't find it there — but a useful related feature does indeed exist.

To find it, log into your TypePad blog's administration pages and click the Design tab. You should be presented with the page shown in Figure 8-13. Here, you want to click Change Content Selections, found in the lower-right corner of Figure 8-13 under Your Content.

On this page, scroll down a little bit, and you should find what's shown in Figure 8-14: a Feeds subheading that, in your case, is probably empty at the moment. If you click Add a new feed, you'll now be presented with a popup dialog box as offered in Figure 8-15.

FIGURE 8-13: Finding the Content Selections panel in TypePad Weblog settings

FIGURE 8-14: Finding the list of feeds under TypePad content selections

FIGURE 8-15: Adding a new sidebar feed in TypePad

Here, you'll want to enter your del.icio.us bookmarks feed into the form field, e.g. `http://del.icio.us/rss/USERNAME`. If you've got a FeedBurner feed to play with, you might also try dropping that URL here for an even richer set of links. Then, once the URL has been submitted, you'll be given the opportunity to set a title for this feed, as well as select a number of items to display.

Once you're done configuring this feed selection to your liking, check out your blog. You should now have a new sidebar section not unlike the one featured in Figure 8-16.

FIGURE 8-16: Finished product of a feed-powered sidebar in TypePad

This is a pretty recent addition to services offered by TypePad so you may experience some occasional hiccups. But, for the most part, this is a quick and easy way to pull RSS feed content from del.icio.us and other sites into your own blog to build a sort of personal portal.

Building a Yummy Bookmark Sidebar in Movable Type

If you're a fan of using Movable Type to maintain and publish your content, you've got a few options with regard to plug-ins and customizations you can use to share your bookmarks. All of the general-purpose techniques in this chapter will work in your templates, but you can also try installing a Movable Type plug-in named Yummy. You can find this plug-in for download here:

```
www.quotesque.net/archives/2005/06/mt-yummy_a_deli.html
```

This plug-in provides a set of new template tags you can easily use to build lists of bookmarks fetched as RSS from del.icio.us using a user name and tags as filters. So, you could publish a sidebar list of all of your bookmarks, all of someone else's bookmarks, all of your bookmarks under a certain tag, or any combination thereof.

Download the plug-in and install it according to the README found along with the plug-in. Once successfully in place, it should appear listed in your blog's control panel, as shown in Figure 8-17.

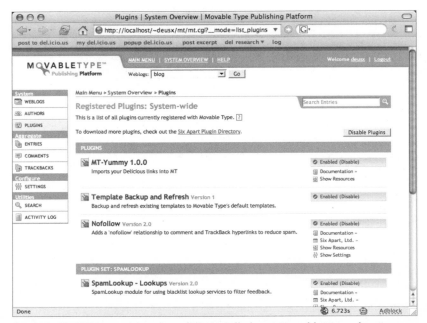

FIGURE 8-17: MT-Yummy is successfully installed as a Movable Type plug-in.

Your next step is to edit one or more of your templates — Figure 8-18 offers a peek at what the HTML might look like for a sidebar list being added to the Main Index template.

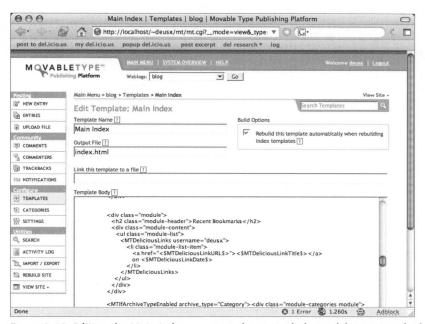

FIGURE 8-18: Editing the Main Index page template to include a sidebar section for bookmarks

The template tags are explained in the plug-in's README file, and your mileage may vary with your site design, but here's a closer look at that HTML:

```
<div class="module">
    <h2 class="module-header">Recent Bookmarks</h2>
    <div class="module-content">
        <ul class="module-list">
            <MTDeliciousLinks username="deusx">
                <li class="module-list-item">
                    <a href="<$MTDeliciousLinkURL$>">
                      <$MTDeliciousLinkTitle$></a>
                    on <$MTDeliciousLinkDate$>
                </li>
            </MTDeliciousLinks>
        </ul>
    </div>
</div>
```

In this snippet, you can see the new tags provided by the plug-in, all prefaced by `MTDelicious`. Using these, you can build any sort of content based on bookmark feeds that you like. And, finally, you can see an example of what this HTML looks like in a sidebar in Figure 8-19.

FIGURE 8-19: Recent Bookmarks now appears in the sidebar of this blog.

Creating New Posts in WordPress from Bookmarks

Just about all of the techniques offered in this chapter so far treat your bookmarks as a separate sort of content with respect to blog entries and the like. The bookmarks are included in a sidebar, or bundled up as a summary blog entry. But, what if you'd like to include bookmarks as first-class individual items right alongside your other content?

If this is what you're after, and you're using WordPress to manage your blog content, check out WordPre.cio.us by Chris Heisel. You can find it located here:

```
http://heisel.org/blog/projects/
```

WordPre.cio.us is a smallish PHP script that integrates with your WordPress installation and, once configured with the URL to an RSS feed at del.icio.us, it can create new blog entries from new bookmarks posted to whatever category you'd like. This script needs to be run on a regular basis in order keep your blog up-to-date with bookmarks, so you should probably schedule a job to hit this PHP page from time to time. For example, here's a suitable crontab entry that does that very thing:

```
0 */2 * * *    curl -s http://example.com/blog/del2wp/del2wp.php
```

This cron entry will fire up the curl command line tool to fetch the preceding URL once every 2 hours, which keeps the blog in relative sync with bookmarks posts.

For an example of this script in use, visit this site:

```
http://hackingfeeds.com/
```

Pictured in Figure 8-20, this is a site that goes mostly neglected, with the exception of bookmarks mirrored from my `hackingfeeds` tag feed. Notice that each of these bookmarks is a separate blog entry, complete with comments and an individual page for the entry. This makes your bookmarks more official citizens of your site, rather than herded up in sidebars or summary posts.

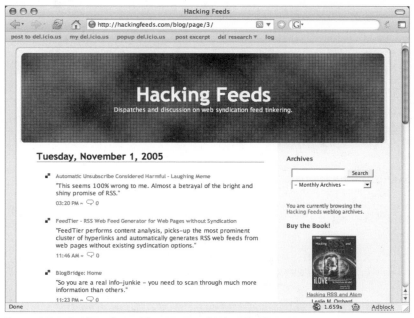

FIGURE 8-20: Bookmarks as blog posts at hackingfeeds.com

Backing Up and Mirroring Your Bookmarks with Python

Many of the approaches shown in this chapter have, in one way or another, depended upon some other Web service besides del.icio.us. But, when it comes to getting your hands on your personal bookmarks — essentially content and data generated by *you* — sometimes it's best to take matters into your own hands and do it yourself. So, the rest of this chapter deals with using the del.icio.us API directly to download, backup, and present your bookmarks.

The first of these tools, a Python program named `ch08_mirror_posts.py`, will use the del.icio.us API to incrementally back up and mirror your bookmarks. As a bonus feature, this program will also parse the XML bookmark data returned by the API and build HTML pages you can use to republish these bookmarks on your own site. In anticipation of that, the HTML will be built using customizable templates that you can tweak and salt to taste.

As always, it's best to download the code for these listings from the book's Web site (www.wiley.com/go/extremetech) — but you're welcome to pop open a text editor and start typing in the program's source code, beginning with Listing 8-1.

Listing 8-1: ch08_mirror_posts.py (Part 1 of 9)

```python
#!/usr/bin/env python
"""
ch08_mirror_posts.py

Download bookmarks from del.icio.us and mirror
them locally as XML and HTML.
"""

# Import some core modules, add the 'lib' directory to
# module search path.
import sys, os, os.path, urllib2, time
from xml.sax import SAXParseException
sys.path.append('lib')

# http://www.aaronsw.com/2002/xmltramp/
import xmltramp

# Details needed to use the del.icio.us API
API_URL    = 'http://del.icio.us/api'
API_USER   = 'your_username_here'
API_PASSWD = 'your_password_here'

# Root path under which all backups will be stored.
POSTS_PATH = 'del-posts'

# Unicode encoding to use while producing HTML.
UNICODE_ENC = 'UTF-8'
```

Listing 8-1 is the preamble to the script, establishing the module imports and configuration constants used later on in the program.

Note that, of the modules used in this program, there's one that you're likely to need to download — unless you already grabbed a copy back in Chapter 3. Namely, that module is xmltramp from Aaron Swartz, available at this URL:

    www.aaronsw.com/2002/xmltramp/

As usual, in Python, you can download this module and leave it in your working directory along with the program. Or, if you notice near the top of this listing, the statement sys.path .append('lib') adds the directory lib to the module search path. So, you could also drop this module into a lib subdirectory after grabbing it, just to keep your working directory clean.

The constants defined in the latter half of Listing 8-1 respectively establish the URL and authentication details for the API; provide a base path under which bookmark data will be stored; and select a Unicode encoding to be used when generating the HTML pages.

Next, in Listing 8-2, you'll see the first of several template strings defined as constants for use in HTML production.

Listing 8-2: ch08_mirror_posts.py (Part 2 of 9)

```
# Overall HTML page template.
HTML_PAGE_TMPL = u"""
<html>
    <head>
        <title>Links for %(date)s</title>
        <meta http-equiv="Content-Type"
            content="text/html; charset=%(unicode_enc)s" />
        <link href="../../../ch08_post_styles.css"
            type="text/css" rel="stylesheet" media="screen" />
    </head>

    <body>
        <h1>Links for %(date)s</h1>
        <ul class="delPosts" id="delPosts-%(date)s">
            %(posts)s
        </ul>
    </body>
</html>
"""
```

What you see in Listing 8-2 is a Python string template containing the shell for an HTML page. If you're not already familiar with string formatting in Python, you might want to consult the docs, here:

```
http://docs.python.org/lib/typesseq-strings.html
```

Basically, this template is a string with named slots, with content eventually provided by a map object. Note that this approach to templating is fairly primitive: It doesn't allow for any logic in the template — just slots for content.

So, the logic to generate something like repeating chunks of HTML — say, for instance, bookmark items — will reside in the program itself. But, that code will use further string templates, as provided in Listing 8-3.

Listing 8-3: ch08_mirror_posts.py (Part 3 of 9)

```python
# HTML template for an individual link.
HTML_LINK_TMPL = u"""
    <li class="delPost" id="del-%(hash)s">
        <span class="delTime">%(time)s</span>
        <a class="delLink" href="%(href)s">%(description)s</a>
        <span class="delExtended">%(extended)s</span>
        <ul class="delTags">
            %(tags)s
        </ul>
    </li>
"""

# HTML template for a tag attached to a link
HTML_TAG_TMPL = u"""
    <li class="delTag">
        <a href="http://del.icio.us/%(user)s/%(tag)s">%(tag)s</a>
    </li>
"""
```

The next two string templates in Listing 8-3 define formatting for bookmarks and tags listed, respectively. Along with the first string template, these templates will be populated, repeated, and nested to build the overall page. You'll be able to customize the HTML in these templates to match whatever site design you like, without necessarily needing to modify the rest of the program.

And, speaking of the program, its main() function begins in Listing 8-4.

Listing 8-4: ch08_mirror_posts.py (Part 4 of 9)

```
def main():
    """
    Backup all of a user's bookmarks by date, attempting to render
    an HTML page of each date along the way.
    """

    # Get ready for calls to the del.icio.us API.
    initApi()

    # Create the backups path, if needed.
    if not os.path.isdir(POSTS_PATH): os.makedirs(POSTS_PATH)

    # Look up all the dates for which this user has bookmarks.
    print "Querying API for posting dates..."
    dates_data = xmlapi('posts/dates')
    open('%s/dates.xml' % POSTS_PATH, 'w').write(dates_data)
```

First up in the main() function begun in Listing 8-4 is a Python docstring, describing the function's purpose. And, being the main driver function of this program, its purpose is synonymous with the purpose of the program itself: to back up your bookmarks and build HTML pages from them.

In preparation for this goal, which will make extensive use of the del.icio.us API, a function initApi() is called. This function's implementation will be revealed shortly — but for now, rest assured that it does things necessary for the use of the API.

Following this, a check is made to see if the bookmarks data directory exists, creating it if it does not. Then, the first call to the API is made, to retrieve a list of dates for which del.icio.us has bookmarks stored for you. The data from this call is stored in the file dates.xml in the root of the backup directory.

The next part of the program, presented in Listing 8-5, begins the logic that actually downloads your bookmarks using the dates data is retrieved.

Listing 8-5: ch08_mirror_posts.py (Part 5 of 9)

```
    # Visit the user's posts for each of the dates.
    for date in xmltramp.parse(dates_data):

        # Grab the date and derive the backup file path.
        dt   = date('date')
        path = date2path(dt)
```

continued

Listing 8-5 *continued*

```
# Skip this date if an XML backup already exists.
if os.path.isfile('%s.xml' % path): continue

# Create the parent directories for backup if necessary.
dir = os.path.dirname(path)
if not os.path.isdir(dir): os.makedirs(dir)

# Catch any errors that happen from here on.
try:

    # Make a query to the API for this date's bookmarks
    print "Backing up %s..." % dt
    posts_data = xmlapi('posts/get?dt=%s' % dt)
    open('%s.xml' % path, 'w').write(posts_data)
```

At the start of Listing 8-5, you can see the first usage of the xmltramp module in extracting the posting dates from the XML data retrieved from the API. If you recall from Chapter 3, the structure of the XML from the posts/dates API call is fairly simple: There's a <dates> tag containing multiple <date> children, each of which provides in attributes a count of posts along with the date itself.

So, xmltramp provides a way to access XML data in a way that behaves a lot like native Python data structures. The object returned by xmltramp.parse(dates_data) represents the root <dates> element, and each object found by iterating over that object as a list represents a <date> child element. Then, for each <date> child, its attributes are available by calling the object as a function. Thus, date('date') retrieves the date attribute of the element (i.e., 2005-01-25).

The retrieved date string is converted to a backup file path prefix via date2path(), which will be defined later. A check is made to see whether the XML data for this date's posts has already been created, causing the loop to skip ahead if so. This presumes that the loop's current date has already been backed up and doing it over again is unnecessary. Because of this check, you'll be able to run this program again and again — say, from a crontab entry — and the backups it makes will be incremental.

 If you run this program early in the day and post further bookmarks later, this loop will miss your new posts because the backed up file will already exist. You may want to delete the current day's backup when running this program, or find another way to handle this situation. As a scheduled job, you might just want to run this program at 11:59 P.M. or so just before the date changes, and things should go pretty smoothly.

As you move through Listing 8-5, if the current date's backup indeed does not yet exist, an effort is first made to ensure the existence of the backup's parent directories. This is where the implementation of date2path() comes in: Dates are hyphen-separated from del.icio.us, but the backup directory structure will be arranged by year, month, and day (e.g., 2005/01/25.xml). The date2path() performs this transformation.

At the tail end of Listing 8-5 is the beginning of a try/except block, meant to catch any HTTP or XML parsing errors that might occur during the course of the backup and otherwise wreck the whole process. First within this block is a call to the posts/get method of the API, using the current date as a parameter. The data retrieved from this call is, at last, written out to disk into the backup path along with a .xml file extension.

Now, with the bookmark data for the date safely backed up, the code in Listing 8-6 will start to work on producing the HTML rendering of the posts.

Listing 8-6: ch08_mirror_posts.py (Part 6 of 9)

```python
# Parse and process each of the link posts retrieved.
posts_out = []
for post in xmltramp.parse(posts_data):

    # Render all of the post's tags using the tag
    # template.
    tags_out = [
        HTML_TAG_TMPL % TemplateSafeDict(
            user = API_USER,
            tag  = tag
        )
        for tag in post('tag').split(' ')
    ]

    # Start building a dict for the link template
    link_ns = TemplateSafeDict(
        tags = ''.join(tags_out)
    )

    # Merge in all the parsed attributes for
    # this post.
    link_ns.update(post._attrs)

    # Render the link post using the template.
    posts_out.append(HTML_LINK_TMPL % link_ns)

    # Print this link's title as progress indicator.
    print "\t%s" % \
        post('description').encode(UNICODE_ENC)
```

A list named `posts_out` is initialized as empty at the beginning of Listing 8-6. This list will contain the rendered HTML fragments for each bookmark post found in the data downloaded from the API. So, the next step is to start processing those posts, via iterating over the parsed XML object produced by a call to `xmltramp.parse(posts_data)`.

Here's where the templating logic starts to appear: Things are taken from the inside out and built in fragments. First, all the tags for the post need to be rendered. Then, the bookmark post itself is rendered, using the product of the tag rendering.

The HTML fragments for tags are generated in a rather compact way — through the use of a *Python list comprehension*. In a nutshell, a Python list comprehension allows you to iterate through a list and produce a new list, after it performs whatever filtering and transformation you desire.

This is where the `for tag in post('tag').split(' ')` statement comes in: The tags for the bookmark are available as a space-separated string. This is split along the spaces into a list. For each individual tag in this list, an instance of the class `TemplateSafeDict` is created using the tag string itself along with the `API_USER` value.

This `TemplateSafeDict` object, whose class will be defined shortly, is basically a Python dictionary but with code added to allow accesses without error to keys that do not exist in the structure. This instance is used with the `%` operator to populate the named content slots in `HTML_TAG_TMPL` corresponding with keys in each instance of `TemplateSafeDict` derived from the list of tags. (If you go back and look at the definition of `HTML_TAG_TMPL` in Listing 8-3, you'll see the slots for `user` and `tag`.)

The end result of this list comprehension, then, is to convert the list of tags into a list of fully populated HTML fragments based on `HTML_TAG_TMPL`.

The next step in the process is to start creating a `TemplateSafeDict` instance named `link_ns` for use in building the next layer of HTML representing the bookmark's contents. This dictionary starts with a `tags` entry, whose value is the set of HTML fragments for tags concatenated into one big string.

Following this is a bit of a hack: The undocumented, ostensibly private member variable `_attrs` of the `xmltramp` object `post` contains all the attributes for this bookmark element in a dictionary. Rather than meticulously extract each interesting attribute and add it to `link_ns`, the `update()` method is used to simply merge them in wholesale.

With this done, an HTML fragment for the bookmark is produced via the `%` operator, populating `HTML_LINK_TMPL` with the contents of `link_ns`. Again, review Listing 8-3 to see what content slots are expected as shared between `HTML_LINK_TMPL` and `link_ns`. Also, you should be somewhat familiar with the structure of a bookmark XML entry from Chapter 3. This stuff all dovetails together fairly nicely.

Once generated, the HTML fragment for the bookmark is appended to the `posts_out` list, a progress message is displayed, and the loop continues. It continues, that is, until all the bookmarks have been processed. Then, you wrap things up in Listing 8-7.

Listing 8-7: ch08_mirror_posts.py (Part 7 of 9)

```
                    # Finally, build the overall page and write it out
                    # to disk
                    page = HTML_PAGE_TMPL % TemplateSafeDict(
                        posts       = ''.join(posts_out),
                        date        = dt,
                        unicode_enc = UNICODE_ENC
                    )
                    page = page.encode(UNICODE_ENC)
                    open('%s.html' % path, 'w').write(page)

            except SAXParseException, e:
                # Rendering fails on XML errors, but at least
                # there's a backup.
                print "\tProblem parsing XML: %s" % e

            except urllib2.HTTPError, e:
                # The API call for posts failed altogether.
                print "\tProblem calling API: %s" %e
```

For those of you typing code in by hand, notice that Listing 8-7 occurs *after the close* of the second loop you've been following so far to produce bookmark HTML fragments. It does, however, remain within the scope of the *first* loop that's running through dates. Because Python eschews braces for syntactic whitespace, this calls for a single outdent. Thus, this code starts at the same indentation level as the statement posts_out = [], back in Listing 8-6.

Indentation matters out of the way, let's see what this code does. This is the grand finale for HTML production: An instance of TemplateSafeDict is created through the use of a concatenation of all bookmark HTML fragments generated, along with the date and desired Unicode encoding. This dictionary is used to build the final HTML page by way of the HTML_PAGE_TMPL string template. It's then encoded to the proper Unicode form and then written out to the backup path in a file with a .html extension (e.g., 2005/01/25.html).

Then, with the work for this loop finally done, the last thing to do in main() is to follow up the try from Listing 8-5 with some exception handling. Here, XML parsing errors are trapped and noted, along with HTTP problems in using the API. It's assumed that these problems are transitory, and so the program reports the issues but continues on with the next date for backup.

All that's left now for this program is to finish up by filling in all of the "to be implemented" functions mentioned so far. For these, continue on to Listing 8-8.

Listing 8-8: ch08_mirror_posts.py (Part 8 of 9)

```python
def initApi():
    """Prepare for calls to the del.icio.us API"""
    # Setup urllib2 for del's Basic Authentication
    auth = urllib2.HTTPBasicAuthHandler()
    auth.add_password('del.icio.us API', 'del.icio.us',
                      API_USER, API_PASSWD)
    urllib2.install_opener(urllib2.build_opener(auth))

def xmlapi(method):
    """Perform a call to the del.icio.us API, returning XML"""
    time.sleep(1) # Enforce the 1 second delay between API calls.
    url = '%s/%s' % (API_URL, method)
    return urllib2.urlopen(url).read()

def date2path(dt):
    """Convert a del.icio.us date into a backup file path."""
    y, m, d = dt.split('-')
    return '%s/%s/%s/%s' % (POSTS_PATH, y, m, d)
```

The first function defined in Listing 8-8 is initApi(). Basically, what it does is prepare Python's urllib2 module with the facility to respond to authentication requests from the del.icio.us API using the user name and password defined at the beginning of the program. This entails installing an HTTPBasicAuthHandler() instance, which is best explained in the documentation for urllib2 located here:

    http://docs.python.org/lib/urllib2-examples.html

Next is the definition of a method called xmlapi(). This is a convenience function that simply serves to tidy up code calling the del.icio.us API, wrapping the HTTP request and fetch, along with a delay mandated by the API documentation. It returns the XML data produced by the API call.

And last, but not least, date2path() is defined. As you've probably already guessed, this function converts a hyphen-separated date string into a file path.

There's one final thing to define, however, and that's the TemplateSafeDict class used throughout the HTML generation in this program. Look for it next, in Listing 8-9.

Listing 8-9: ch08_mirror_posts.py (Part 9 of 9)

```python
class TemplateSafeDict:
    """A dict-alike that's safe for dumb templates."""
```

Listing 8-9 *continued*

```python
    def __init__(self, **kwargs):
        """Initialize the new dict."""
        self.data = dict(**kwargs)

    def update(self, data):
        """Update the dict with new data."""
        self.data.update(data)

    def __repr__(self):
        """Return the dict's representation."""
        return repr(self.data)

    def __setitem__(self, key, val):
        """Set a value in the dict."""
        self.data[key] = val

    def __getitem__(self, key):
        """
        Get a value from the dict by key.  If no such key exists,
        just return a blank string.  Useful for dumb templates.
        """
        if key in self.data:
            return self.data[key]
        else:
            return u''

# If being run as a script, fire up the main function.
if __name__ == '__main__': main()
```

Essentially, what `TemplateSafeDict` in Listing 8-9 implements is a read-only proxy object for a Python dictionary. You can read up on what all the magic double-underscore methods do in Python here:

```
http://docs.python.org/ref/sequence-types.html
```

The one real special feature of this object is in the `__getitem__()` method. Normally, when an attempt is made to access a dictionary key that does not exist, an exception is thrown. But, when rendering a template, it is more desirable to simply return an empty string and continue on. That's what this method enables.

So, our dumb templates defined at the start of the program can include content slots for keys that need not necessarily exist in the dictionary used to populate them. This, then, has practical value in cases where a bookmark may have a title or description defined, but no extended notes field supplied. Instead of needing any elaborate logic to test for the existence of an extended notes field, our template can remain simple and just include an empty element where no extended notes are available.

Running the Program

That's the end of the program, so it's time to try it out. You should be able to run it with a simple command line invocation of `python ch08_mirror_posts.py`, or even execute it directly from a UNIX shell if you've set the proper permissions. If all goes well, you should see something like Figure 8-21 take shape in your terminal window.

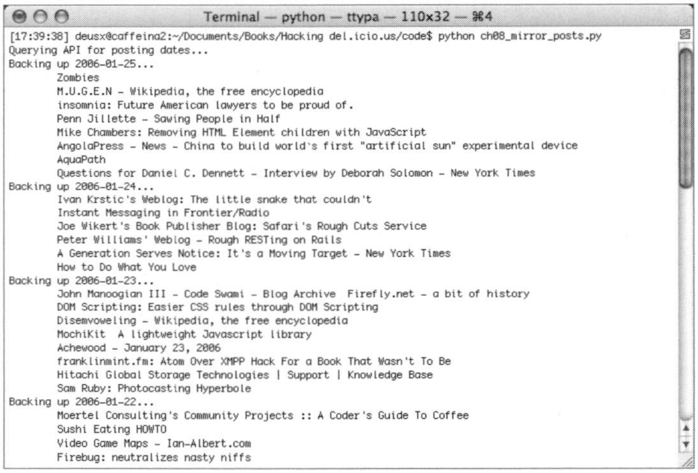

```
[17:39:38] deusx@caffeina2:~/Documents/Books/Hacking del.icio.us/code$ python ch08_mirror_posts.py
Querying API for posting dates...
Backing up 2006-01-25...
        Zombies
        M.U.G.E.N — Wikipedia, the free encyclopedia
        insomnia: Future American lawyers to be proud of.
        Penn Jillette — Sawing People in Half
        Mike Chambers: Removing HTML Element children with JavaScript
        AngolaPress — News — China to build world's first "artificial sun" experimental device
        AquaPath
        Questions for Daniel C. Dennett — Interview by Deborah Solomon — New York Times
Backing up 2006-01-24...
        Ivan Krstic's Weblog: The little snake that couldn't
        Instant Messaging in Frontier/Radio
        Joe Wikert's Book Publisher Blog: Safari's Rough Cuts Service
        Peter Williams' Weblog — Rough RESTing on Rails
        A Generation Serves Notice: It's a Moving Target — New York Times
        How to Do What You Love
Backing up 2006-01-23...
        John Manoogian III — Code Swami — Blog Archive  Firefly.net — a bit of history
        DOM Scripting: Easier CSS rules through DOM Scripting
        Disemvoweling — Wikipedia, the free encyclopedia
        MochiKit  A lightweight Javascript library
        Achewood — January 23, 2006
        franklinmint.fm: Atom Over XMPP Hack For a Book That Wasn't To Be
        Hitachi Global Storage Technologies | Support | Knowledge Base
        Sam Ruby: Photocasting Hyperbole
Backing up 2006-01-22...
        Moertel Consulting's Community Projects :: A Coder's Guide To Coffee
        Sushi Eating HOWTO
        Video Game Maps — Ian-Albert.com
        Firebug: neutralizes nasty niffs
```

FIGURE 8-21: Watching a run of ch08_mirror_posts.py in progress

When the program has completed, you should have a directory structure organized by date of XML and HTML files representing all of your bookmarks. For example, if you have the `tree` command in your shell, if you run it you should get a result something like this:

```
[17:44:33] deusx@caffeina2:code$ tree del-posts/
del-posts/
|-- 2005
|   |-- 10
|   |   |-- 19.html
|   |   |-- 19.xml
|   |   |-- 20.html
|   |   |-- 20.xml
|   |   |-- 21.html
|   |   |-- 21.xml
...
```

Now, try viewing one of those HTML files in your browser. It'll look something like Figure 8-22. Looks pretty ugly, doesn't it? That's because we've missed a piece of the puzzle: CSS.

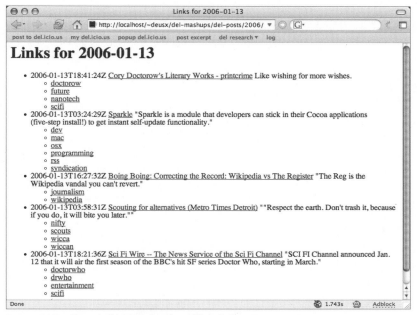

FIGURE 8-22: Unstyled HTML produced by ch08_mirror_posts.py

You might have noticed the reference to ch08_post_styles.css back in Listing 8-2. Every HTML file produced by the program links to this stylesheet in its header. Check out Listing 8-10 for a complete set of CSS styles applicable to this HTML. In fact, if you put this file one directory above the posts backup directory, all of the HTML files should include it.

Listing 8-10: ch08_post_styles.css

```
body, div, span, p, li { font: 12px arial; }
ul.delPosts { margin: 2ex; }

li.delPost {
    list-style: none;
    clear: both;
    margin: 2em;
    margin-bottom: 2em;
    padding-bottom: 2em;
}
```

Listing 8-10 *continued*

```css
span.delTime {
    float: right;
    font-weight: italic;
    font-size: x-small;
}

a.delLink {
    display: block;
    font-weight: bold;
    margin-left: -2em;
    padding-bottom: 0.5em;
}

ul.delTags {
    list-style: none;
    clear: both;
    margin: 0;
    padding: 0;
    padding-top: 0.5em;
}

li.delTag {
    font-size: x-small;
    float: left;
    width: 15ex;
    margin: 0.25em;
    padding: 0.25em;
    border: 1px solid #ccc;
    background-color: #f0f0f0;
}

li.delTag a {
    display: block;
    width: 100%;
}
```

There's nothing that says you have to use these CSS styles for your bookmarks because you should be able to tailor the HTML and CSS produced by this program to blend in with your existing site and content. The styles in Listing 8-10 at least illustrate what can be applied to the HTML as provided in this program's out-of-box templates. Check out Figure 8-23 to see how things change once this CSS is brought into the picture.

FIGURE 8-23: Freshly styled HTML, courtesy of ch08_post_styles.css

Browsing Your Bookmarks with Ajax

So, now that you've got all your bookmarks backed up as XML and HTML. With a little CSS, you can polish up the HTML for nicer viewing in a browser — but what can you do with all that XML?

Well, although having all those static HTML renderings of your links is nice, how about building something a little more dynamic? With a little help from Ajax, you can turn that pile of XML data into an interactive database. This next mashup will allow you to build a JavaScript-powered mini-browser for all of your downloaded bookmarks. Check out Listing 8-11 for the beginnings of this new project, ch08_post_browser.html.

Listing 8-11: ch08_post_browser.html

```
<html>
    <!--

        ch08_post_browser.html

        Bare-bones HTML to play host to the browser JavaScript.
    -->
    <head>
```

continued

Listing 8-11 *continued*

```
        <title>del.icio.us mini-browser</title>

        <!-- http://www.mochikit.com/ -->
        <script src="MochiKit/MochiKit.js"
                type="text/javascript"></script>

        <script src="ch08_post_browser.js"
                type="text/javascript"></script>

        <link href="ch08_post_styles.css"
                type="text/css" rel="stylesheet" />

    </head>
    <body>

        <form id="main">
            <select id="date_selector">
                <option value="">No dates loaded</option>
            </select>
            <select id="tag_selector">
                <option value="">No tags loaded</option>
            </select>
        </form>

        <div id="links">No links loaded.</div>

    </body>
</html>
```

In Listing 8-11, you're given some very simple HTML to start things off. There's not much here because just about everything will be built on-the-fly in JavaScript code. The tags that do appear here are mostly just to give the JavaScript some user interface controls and areas into which new content will be injected.

This HTML also pulls in the JavaScript and CSS meant to help power this browsing interface. Of particular interface is the include for MochiKit, a set of JavaScript modules that you'll need to download before you go on. Check out the MochiKit project page here:

```
www.mochikit.com/
```

When you download and unpack the archive from the site, you'll find a version of the libraries in separate and modular form, as well as a single packed JavaScript library. It's this packed version that gets included in Figure 8-11.

MochiKit is a very useful set of extensions for JavaScript that makes it easier to deal with lists, loops, Ajax, and page content creation. You'll see all of these things employed in this browser, so you may want to dig a little deeper into this package and see all that it has to offer.

Forging ahead, take a look at Listing 8-12 for the beginning of ch08_post_browser.js, where the functionality of the bookmark browser is implemented.

Listing 8-12: ch08_post_browser.js (Part 1 of 8)

```
/**
    ch08_post_browser.js

    Implementation of an AJAX-powered date and tag browser for
    del.icio.us posts, with optional support for a PHP proxy or
    static captures of API data.
*/
var USE_PROXY  = false;
var STATIC_URI = "del-posts";

/**
    Initialize the browser, load up the list of dates.
*/
function init() {
    // Insert loading messages into the selectors.
    setOptions('date_selector', [['Loading dates...', '']]);
    setOptions('tag_selector',  [['Loading tags...', '']]);

    // Switch between proxy and static API URLs for dates
    var dates_url = (USE_PROXY) ? PROXY_URI+'/posts/dates' :
                               STATIC_URI+'/dates.xml';

    // Fire up the request for dates...
    var d = doSimpleXMLHttpRequest(dates_url);
    d.addCallback(datesFetched);
    d.addErrback(function() {
        setOptions('date_selector', [['Dates not loaded.', '']]);
    });

    // Switch between proxy and static API URLs for tags
    var tags_url = (USE_PROXY) ? PROXY_URI+'/tags/get' :
                               STATIC_URI+'/tags.xml';

    // Fire up the request for tags...
    var d = doSimpleXMLHttpRequest(tags_url);
    d.addCallback(tagsFetched);
    d.addErrback(function() {
        setOptions('tag_selector',  [['Tags not loaded.', '']]);
    });
}
addLoadEvent(init);
```

First up in Listing 8-12 is the assignment of two constants: USE_PROXY and STATIC_URI. There will be mentions of proxy support throughout this code, but you won't see it come into play until the final mashup of this chapter. So don't worry about it too much yet. Initially, this code is meant to access the static tree of XML bookmark data fetched by ch08_mirror_posts.py.

The init() function is defined in Listing 8-12, which begins the process of building the browser application. The first thing it does is swap loading messages into the options for date and tag selection menus provided in the HTML. Next, the doSimpleXMLHttpRequest() function provided by MochiKit is used to initiate HTTP GET requests to fetch both dates and tags.

Because this process of fetching new content via XMLHttpRequest is asynchronous, call-back functions are needed in order to process the fetched data when it arrives, or handle any error conditions that occur along the way. In the case of errors, the respective loading messages in the select menus are simply replaced with failure messages. On the other hand, the functions datesFetched() and tagsFetched() are called for the arrival of date and tag data, respectively.

You can find both of these functions defined next in Listing 8-13.

Listing 8-13: ch08_post_browser.js (Part 2 of 8)

```
/**
    Process the list of dates when it arrives, populate the
    drop-down menu and wire it up to react to selections.
*/
function datesFetched(req) {
    var xml      = req.responseXML;
    var dates    = xml.getElementsByTagName('date');
    var date_cnt = 0;

    // Add the dates fetched as select options.
    setOptions('date_selector',
        map(function(date) {
            var date_txt  = date.getAttribute('date');
            var count_txt = date.getAttribute('count');
            return [date_txt+' ('+count_txt+')', date_txt];
        }, dates)
    );

    // Register the selector change handler.
    $('date_selector').onchange = dateSelected;

    // Start things off by loading up the first set of links.
    return $('date_selector').onchange();
}
```

Listing 8-13 *continued*

```
/**
    Process the list of tags when it arrives, populate the
    drop-down menu and wire it up to react to selections.
*/
function tagsFetched(req) {
    var xml     = req.responseXML;
    var tags    = xml.getElementsByTagName('tag');
    var tag_cnt = 0;

    // Add the tags fetched as select options.
    setOptions('tag_selector',
        map(function(tag) {
            var tag_txt  = tag.getAttribute('tag');
            var count_txt = tag.getAttribute('count');
            return [tag_txt+' ('+count_txt+')', tag_txt];
        }, tags)
    );

    // Register the selector change handler.
    $('tag_selector').onchange = tagSelected;
}
```

Note that both `datesFetched()` and `tagsFetched()` are nearly identical in Listing 8-13. They're just different enough that, for the sake of clarity, they're separate functions here. But, their purposes are also nearly identical:

These functions process the respective XML structures fetched from the del.icio.us API for date and tag listings, in order to populate the date and tag drop-down menus with selections. Then, they set each menu's `onchange` handler to fire off the appropriate callback script to handle loading in a set of bookmarks appropriate to the date or tag selected. One of the biggest differences between the two is that `datesFetched()` is built to load up the first day worth of bookmarks once it's finished processing as a way of kicking off the browser display.

In each of these functions, the `setOptions()` function is used, which will be implemented in this script later on. However, the `map()` function comes courtesy of MochiKit. It works somewhat like list comprehensions in Python: Feed a list in, transform each of its elements with an anonymous function, return a list of transformed elements.

In this case, each of the dates or tags and their respective bookmark counts are turned into label/value pairs in a list to be used by `setOptions()` in building the selection menu.

Next, in Listing 8-14, the `dateSelected()` and `tagSelected()` functions are examined.

Listing 8-14: ch08_post_browser.js (Part 3 of 8)

```
/**
    React to a new selection by loading up posts for the date.
*/
function dateSelected() {
    // Get the selected date from the drop down.
    var date = this.options[this.selectedIndex].value;
    var url;
    if (USE_PROXY) {
        // Use a proxy-based URL.
        url = PROXY_URI+'/posts/get?dt='+date
    } else {
        // Use a static file path URL.
        var path = date.split('-').join('/');
        url = STATIC_URI + '/' + path + '.xml';
    }
    loadPosts(url);
}


/**
    React to a new selection by loading up posts for the tag.
*/
function tagSelected() {
    // Get the selected tag from the drop down.
    var tag = this.options[this.selectedIndex].value;
    var url;
    if (USE_PROXY) {
        // Use a proxy-based URL.
        url = PROXY_URI+'/posts/all?tag='+tag
    } else {
        // Use a static file path URL.
        var path = tag.split('-').join('/');
        url = STATIC_URI + '/' + path + '.xml';
    }
    loadPosts(url);
}
```

Once more, note the similarity of the two functions in Listing 8-14. This is because the API and data for both date and tag listings are very similar. Because both of these functions are called in response to a change in selection on the date or tag menu, the first thing done is to extract the current value of the respective selection field. This value is then used in building a URL with which to fetch fresh bookmarks.

Here you see evidence of proxy support in URL construction — but again, don't worry about it too much yet. You may be interested to note that the proxy support looks more like direct usage of the del.icio.us API, while non-proxy implementation is meant to work against the static backup data fetched by `ch08_mirror_posts.py`.

In Listing 8-15, you take a look at the `loadPosts()` function.

Listing 8-15: ch08_post_browser.js (Part 4 of 8)

```
/**
    Given a URL, initiate the process of loading a new set of
    bookmark posts into the browser.
*/
function loadPosts(url) {
    // Initiate a GET request for the posts.
    setContent($('links'), 'Loading posts...');
    var d = doSimpleXMLHttpRequest(url);
    d.addCallback(postsFetched);
    d.addErrback(function(rv) {
        setContent($('links'), 'Problem loading '+url+'!');
    });
}


/**
    Process the arriving posts data, rebuild the list of links
    shown on the page.
*/
function postsFetched(req) {
    // Get the incoming XML, extract user name and list of posts.
    var xml   = req.responseXML;
    var user  = getNodeAttribute(xml.firstChild, 'user');
    var posts = xml.getElementsByTagName('post');

    // Build the HTML list of posts using buildPostItem
    var posts_list =
        UL({'class':'delPosts'},
            map(function(post) {
                return buildPostItem(user, post);
            }, posts)
        );

    // Replace the existing list of links on page.
    setContent($('links'), posts_list);
}
```

A pair of functions is defined in Listing 8-15: `loadPosts()` and `postsFetched()`. Again, this is because of the asynchronous nature of Ajax communications and the need for callbacks.

The `loadPosts()` function first inserts a loading message into the content area where bookmarks will be loaded. Then, it starts a request via `doSimpleXMLHttpRequest` with `postsFetched()` registered as the callback method when content is ready. Alternatively, on errors, a failure message is inserted into the link container.

The `postsFetched()` function begins the process of building new HTML content from the del.icio.us API bookmark data. It starts by building a `<ul>` element with a CSS class name of `delPosts`, using another MochiKit convenience, the `UL()` function. MochiKit is full of these tools and shortcuts to make this method of dynamic content construction easier.

Inside the `UL()` function call, the work of creating the individual `<li>` child elements is farmed out to a function called `buildPostItem()`. This is done by using `map()` to apply `buildPostItem()` on each of the `<post>` elements found in the bookmarks data. This function is defined next, in Listing 8-16.

Listing 8-16: ch08_post_browser.js (Part 5 of 8)

```
/**
    Given a user name and a post node, build the HTML
    for a single bookmark post.
*/
function buildPostItem(user, post) {

    // Extract the attributes from the post.
    var data = extractFromPost(post);

    // Build the link post list item.
    var item =
        LI({'class':'delPost'},

            SPAN({'class':'delTime'}, data['time']),

            A({'class':'delLink', href:data['href']},
                data['description']),

            SPAN({'class':'delExtended'}, data['extended'])
        );

    // Add tag links, if any tags attached.
    var tags = data['tag'].split(' ');
    if (tags) {
        var tags_list = buildTagList(user, tags);
        appendChildNodes(item, tags_list);
    }

    return item;
}
```

In Listing 8-16, the function `buildPostItem()` is defined. This function is at the core of building the HTML content for each bookmark displayed on the page. It attempts to closely mimic the same HTML built by `ch08_mirror_posts.py`, but this time everything's done on-the-fly in the browser.

First, the `extractFromPost()` function is called, which extracts the attributes from the bookmark `<post>` passed in as a parameter. Then, an `<li>` element is constructed, with child elements constructed to contain the date, link, title, and extended notes. Each of these child elements is assigned a CSS class and filled with content from the extracted post data.

Next, the bookmark data is checked for tags. If tags are present, the `buildTagList()` function is called to construct another HTML list of tag links. Then, at the end, the finished bookmark item element is returned.

Continue on to Listing 8-17, where the `extractFromPost()` function is presented.

Listing 8-17: ch08_post_browser.js (Part 6 of 8)

```
/**
    Given an XML node representing a bookmark post, extract all
    the attributes containing the bookmark's details.
*/
function extractFromPost(post) {
    var data = {};
    forEach(
        ['time','href','description','extended','tag'],
        function(k) { data[k] = getNodeAttribute(post, k) }
    );
    return data;
}
```

The `extractFromPost()` function in Listing 8-17 is pretty simple: Using the MochiKit `forEach()` function, a list of post attribute names is traversed to copy each corresponding node attribute into a JavaScript object. This is basically a convenience function to ease the use of post attributes in building content.

Next, in Listing 8-18, you'll see what makes the `buildTagList()` function tick.

Listing 8-18: ch08_post_browser.js (Part 7 of 8)

```
/**
    Given a user name and a list of tags, build an HTML list of
    tag links.
*/
function buildTagList(user, tags) {
    return UL({ 'class':'delTags' },
```

continued

Listing 8-18 *continued*

```
        map(function(tag) {
            var href = 'http://del.icio.us/'+user+'/'+tag;
            return LI({'class':'delTag'}, A({href:href}, tag));
        }, tags)
    );
}
```

Found in Listing 8-18, `buildTagList()` is another pretty straightforward convenience function used to build an HTML list of tag links. It uses the `map()` function and DOM helper functions to transform tag names into `<li>` elements, each containing a tag link element. This list of elements is used as the children of a parent `<ul>` element, which is returned as the final product of this function.

Finally, this JavaScript is wrapped up in Listing 8-19 with two more function definitions.

Listing 8-19: ch08_post_browser.js (Part 8 of 8)

```
/**
    Set the options for a given select identified by ID.
*/
function setOptions(sid, data) {
    var opts = $(sid).options;
    opts.length = 0;
    forEach(data, function(d) {
        opts[opts.length] = new Option(d[0], d[1]);
    });
}

/**
    Completely replace the content of a given parent with the
    children supplied.
*/
function setContent(node, children) {
    while (node.firstChild)
        node.removeChild(node.firstChild);
    appendChildNodes(node, children);
}
```

The two functions defined in Listing 8-19 are very close cousins in terms of functionality: The `setOptions()` function was used very early on in the script. Basically, it clears out all of the options from an HTML `<select>` element and, using a two-dimensional array passed in as a parameter, inserts a brand new set of options.

After this, the `setContent()` function is defined. This function serves to clear out all of the content found in a given page element, replacing it with the content passed in as a parameter.

Trying Out the Bookmark Browser

With the completion of the browser's implementation, it's time to try it out. It's best for this JavaScript, the associated HTML, and the CSS to all live in the parent directory under which your bookmark backup folder lives. The `STATIC_URI` constant at the start of `ch08_post_browser.js` can be tweaked to reflect a different location of this directory, but the examples here assume everything's all in the same place.

So, once everything's in the right place, load up `ch08_post_browser.html` in your Web browser. It's hard to depict the dynamic nature of this thing as an application through screenshots — but, if everything is in working order, you should first see a screen like Figure 8-24 as the JavaScript starts up and initiates fetches to pull in your bookmark dates and tags. Once everything has loaded, the page should appear loaded with bookmarks, as in Figure 8-25.

You may notice that in this initial stage, tags are not loaded. This is because tags were not included in the backup process implemented in `ch08_mirror_posts.py`. I'll leave it as a project for you to improve the backup program to download tags and possibly fetch each of your tags' set of bookmarks separately. However, the tag selection function will become useful with the introduction of this chapter's final program.

FIGURE 8-24: Bookmark browser loading in progress

FIGURE 8-25: Bookmark browser loading has completed and fresh links are displayed.

But for now, try playing with the date selector. Each time you choose a new item from the menu, that date's bookmarks are dynamically fetched and built into links on the page. With a little more work and CSS tweaking, you could use this code along with your bookmark backups to build the ultimate blog links sidebar.

Building a Caching API Proxy Using PHP

Presenting dynamically fetched bookmarks from your static backups is a pretty neat trick, but it's limited to the data set grabbed during the backup process. Although the JavaScript code can support it, you've already seen that it can't use tags yet because the backup program didn't fetch them. While it's great to have a tool to back up your bookmarks, it quickly gets limiting when unanticipated use cases arise as you try to use it as a database or a replacement for the del.icio.us API. You'll constantly need to update the tool to fetch different combinations of API calls and queries.

So, why not just use the del.icio.us API in the Ajax-powered bookmark browser? Well, the answer is two-fold: First, there are cross-domain security limitations that prevent the use of `XMLHttpRequest` to make requests to other servers — and that includes calls to the del.icio.us API from a page hosted on your own servers. And second, one of the goals of the latter part of this chapter is to reduce reliance on the del.icio.us servers by using data on servers you control.

Another approach to these concerns is to build a caching proxy in front of the del.icio.us API. Instead of grabbing all of the data you could possibly need up front in a backup script, emulate the del.icio.us API to allow all of the same calls and cache the results of all calls locally. With this approach, you'll gradually build a cache of all of your del.icio.us bookmarks that naturally reflects usage patterns, while at the same time being able to more easily support unanticipated API call combinations.

For this proxy, we're going to need PHP. Whereas the backup program in Python could run on the command line, this proxy needs to run on the Web. So, check out Listing 8-20 for the start of this proxy script in PHP.

Listing 8-20: ch08_api_cache.php (Part 1 of 6)

```php
<?php
    /**
        ch08_api_cache.php

        Provide a caching proxy in front of the del.icio.us API
        for use by the AJAX browser.
    */

    define('DEL_API',        'del.icio.us/api');
    define('DEL_USER',       'your_username_here');
    define('DEL_PASSWD',     'your_password_here');
    define('DEL_POSTS_PATH', 'del-posts');
    define('DEL_CACHE_AGE',  '3600');

    // http://sourceforge.net/projects/snoopy/
    require_once 'includes/Snoopy.class.php';
```

In Listing 8-20, the PHP script starts with a descriptive comment and a set of configuration defines. These include the original del.icio.us API URL, your user name and password, the path where the cache should be built, and a maximum age (in seconds) before considering a file in the cache as stale and in need of a fresh fetch.

Note that the cache path is the same as that used by ch08_mirror_posts.py — these two programs are not mutually exclusive: You can use the backup script to seed and regularly refresh data in the backup/cache, while the proxy will follow the same directory structures. Just make sure all your file permissions are set so that both the Python program and PHP page can read and write in this directory.

At the end of Listing 8-20, code for the Snoopy Web client is required for the page. You'll need to download this package from the following Web page:

```
http://sourceforge.net/projects/snoopy/
```

Snoopy is a pretty reliable HTTP client class that works where many other means for fetching URLs fail. If you know a bit of PHP, you can skip this download and swap out the Snoopy usage later in the listings to simplify dependencies. But, it's safe to just grab Snoopy and let it do what it does best.

In Listing 8-21, the code starts to get down to the business of being a proxy.

Listing 8-21: ch08_api_cache.php (Part 2 of 6)

```php
if (isset($_SERVER['PATH_INFO'])) {

    // Assume all requests with a path result in XML.
    header('Content-Type: text/xml');

    $path = $_SERVER['PATH_INFO'];
    switch($path) {

        // Proxy through requests for dates
        case '/posts/dates':
            echo delAPI($path, DEL_POSTS_PATH.'/dates.xml');
            exit;

        // Proxy through requests for tags
        case '/tags/get':
            echo delAPI($path, DEL_POSTS_PATH.'/tags.xml');
            exit;
```

First thing in Listing 8-21, a check is made for the server variable PATH_INFO. All del.icio.us API calls take the form of some combination of paths leading from the URL prefix http://del.icio.us/api, so this is an attempt to handle extra paths from this script's URL in the same way as del.icio.us API calls. So, for example, while the del.icio.us API call for dates looks like this:

```
http://del.icio.us/api/posts/dates
```

the same call through this proxy might look like this:

```
http://example.com/ch08_api_cache.php/posts/dates
```

So, ideally, you'll just need to swap out the API URL prefix for the URL where you install this PHP script.

The rest of the code in Listing 8-21 performs a switch on the PATH_INFO value, providing proxy points for retrieving dates and tags. The function delAPI(), which will be defined toward the end of the script, performs the call to the del.icio.us API and manages the cache, deciding whether a fresh request needs to be made or whether cached data will suffice. The first parameter to this function is the path of the call, while the second establishes a filename in the cache for the call's data.

In Listing 8-22, proxying calls get a little more complex.

Listing 8-22: ch08_api_cache.php (Part 3 of 6)

```php
// Proxy through requests for post gets
case '/posts/get':

    // Pass the query string on through to API
    $path .= '?'.$_SERVER['QUERY_STRING'];

    // Cache filename starts at root
    $get_fn = DEL_POSTS_PATH;

    // Build the date into the cache path.
    if (isset($_GET['dt'])) {
        $pat = '/(\d{4})-(\d{2})-(\d{2})/';
        if (preg_match($pat, $_GET['dt'], $parts)) {
            $parts = array_slice($parts, 1);
            $get_fn .= '/'.join('/', $parts);
        }
    }

    // Build tag filters into the cache path.
    if (isset($_GET['tag'])) {
        $bad = array(' ','/');
        $tag = str_replace($bad, '-', $_GET['tag']);
        $get_fn .= '/'.$tag;
    }

    // If neither date nor tags found, assume index
    if ($get_fn == DEL_POSTS_PATH) {
        $get_fn .= 'index';
    }

    // Tack a .xml extension onto the end of the path
    $get_fn .= '.xml';

    // Dispatch off to the API.
    echo delAPI($path, $get_fn);
    exit;
```

Here in Listing 8-22, the posts/get call is handled. Two things here make this a little more complicated than dealing with the list of dates or tags.

First, the query parameters making up the bookmark fetch call need to be passed along to the del.icio.us API. This isn't too difficult, but it needs doing.

And second, this code does the work of translating from query parameters to a cache filename path. It handles turning dates into paths, as well as adding the ability to cache tag collections and tags filtered by date. However, because this code is using input supplied from the Web — which is potentially untrustworthy — a little bit of effort needs to be put into making sure a date is a date and not simply slicing on hyphens and building a file path. So, a regular expression is used to extract the expected date segments and a few safeguards are applied to tags in building paths.

Listing 8-23 provides the last proxied API call in this script.

Listing 8-23: ch08_api_cache.php (Part 4 of 6)

```
// Proxy through requests for all posts
case '/posts/all':

    // Pass the query string on through to API
    $path .= '?'.$_SERVER['QUERY_STRING'];

    // Cache filename starts at root
    $get_fn = DEL_POSTS_PATH.'/all';

    // Build tag filters into the cache path.
    if (isset($_GET['tag'])) {
        $bad = array(' ','/');
        $tag = str_replace($bad, '-', $_GET['tag']);
        $get_fn .= 'tags/'.$tag;
    } else {
        // We're going to fetch everything...
        $get_fn .= '/00index';
    }

    // Tack a .xml extension onto the end of the path
    $get_fn .= '.xml';

    // Dispatch off to the API.
    echo delAPI($path, $get_fn);
    exit;
    }

}
```

Listing 8-23 shows code to handle the posts/all call to the API. This is a call that wasn't used in the backup script, but can be employed to fetch all bookmarks at once, or selectively filter on tags. Of all calls, this one benefits from caching because it can return a large amount of data from del.icio.us. However, it can be very useful in dealing with queries involving tags.

For the most part, however, this part of the script works in much the same way as the code handling posts/get does.

And that's it for API methods handled by the proxy. The list implemented here is far from complete, but the pattern for adding more calls should be fairly clear. For the purposes of this chapter, however, this should be enough of a proxy to turn on the rest of the features of the Ajax bookmark browser.

And finally, you get into the meat of the cache handling with the definition of delAPI() in Listing 8-24.

Listing 8-24: ch08_api_cache.php (Part 5 of 6)

```
/**
    Perform a request on the del.icio.us API, with an
    attempt to use cached data first.
*/
function delAPI($path, $fn) {

    // Attempt to serve up non-stale data from cache.
    $now = time();
    if (is_file($fn)) {
        $age = $now - filemtime($fn);
        if ($age < DEL_CACHE_AGE) {
            return file_get_contents($fn);
        }
    }

    // Create the cache path, if necessary.
    $dir = dirname($fn);
    if (!is_dir($dir)) {
        $curr  = DEL_POSTS_PATH;
        $local = str_replace($curr.'/', '', $dir);
        $parts = explode('/', $local);
        while (count($parts) > 0) {
            $curr .= '/' . array_shift($parts);
            if (!is_dir($curr)) mkdir($curr);
        }
    }

    // Cache is stale, so fetch fresh from the API
    $base = 'http://'.DEL_USER.':'.DEL_PASSWD.'@'.DEL_API;
    $client = new Snoopy();
    $client->fetch($base.$path);

    // Grab the data from the fetch, cache it, return it.
    $data = $client->results;
    file_put_contents($fn, $data);
    return $data;

}
?>
```

The implementation for delAPI() is provided in Listing 8-24. The first thing this function does is attempt to locate a file for the API request. Then, if it has found one, it checks the age of this file. If the file is not old enough to be stale, the data is loaded up and returned.

However, if the file is missing or old enough to need a refresh, the next thing that happens is a search for the parent directory for the potential cache file. If the parent path doesn't exist, it's created, including all folders along the way. This ensures that all the path components of a new day's cache file will be created.

Then, the del.icio.us API URL is constructed and a Snoopy instance is created and used to fetch the URL. The data from this HTTP GET is loaded up and stored away in the cache file for use next time. Finally, the fetched data is returned.

Now, there's one last bit to this script in Listing 8-25, and you'll be ready to take it for a spin.

Listing 8-25: ch08_api_cache.php (Part 6 of 6)

```html
<html>
    <head>
        <title>del.icio.us mini-browser</title>

        <!-- http://www.mochikit.com/ -->
        <script src="MochiKit/MochiKit.js"
                type="text/javascript"></script>

        <script src="ch08_post_browser.js"
                type="text/javascript"></script>

        <link href="ch08_post_styles.css"
            type="text/css" rel="stylesheet" />

        <script>
            var USE_PROXY = true;
            var PROXY_URI = location.href;
        </script>

    </head>
    <body>

        <form id="main">
            <select id="date_selector">
                <option value="">No dates loaded</option>
            </select>
            <select id="tag_selector">
                <option value="">No tags loaded</option>
            </select>
        </form>

        <div id="links">No links loaded.</div>

    </body>
</html>
```

If you'll notice, the final part of ch08_api_cache.php in Listing 8-25 is nearly identical to ch08_post_browser.html. This is intentional, so that when the PHP script is loaded up without any additional path information, the bookmark browser code is loaded up by default. This, then, makes the page self-referential in that viewing the proxy page pulls up code that makes calls back to itself.

The one difference in this HTML from ch08_post_browser.html is in the final bit of JavaScript at the end of the page header. Here, the Ajax browser's USE_PROXY constant is flipped to true, and the PROXY_URI is set to the location of the current page. This, then, calls into action all the proxy support bits that you've been heretofore instructed to ignore.

Trying Out the Bookmark Browser with Proxy Support

Now, everything comes full circle, and you can use all of the features of the Ajax bookmark browser in conjunction with this new PHP caching proxy. If you place this PHP script into the same directory along with the HTML, CSS, JS, and bookmark backups you've been working with so far in this chapter, you should see a view like Figure 8-26 when you load up the page.

Your tags should load up into the second selection field, and when you choose one from the list, you should see the appropriate bookmarks.

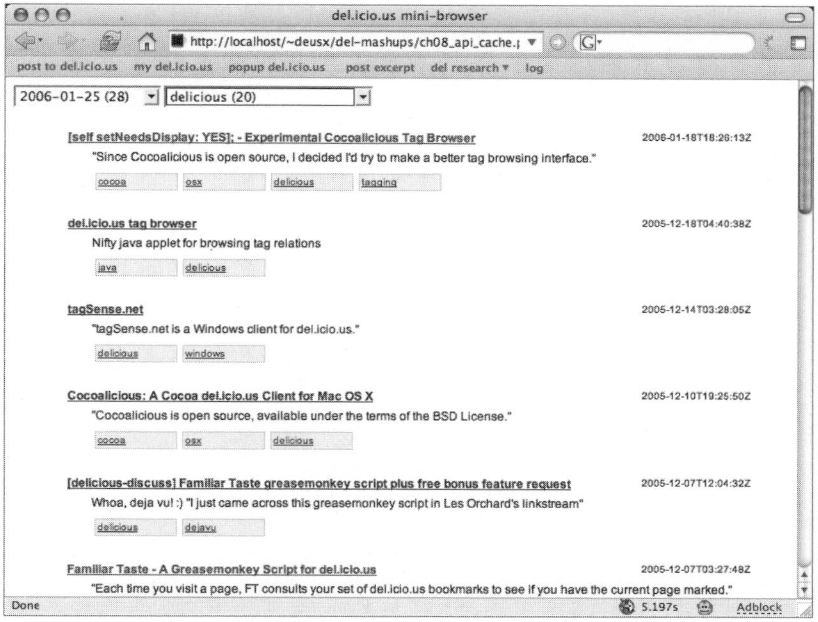

FIGURE 8-26: Bookmark browser with proxy-powered tag filtering support enabled

Summary

So, now you should have a pile of tools available to get your bookmarks out of del.icio.us and into just about whatever form you'd like. This chapter showed you several different ways to include links from del.icio.us into HTML sidebars and RSS feeds, as well as providing you with some code to back up and mirror your links. This chapter also gave you a small Ajax-powered bookmark browser on which you can build an interactive view on your links. And finally, to help enhance your backups and to better power the Ajax browser, you saw code for a PHP cache in front of the del.icio.us API.

The techniques described in this chapter are far from comprehensive with respect to what you can do and find on the Web, but they should give you an idea of what you can do and where you can go from here.

In the next chapter, we move from getting your links out of del.icio.us and toward getting del.icio.us *more* involved with your Web site and blog.

Getting del.icio.us into Your Blog

The goal of the previous chapter was to provide you with tools to help you get your bookmarks out of del.icio.us and explore ways to maintain some independence from the service. This chapter, on the other hand, shows you ways to make links to your own content easier to bookmark, as well as how to get del.icio.us *further* integrated into your sites and pages.

Beyond simple sidebars that can pull your personal bookmarks into templates and pages you control, you can use the same data access and API methods to call up lists of others' bookmarks found to be related to your content. And, thanks to the predictable construction of URLs used by del.icio.us for posting new bookmarks and requesting filtered views of bookmarks, you can easily template the generation of these links within the context of blog posts and other managed content on your site.

Going beyond this even, you can also take advantage of some of the data feeds offered by del.icio.us to include even more bookmarking context in your site.

Adding "Bookmark This" to Movable Type Posts

One of the first ways you can further integrate del.icio.us into your site is by making your content more easily bookmarked. If you can provide permanent URLs — or *permalinks* — for each individual item of content you're halfway there. Most blogging packages offer this feature, and it's just a good common practice for publishing on the Web because it provides a way to unambiguously refer to and identify pieces of your content. This, of course, is the entire point of del.icio.us.

So, given permalinks to your content, visitors can use the standard bookmarklets provided by del.icio.us without much fuss. You can take it a step further by providing ready-to-click buttons or links to the del.icio.us bookmark posting form with your content's permalink URL and title pre-populated in the item fields. By placing this link right next to your content, you can make it even easier — and more likely — for your readers to add your URLs to their collections.

And, getting added to bookmark collections can help attract more people to check out your site. As you've already likely experienced from using del.icio.us, seeing a bookmark in a friend's collection is a better recommendation than any banner ad can supply. One of the earliest tips for blog entry bookmarking came from the del.icio.us blog itself, in the form of a small addition for Movable Type blogs. You can read all about it here:

```
http://blog.del.icio.us/blog/2005/05/bookmark_this.html
```

It helps if you know a bit about customizing templates for your Movable Type blog, but there's not much to this change. Just log in to your blog's management pages, navigate to the settings for the blog you want to customize, and click the Templates item in the Configure section of the left navigation bar. From here, you can edit both the Main Index and Individual Entry Archive templates to add the following bit of HTML template code:

```
<a href="http://del.icio.us/post?url=<$MTEntryPermalink encode_url=
"1"$>&title=<$MTEntryTitle encode_url="1"$>">Bookmark This</a>
```

This template code builds a link to the del.icio.us bookmark posting form for the currently logged in user, pre-populated with the blog entry's title and permalink URL. By using the `encode_url` option in both of the Movable Type template tags, any sensitive characters are escaped in the constructed URL intended to pass the two values. You may want to review Chapter 2 for a refresher on just which form fields are available for pre-population in this fashion.

If you're still using the default templates, one of the best spots to insert this code is in a paragraph toward the end of the entry text with a CSS class of `entry-footer` (see Figure 9-1).

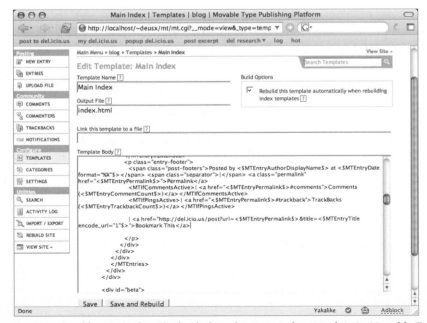

FIGURE 9-1: Adding a Bookmark This link to the Main Index template in Movable Type

This is where the entry permalink is located, as well as a count of comments and trackback pings. Once you've added this code to your templates and saved them, use the Rebuild Site button in the management interface to generate new HTML pages for your entries. Once this process has finished, you should start seeing Bookmark This links added to all of your entries (see Figure 9-2).

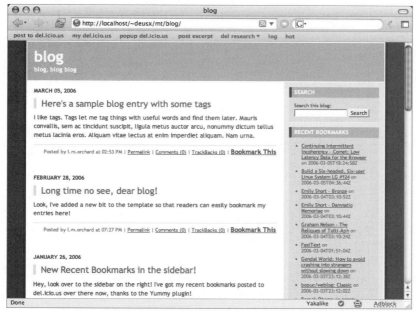

FIGURE 9-2: Main blog index in Movable Type with newly added Bookmark This links

Template Tweaks for Easy Bookmarks in WordPress

As with Movable Type, one of the quickest ways to enrich blog posts in WordPress with bookmarking links is with a template modification. And again, it helps if you have some familiarity with the template code behind the theme you're using for your WordPress blog. For now, I'll assume that you're using the default Kubrick theme that comes out-of-the-box with WordPress 2.0.

There are basically two ways to edit themes in WordPress: If the Web server on which your instance of WordPress is running can write to the files under your installation directory — specifically under the `wp-content/themes` directory — you can use the built-in Theme Editor under the Presentation tab in the admin interface to make these changes (see Figure 9-3).

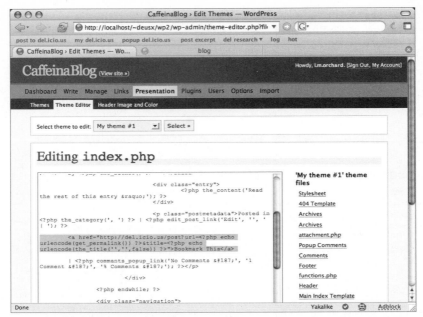

FIGURE 9-3: Adding a Bookmark This link to the Main Index template in WordPress

On the other hand, if WordPress cannot write to its own files, you'll need to edit the template files in your favorite text editor and upload the changes into your WordPress installation via FTP or some other means provided by your hosting service. You can find template files located at the sub-directory path wp-content/themes. From here, you should find one more child directory named default — there may be more folders here, depending on other themes you may have installed or which may have come bundled with your WordPress installation.

Once you're able to edit themes, one of the standard template files you can find in the default theme is index.php. Here, you'll find the template code used to render the front page of your blog, among a few others. Open this file in your editor and, around line 17, you'll find a paragraph with a CSS class of postmetadata. It should look something like this:

```
<p class="postmetadata">Posted in <?php the_category(', ') ?> |
<?php edit_post_link('Edit', '', ' | '); ?>  <?php comments_
popup_link('No Comments &#187;', '1 Comment &#187;', '% Comments
&#187;'); ?></p>
```

This line constructs links to the post's categories and comments, and constructs an editing link for logged-in users. I hope you can decipher the purpose of each bit of this line's template code without much problem. Here, you can insert a bit of HTML that will get appended to each blog entry as it's rendered out to the page. So, to add a handy Bookmark This link after each entry, you'll need this bit of template code:

```
<a href="http://del.icio.us/post?url=<?php echo urlencode(get_
permalink()) ?>&title=<?php echo urlencode(the_title('','',
false)) ?>">Bookmark This</a>
```

Insert this link template anywhere in the `postmetadata` paragraph — personally, I prefer to paste it in just before the `comments_popup_link` tag. Basically, just like the Movable Type template code, this constructs a URL to the del.icio.us bookmark post form with URL and title pre-populated from URL-encoded versions of the current post's permalink and title. Finally, you can see the results of this addition in Figure 9-4.

Note that this link doesn't spawn a popup window or anything fancy — it simply takes users straight to a pre-populated bookmark form, where they can add tags or edit the notes and title before submitting the new link to their collection.

FIGURE 9-4: WordPress blog entries with added Bookmark This template links

Using the Sol-Delicious Plug-in for WordPress

Another way to add Bookmark This links to WordPress blog posts is by using the Sol-Delicious plug-in by Bas Wenneker, found here:

```
http://solutoire.com/?page_id=13
```

You can find the zip file archive containing the plug-in, as well as short instructions on how to install it. There's not much to it, however: Grab the zip archive, unpack it, and copy the plug-in file named `sol-delicious.php` into your `wp-content/plugins` directory. Then, you'll need to visit your blog's administration interface and activate the new plug-in (see Figure 9-5).

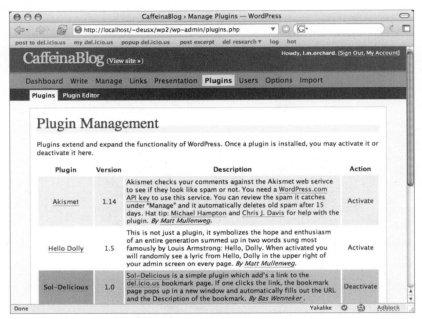

FIGURE 9-5: Activating the Sol-Delicious plug-in in WordPress

Once the plug-in has been installed and activated, you'll have a new template tag available to use as a replacement for the hand-built HTML template code provided just a few paragraphs ago:

```
<?php sol_del(' ','Add to del.icio.us',' | ') ?>
```

This template tag takes three arguments: text meant to appear before the link, text for within the link, and some text to be appended after the link. Through this new template tag, the Sol-Delicious plug-in will do basically everything that the hand-built HTML above does — it just does it with less template code, which is a bit simpler to manage for you.

Using the Notable Plug-in for WordPress

As you'll read in the final chapters of this book, del.icio.us is not without competitors in the social bookmarking space. If you'd like to hedge your bets and include bookmark buttons to many of these services all at once, check out Cal Evans's WordPress plug-in called Notable:

```
www.calevans.com/view.php/page/notable
```

From this page, you can download a zip archive in which you'll find a folder intended to be copied into your `wp-content/plugins` directory. Once in place, you can activate Notable in your blog's administrative interface just like any other WordPress plug-in.

However, there's an additional step with this plug-in: Navigate over to the Options section in your admin pages, and then to the Notable tab, where you'll be greeted with the configuration options shown in Figure 9-6. Here, you can choose which icons from a list of bookmarking sites you'd like to include in your entries, along with a path to icon images included with the plug-in.

FIGURE 9-6: Configuring the Notable plug-in in WordPress

After activation and configuration, you'll get this new template tag available for use:

```
<?php wp_notable(); ?>
```

You can stick this tag into the `postmetadata` section of your `index.php`, just like the previous plug-in. This time, however, instead of a text link you should see a series of icons (see Figure 9-7) — each of these leads to a posting form at a different bookmarking site, with title and URL pre-populated from the current post's data.

FIGURE 9-7: Bookmarking icons added with the Notable plug-in in WordPress

Using the Sociable Plug-in for WordPress

Just as del.icio.us is not alone in its field, the Notable plug-in itself is not free from competition. Another WordPress plug-in with very similar functionality is Sociable, available for download here:

```
www.maxpower.ca/sociable/2006/01/26/
```

Again, this plug-in can be acquired as a zip archive that contains a folder to be placed in your `wp-content/plugins` directory and activated in your blog's admin pages. However, unlike Notable, Sociable does not offer an options screen as of this writing. Instead, you can choose which bookmarking services to show by way of the template tag it makes available for use, like so:

```
<?php wp_sociable('delicious,simpy,digg,spurl'); ?>
```

Once the plug-in is activated and the new tag has been added to your blog template, you'll see results very similar to Figure 9-7 appearing in your pages.

Build Bookmarking into Your Feed with FeedBurner

You were introduced to a few of the features of FeedBurner in the previous chapter — with an eye toward splicing your bookmark posting stream into your feeds, as well as for building sidebar lists from your links. Another relatively new feature from FeedBurner — called FeedFlare — takes things in the opposite direction.

With FeedFlare activated for one of your feeds, FeedBurner can inject "Add to del.icio.us" links into items. These links are visible in the feed readers of your subscribers, available for quick access from most aggregators. If you haven't already, pay a visit to FeedBurner and set up one of your feeds for burning here:

```
www.feedburner.com/
```

Once you've got a feed configured at FeedBurner, you can find the FeedFlare feature in the Services section under the Optimize tab (see Figure 9-8). Here, you can select Add to del.icio.us along with an array of other link injection options. Simply check the boxes for the links you want added, drag the links into your desired order, and activate the feature.

FIGURE 9-8: Activating FeedFlare on a feed in FeedBurner

With FeedFlare activated, you can take a look at the injected links in the feed by subscribing to it in an aggregator. Or, even better: if you activate the BrowserFriendly feature, FeedBurner applies a browser-friendly stylesheet to the feed — allowing you to view the feed directly in your browser, as in Figure 9-9. Along with making the feed more convenient to view and subscribe for your site visitors, this feature will help you preview changes you make to the feed and FeedBurner settings.

FIGURE 9-9: Viewing a styled FeedBurner feed with "Add to del.icio.us" links injected

Injecting Bookmark Links with Unobtrusive JavaScript

If your blog or content management system doesn't allow for easy customization of individual content items or posts on the server side, you can try a few customization tricks on the client side. As long as you can find a way to get a `<script>` tag inserted somewhere into the page, you can leverage unobtrusive JavaScript techniques to restyle and modify the page after it has been loaded and rendered. Of course, this approach counts on the availability of enabled JavaScript on your visitors' browsers — but there should be enough of a majority of your audience who meet this requirement to make this a useful trick.

One example of a blog publishing system that allows general template customization, but not necessarily per-item formatting changes, is the OPML Community Server used in tandem with the OPML Editor. You can read more about the OPML Editor and the Community Server here:

```
http://support.opml.org/
```

As of this writing, the OPML Community Server allows users with hosted blogs to edit an overall HTML template (see Figure 9-10), but the rendering of individual entries posted to the server is under the control of the community server code and not currently open to alteration by community members.

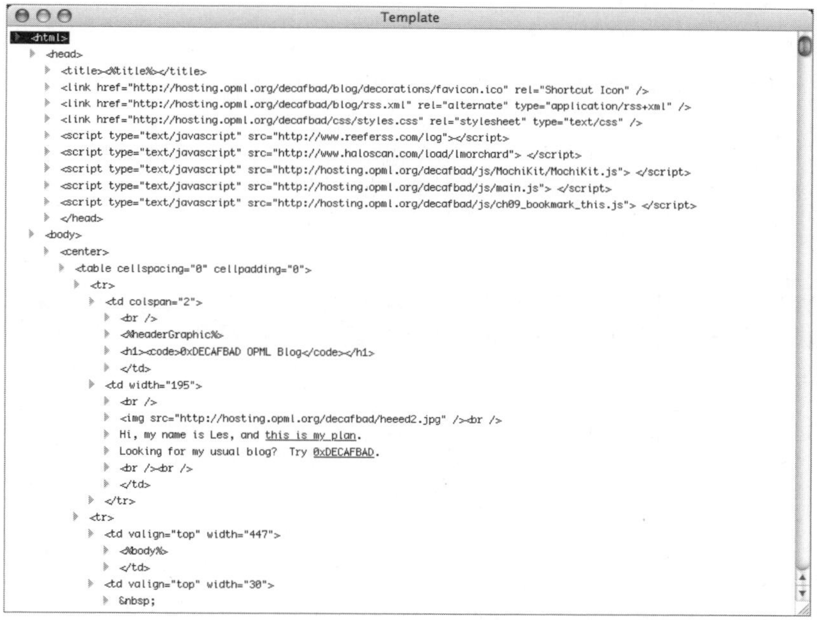

FIGURE 9-10: Editing the page template for an OPML Community Server blog

Fortunately, the page template allows for the inclusion of any arbitrary CSS styles and JavaScript code. And, as for the rendering of individual entries, the HTML produced by the server follows a regular and predictable structure. This means that JavaScript code included on the page can search for this pattern in the loaded page DOM and perform manipulations just after the page has loaded, which includes the injection of Bookmark This links.

So, to get started, you can begin creating a JavaScript include named `ch09_bookmark_this.js` with the code in Listing 9-1. (You can download all the source code for this chapter from the book's Web site at www.wiley.com/go/extremetech.) When finished, you'll be able to use this code to customize per-item display of OPML Community Server blogs, including an icon that links to a pre-populated del.icio.us bookmark posting form.

Listing 9-1: ch09_bookmark_this.js (Part 1 of 5)

```
/**
    ch09_bookmark_this.js

    Inject del.icio.us bookmark links into an OPML blog page.
*/
var DEL_LINK_TITLE  = "Bookmark this at del.icio.us!";
var DEL_ICON_WIDTH  = 10;
var DEL_ICON_HEIGHT = 10;
var DEL_ICON_SRC    =
    'http://decafbad.com/2006/02/delicious.tiff';
```

The JavaScript include in Listing 9-1 starts off with a comment identifying the file and its purpose, as well as a few constants defining a title and image parameters for use a little later in constructing the bookmark links to be injected into the page for each blog post. The actual page manipulation starts next in Listing 9-2.

Listing 9-2: ch09_bookmark_this.js (Part 2 of 5)

```
function bookmarkThisInit() {

    // Iterate through all the images found on the page.
    var imgs = document.getElementsByTagName('img');
    for (var i=0, img; img=imgs[i]; i++) {

        // Does the alt text contain "Permanent link"?
        if ( /Permanent link/.test(img.alt) ) {

            // Grab the actual permalink, along with its URL.
            var perma     = img.parentNode;
            var perma_url = perma.href;
```

In Listing 9-2, a function named `bookmarkThisInit()` is defined. The first thing that happens in this function is a call to `document.getElementsByTagName()`, searching the browser DOM for all the image tags on the page. The images returned by this method are each then processed, searching for those with an alt text attribute containing the phrase "Permanent link." For each of these matching images, it's assumed that the immediate parent node is a hyperlink — that's the permalink itself. This hyperlinks node is found, and the URL to which it links is extracted.

For OPML Community Server blogs, the permalink for every item includes an image whose alt text contains the phrase "Permanent link." If you view source on one of these blogs, you can find images with this text repeated throughout the page. Keep an eye out for this sort of regular pattern, if you want to customize this script for a different content management system. Using a search strategy like this, you can dig up just about any reoccurring configuration of markup on a page and perform modifications from there.

This script will get around to making just that sort of change — but there's a little more preparation in order first, offered in Listing 9-3.

Listing 9-3: ch09_bookmark_this.js (Part 3 of 5)

```
// Find a title for this permalink, based on the
// post title or anchor name.
var bs = perma.parentNode.getElementsByTagName("b");
var title = (bs.length) ?
    bs[0].firstChild.nodeValue :
    perma.parentNode.firstChild.name;

// Include the document title, for good measure.
title += " - " + document.title;

// Construct a del.icio.us posting form URL.
var del_url = "http://del.icio.us/post";
del_url += "?url=" + encodeURIComponent(perma_url);
del_url += "&title=" + encodeURIComponent(title);
```

The code in Listing 9-3 serves to construct a del.icio.us bookmark posting form URL. The permalink URL to the blog entry was easy to find — it was the target of the permalink parent node for each of the matching images found in the page. The title, however, is a bit more challenging to find.

On OPML Community Server blogs, there are basically two types of entries: full essay-style entries with titles, and smaller standalone entries consisting of just a paragraph or so. For the entitled essays, the title itself is contained within a bold tag found as a sibling to the permalink. For the smaller entries, there's an anchor tag present at the start of the text whose timestamp-based name you can use as a stand-in for the title. So, the first few lines of Listing 9-3 attempt to dig up a suitable title for both of these entry varieties.

Having found a primary title, the code next appends the document title to the string in order to identify the blog itself. This is concatenated with the entry permalink URL — both escaped for sensitive characters with calls to encodeURIComponent() — and a del.icio.us posting form URL is constructed. This URL is put to good use in Listing 9-4.

Listing 9-4: ch09_bookmark_this.js (Part 4 of 5)

```
                 // Build the link icon.
                 var del_img = document.createElement("img");
                 del_img.setAttribute("width",  DEL_ICON_WIDTH);
                 del_img.setAttribute("height", DEL_ICON_HEIGHT);
                 del_img.setAttribute("src",    DEL_ICON_SRC);
                 del_img.style.border = "none";

                 // Build the link element for injection.
                 var del_link = document.createElement("a");
                 del_link.setAttribute("href",  del_url);
                 del_link.setAttribute("title", DEL_LINK_TITLE);
                 del_link.style.marginLeft  = DEL_ICON_WIDTH+"px";
                 del_link.style.marginRight = DEL_ICON_WIDTH+"px";

                 // Add the link icon into the link, then add the link.
                 del_link.appendChild(del_img);
                 perma.parentNode.appendChild(del_link);

            }
        }
    }
```

Now that the script has a handle on the permalink, and a del.icio.us posting form URL constructed, it's time to build and insert the Bookmark This button. In Listing 9-4, a new image element is created with a call to `document.createElement()`. This element is then assigned a width, height, and source URL from the constants defined at the start of the script back in Listing 9-1.

After building the image, a hyperlink element is created and given a title and the posting form URL. There's a little style fudging going on here, with a margin added to the link so that the icon has a bit of space around it — but you may want to change or remove this bit of code.

With icon and link elements in hand, the icon is placed inside the link, and the link is appended as a new child to the permalink's parent element. This will place the del.icio.us bookmarking icon either at the end of the blog post title, or the end of the entry itself.

Finally, in Listing 9-5, you see how this whole process is made unobtrusively active.

Listing 9-5: ch09_bookmark_this.js (Part 5 of 5)

```
// See: http://simon.incutio.com/archive/2004/05/26/addLoadEvent
function addLoadEvent(func) {
    var oldonload = window.onload;
    if (typeof window.onload != 'function') {
        window.onload = func;
    } else {
        window.onload = function() {
            oldonload();
            func();
        }
    }
}

addLoadEvent(bookmarkThisInit);
```

The function defined in Listing 9-5, `addLoadEvent()`, comes courtesy of Simon Incutio. You can read all about it in this blog entry:

    http://simon.incutio.com/archive/2004/05/26/addLoadEvent

Basically, this function allows the registration of a call to a function after the page has loaded, without clobbering any other preexisting calls registered. If you're using a JavaScript library that already offers this method — such as MochiKit — you may want to omit the function definition itself. However, the call to `addLoadEvent()` at the very end of this script sets things up so that `bookmarkThisInit()` gets called as soon as everything in the page finishes loading.

This is where the technique gets its "unobtrusive" moniker: In order to use this script on a page, all you need to do is include it on the page. Because it does its work without any further code on the page, and without clobbering other running scripts, there's nothing else you need to worry about besides the include itself.

If all has gone well, you should be able to see new little del.icio.us icon links appearing next to blog entries, as shown in Figure 9-11. As of this writing, you can see this script actively demonstrated on this blog:

    http://blogs.opml.org/decafbad/

I hope this code can offer a few ideas for use on whatever site you find a need to customize — the technique is handy for, but not limited to, OPML Community Server blogs.

FIGURE 9-11: Bookmark This links with del.icio.us icons added to an OPML blog

Including Related Links with Tags and JSON

Although the previous chapter offered some help to get your links out of del.icio.us and displayed on your blog, you can use tagging to integrate bookmarks even further into your blog. By attaching tags to your own blog posts or content items on your site, you can relate these to bookmarks posted to your del.icio.us collection. Simply use the same tagging vocabulary on both your own site and on your del.icio.us bookmarks, and the shared tags can be used as convenient intersection points for presenting related materials.

In this section, I show you first how to get tagging integrated into a Movable Type or WordPress blog. Then, I show you how to use those tags to dynamically pull tag-related links into your pages.

Tagging Posts in Movable Type

Tagging your entries is another small way you can build more ties between a Movable Type blog and del.icio.us. In the normal use case, tags on blog entries can serve as an alternative to categories local to the blog itself — but you can also use these tags to relate your entries to tags in your collection on del.icio.us. To start using tags on a Movable Type blog, check out Brad Choate's Tags Power Tool, described and available for download here:

```
www.sixapart.com/pronet/plugins/plugin/tags.html
```

This is a pretty easy plug-in to install, and it comes with full instructions on where to place the handful of relevant files. Once you've gotten it installed, you'll find that the Keywords field on your entry editing page has been replaced by a Tags field (see Figure 9-12). You can use this field in much the same way as you do on del.icio.us: freeform, space-separated tags entered here will be attached to each of your entries in place of categories and keywords. In fact, the plug-in will automatically create new categories for tags when necessary, and assign the entry's category to the first tag used in the list.

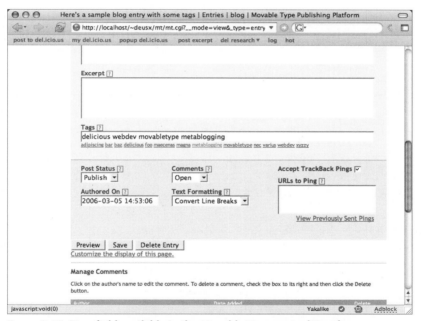

FIGURE 9-12: Tags field available in the Movable Type post editing form

After getting the plug-in installed and attaching tags to a few of your entries, the next step is to include display of the tags in your blog templates. The Tags Power Tool plug-in provides a set of new template tags for your use in accomplishing this.

Listing 9-6 offers some sample code you could insert into your Main Index template within the `entry-footer` section, just like the Bookmark This link offered earlier in this chapter. This code will result in a simple, horizontal list of tags attached to the entry, each linked to the appropriate tag in your del.icio.us bookmark collection.

Listing 9-6: Template code to list tags in Movable Type

```
<style type="text/css">
  .tag {
    padding: 0 0.5em 0 14px;
    margin: 0;
    background-image: url(http://decafbad.com/2006/03/del-small.tiff);
    background-position: top left;
    background-repeat: no-repeat;
  }
</style>

<br />

<MTEntryTags>
    <span class="tag">
      <a rel="tag"
         href="http://del.icio.us/deusx/<$MTTagName$>"><$MTTagName$></a>
    </span>
</MTEntryTags>
```

You can see a preview of how this will appear, in Figure 9-13. Once added, these links can provide a quick path to further links of interest from your blog entries, as well as help you categorize your own entries along similar lines as your tag vocabulary in use on del.icio.us.

Tagging Posts in WordPress

With WordPress 2.0, entering categories is a lot more like entering tags than in previous versions. In the past, categories needed to be painstakingly created one at a time and selected with a list of check boxes. With the newest versions, however, categories can be supplied as a comma-separated list (see Figure 9-14), which makes things almost as easy as del.icio.us tags. Entering the name of a new category here will cause it to be automatically created in the database, once the entry has been posted. So, while there has been a handful of tagging plug-ins made available for WordPress, this revised implementation of the built-in categories is worth sticking with for use here.

 On the Web

On the other hand, if you haven't upgraded to WordPress 2.0, you might just want to take a look at a few of the tagging plug-ins available for WordPress 1.5 and later.

Bunny's Technorati Tags is a good option that's simple to install and doesn't require any database options. You can find it available here:

```
http://dev.wp-plugins.org/wiki/BunnysTechnoratiTags
```

On the other hand, Ultimate Tag Warrior does require the addition of a new table to your WordPress database, but it offers a few more user interface bells and whistles. Check it out here:

```
www.neato.co.nz/ultimate-tag-warrior/
```

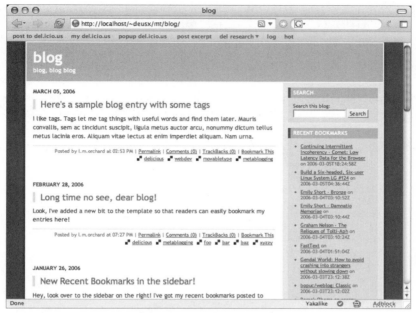

FIGURE 9-13: Entries with tags displayed in Movable Type

FIGURE 9-14: Assigning categories to a post in WordPress

Now, if you look through some of your WordPress templates — index.php in particular —
you'll see the template tag the_category() used to list links to post categories. The formatting options offered by this tag are a bit limited, so Listing 9-7 offers a much more verbose yet
flexible replacement for this tag. With this code, you get both del.icio.us tag links and blog category links. Check out Figure 9-15 for an example peek at how this code looks in a template.

Listing 9-7: Listing categories in WordPress with del.icio.us tags

```php
<?php
    foreach ( (get_the_category()) as $cat ) {
        $cat_name = $cat->cat_name;
        $del_url  = "http://del.icio.us/deusx/$cat_name";
        $cat_url  = get_settings('home')."/category/$cat_name/";
        ?>
        <span class="tag">
            <a rel="tag" href="<?php echo $del_url ?>">
<img src="http://decafbad.com/2006/03/del-small.tiff" border="0" /></a>
            <a href="<?php echo $cat_url ?>"><?php echo $cat_name ?></a>
        </span>
        <?php
    }
?>
```

FIGURE 9-15: Entries with tags displayed in WordPress

Using Tags and JSON Feeds to Display Related Links

Now that you've got the means to attach tags to your posts in a Movable Type or WordPress blog, you can use these to display del.icio.us bookmarks related to posts by tags. To keep things fairly agnostic with respect to either of these blog packages — or whatever other content management system you may be using — you'll implement this using JSON feeds and DOM content injection, with a minimum of system-specific template code.

Because of the potential for complexity in this little project, we'll make use of the MochiKit JavaScript library again. MochiKit offers a very nice set of HTML DOM construction tools, which makes the dynamic generation of content in JavaScript a breeze. This kit was introduced in the previous chapter, but if you need a refresher you can visit the home page here:

```
www.mochikit.com/
```

Now, check out Listing 9-8 for the first part of the JavaScript include that will power these tag-related links, named ch09_delicious_related.js.

Listing 9-8: ch09_delicious_related.js (Part 1 of 4)

```
/**
    ch09_delicious_related.js

    Facilitates the injection of related links by tag from
    del.icio.us JSON feeds.
*/
DeliciousRelated = {

    JSON_BASE_URL: 'http://del.icio.us/feeds/json/deusx',
    MAX_LINKS:     5,
```

Listing 9-8 starts off with a descriptive comment and the opening lines of a JavaScript object literal constructing the DeliciousRelated package. Here, two package constants are defined:

- JSON_BASE_URL: This is a base URL prefix used in finding JSON feeds, in which you should replace deusx with your own del.icio.us user name.

- MAX_LINKS: This is a limit to the maximum number of related links to display per tag on the page.

Continuing on to Listing 9-9, you can find the code used in initializing this package on page load, as well as how related links are scheduled for loading.

Listing 9-9: ch09_delicious_related.js (Part 2 of 4)

```
// Array of jobs scheduled to run at page load
_jobs: {},

/**
    On window load, fire off all the scheduled jobs.
*/
init: function() {
    for(jid in this._jobs)
        this._jobs[jid].load();
},

/**
    Given a job / element ID and a del.icio.us tag,
    schedule a job to load up links for the tag.
*/
register: function(jid, tag) {
    var _dr = this;
    this._jobs[jid] = {
        jid: jid,
        tag: tag,

        load: function()
            { _dr.loadTag(this) },
        loaded: function(posts)
            { _dr.tagLoaded(this, posts) }
    }
},
```

In Listing 9-9, two package functions are defined: `init()` and `register()`.

The `init()` function will be called upon the completion of page load, and it serves to iterate through a set of scheduled job objects, calling a `load()` method on each.

The `register()` function is responsible for creating and scheduling the jobs fired off by `init()`. In a nutshell, it will be used in HTML template code like so:

```
<ul class="relLinks" id="delRel-<$MTTagName$>">
  <script type="text/javascript">
    DeliciousRelated.register(
      "delRel-<$MTTagName$>", "<$MTTagName$>"
    )
  </script>
</ul>
```

When used in the page code, `register()` expects two parameters: the ID of an HTML DOM element into which content should be injected, and the name of a del.icio.us tag from which to load bookmarks and generate the content for injection.

This pair of functions, `init()` and `register()`, allows for the simple usage of this package in template code while it's building the page — yet defers the actual execution of JSON data fetches until the page has finished loading and the HTML DOM has been completely built. Shortly, you'll see expanded examples of this function used in HTML template code.

Next, in Listing 9-10, you see the definition of `loadTag()`, the package function called by the `load()` method of scheduled job objects.

Listing 9-10: ch09_delicious_related.js (Part 3 of 4)

```
/**
    Initiate the loading of JSON link data for a
    scheduled job.
*/
loadTag: function(job) {
    var cb_ref = "DeliciousRelated._jobs['"+job.jid+"'].loaded";

    var json_url = this.JSON_BASE_URL;
    json_url    += '/'+job.tag;
    json_url    += '?callback='+encodeURIComponent(cb_ref);

    var script_ele  =
        createDOM('script',
            { 'type': 'text/javascript', 'src':json_url });

    document.getElementsByTagName("head")[0].appendChild(script_ele);
},
```

The `loadTag()` function defined in Listing 9-10 performs the task of building the URL to a JSON feed at del.icio.us, and injecting the `<script>` element necessary to cause the browser to dynamically load this JSON feed. As arguments, it takes a reference to the scheduled job for which the content should be loaded. This job object contains the name of the tag and the job ID as properties.

The tag name is used to build the JSON URL path. The job ID is used to build a string reference to the job's `loaded()` method, which is supplied as the `callback` query parameter attached to the JSON URL. This results in the returned data from del.icio.us being wrapped in a call to this method. Thus, this is a way to asynchronously signal when the JSON request has completed, and trigger processing of the fetched bookmark data.

Note   The technique employed here to communicate between the browser and the RSS-to-JSON script on the server is known as JSONP — or, JSON with Padding. You can read what MochiKit's Bob Ippolito has to say about this technique in his proposition here:

```
http://bob.pythonmac.org/archives/2005/12/05/
remote-json-jsonp/
```

The `loaded()` method of scheduled job objects calls the package function `tagLoaded()`. Listing 9-11 offers the definition of this function.

Listing 9-11: ch09_delicious_related.js (Part 4 of 4)

```
/**
    Handle the completion of loading JSON link data,
    inject list links for each post found.
*/
tagLoaded: function(job, posts) {
    var list = $(job.jid);
    for (var i=0, post; i<this.MAX_LINKS && (post=posts[i]); i++) {
        list.appendChild(
            LI({}, A({'href':post.u}, post.d))
        );
    }
}

};

// Schedule the package init to fire at window load.
addLoadEvent(function() { DeliciousRelated.init() });
```

As you can see in Listing 9-11, there's not much to the implementation of `tagLoaded()`.

First, the `$()` convenience function from MochiKit is used to look up the HTML DOM element specified by a scheduled job object. This scheduled job is supplied as the function's first parameter.

A list of del.icio.us posts is supplied as the second parameter for this function, having been fetched via JSON and passed from the scheduled job's `loaded()` method. A loop iterates through this list of posts, up to the end of the list or until the maximum number of links has been reached. Each of these posts is wrapped up in an HTML list element and hyperlink, using the URL and description in each post, and injected into the page as children of the schedule job's specified list element.

All of this results in the first few bookmarks in the tag being displayed on the page in the appropriate spot.

Using the Related Links Script with Movable Type

Now, it's time to put this script to real use in your blog. First, let's take a look at how to use it with Movable Type. As before, it's best if you know your way around editing templates in Movable Type, and this code is best used on an individual archive page for a post. You can stick these links wherever you like, although they may work best in a spot below the post — or even in a sidebar area.

The first thing you need to do, however, is include the script itself in the header of your template with a tag like the following:

```
<script type="text/javascript" src="/js/ch09_delicious_related.js" />
```

Next, you need to include calls to `DeliciousRelated.register()` in your page where tag links should appear. Check out Listing 9-12 for some sample template code integrating this JavaScript include with the Tags Power Tool template tags.

Listing 9-12: Using DeliciousRelated in a Movable Type template

```
<ul class="relatedTags">
  <MTEntryTags>
    <li id="tag-<$MTTagName$>">
      <a rel="tag" href="http://del.icio.us/deusx/<$MTTagName$>">
        <$MTTagName$>
      </a>
    </li>
    <ul class="relLinks" id="delRel-<$MTTagName$>">
      <script type="text/javascript">
        DeliciousRelated.register(
          "delRel-<$MTTagName$>", "<$MTTagName$>"
        )
      </script>
    </ul>
  </MTEntryTags>
</ul>
```

The template snippet in Listing 9-12 illustrates how you can use the additional template tags supplied by the installation of the Tags Power Tool to construct some HTML into which the JavaScript can inject links related by tag to the current blog post. This results in a list of tags; under each is a list of bookmarks, as shown in Figure 9-16.

Again, although this screenshot depicts the list of related links in the middle of the page, you may want to consider constructing a sidebar section for these links if you'd like them to be a little less obtrusive in your page layout.

Using the Related Links Script with WordPress

Using the related links JavaScript with WordPress works in much the same way as the Movable Type templates, as well as the template code for including del.icio.us tag links presented earlier in this section.

FIGURE 9-16: Related links listed by tag in a Movable Type entry

First, remember to include a reference to the JavaScript in your theme's `header.php` template like so:

```
<script type="text/javascript" src="/js/ch09_delicious_related.js" />
```

Next, take a look at Listing 9-13 for some example template code to work these related links into your blog theme templates.

Listing 9-13: Using DeliciousRelated in a WordPress template

```php
<ul class="relatedTags">
<?php
  foreach ( (get_the_category()) as $cat ) {
    $cat_name = $cat->cat_name;
    $del_url  = "http://del.icio.us/deusx/$cat_name";
    $cat_url  = get_settings('home')."/category/$cat_name/";
    ?>
    <li class="relTag">
      <a rel="tag" href="<?php echo $del_url ?>">
        <?php echo $cat_name ?>
      </a>
      <ul class="relLinks"
```

Listing 9-13 *continued*

```
            id="delRel-<?php echo $cat_name ?>">

            <script type="text/javascript">
              DeliciousRelated.register(
                "delRel-<?php echo $cat_name ?>",
                "<?php echo $cat_name ?>"
              )
            </script>

        </ul>
      </li>
      <?php
    }
  ?>
  </ul>
```

In Listing 9-13, you can find some WordPress template code that constructs a list of tags with associated related links for the current blog post. This code probably goes best in either the `single.php` or `comment.php` templates from the default theme, although you could likely fit it into the `sidebar.php` template. Figure 9-17 offers an example of what this template code produces in the page.

FIGURE 9-17: Related links listed by tag in a WordPress entry

You should play with the placement and styling of these links with CSS until you find a way to present them that works with your blog's design. This script can offer a good way to help build more connections between your content and your bookmarks on del.icio.us.

Turning Bookmarks into Comments with RSS and JSON

One feature on most blogs is the integration of comments along with entries. There's usually a template tag for including the count of comments for a particular entry, as well as a link to the list of comments and a comment form for the entry. Usually, this comment facility is built right into the software package itself — although occasionally it's provided by a third-party service. In a sense, bookmarks posted to del.icio.us from your content are like comments — wouldn't it be nice if you could pull them easily into that context? This sounds like the start of a project that could use some thinking through.

Thinking About the Problem

As you may remember from Chapter 4, one of the varieties of RSS feeds offered by del.icio.us lists bookmarks posted for a given URL. Using these feeds, you can request lists of bookmarks for the URLs of your site. In a sense, these are like comments made on content at your site.

So, through these per-URL RSS feeds, you've got access to the relevant bookmark data. Now, how can these bookmarks be brought into the context of your content? One way to do it would be on the server side: Fetch the appropriate RSS feed for the page being served up, and present the bookmarks found for that URL. Depending on your blogging package, however, this can offer a varying degree of difficulty.

If you've got a WordPress blog, every page is dynamically built at the time of serving it — so you can read in the RSS feed for that page fresh with every visit. Once the feed has been fetched, you can parse the feed data and display a list of the bookmarks found, thus presenting del.icio.us bookmarks from others in a way not unlike contents posted to your blog.

On the other hand, for a Movable Type blog, pages are built only at the time content changes. So, the bookmarks display could go quickly stale between visits. On the bright side, however, at least your Movable Type server won't get banned from accessing del.icio.us data: Making a request for RSS feeds with every page hit on a WordPress blog will quickly see your site running afoul of the usage limits at del.icio.us.

Gluing the Pieces Together

Thus far, you've learned several key points concerning using del.icio.us bookmarks as comments in your blog entries:

- Use del.icio.us RSS feeds to request up-to-date lists of others' bookmarks relevant to your page URLs.

- Mind usage constraints imposed by del.icio.us in accessing these bookmarks' RSS feeds

- You'll need to have easy integration with whatever content management or blogging system is in use at your site.

For some sites and blogs, comments are provided by a separate package or service. For example, check out the HaloScan weblog commenting and trackback service located here:

```
http://haloscan.com/
```

HaloScan is an easy-to-integrate solution for comments and trackbacks with free and for-pay options. On most sites, all it takes is a simple JavaScript include and some template tweaks to enrich a site with commenting features. So, HaloScan helps integrate feedback into sites where the content management software does not provide this service.

Taking a hint from HaloScan, what if you did some of work of displaying del.icio.us bookmarks on the client side in the browser through Ajax or some other JavaScript techniques? You've already seen the use of unobtrusive JavaScript in this chapter to insert simple Bookmark This buttons in your content — why not take this technique further and inject even more information into your pages? There's just one snag, however: RSS feeds from del.icio.us come from a different domain than where your site is hosted — unless you happen to run the del.icio.us blog itself. And, because Ajax technology is restricted for security reasons to making requests only to the domain from which the page was loaded, JavaScript on your site's pages cannot access RSS feeds from del.icio.us.

So, don't make your requests to del.icio.us directly — access that data through a proxy resident on your server. In the previous chapter, you saw how this could be done with a caching proxy written in PHP and sitting in front of the del.icio.us API to enable a dynamic Ajax-powered bookmark browser. What if you could take a similar approach here? And, while you're at it, why not make things easier by swapping out XML for JSON?

Take a look at the FeedMagick project, located here:

```
http://decafbad.com/trac/wiki/FeedMagick
```

FeedMagick is a Web-based package written in PHP that's useful for filtering and manipulating RSS/Atom syndication feeds. And, one of the scripts included with this package turns RSS feeds into JSON — simply provide the URL to an RSS feed, and it uses MagpieRSS to parse the feed, and subsequently serves up a JSON data structure based on the content from the feed. And the best part for this project? JSON can be served up from any domain you like — your own or from a third-party service — because JSON isn't bound by the same security restrictions as the XmlHTTPRequest object.

And, here's one more very important benefit to using a package like FeedMagick: Most of the scripts in FeedMagick operate from a cache — that is, when you use FeedMagick to get JSON from RSS feeds, the RSS feeds are cached just like the caching proxy did in the previous chapter. This will greatly reduce the number of times the del.icio.us servers will be accessed and thus greatly reduce the chances that your server will be throttled or banned for overzealous usage.

Note The RSS-to-JSON facilities of FeedMagick will be used in this chapter, but be aware that it's not the only show in town when it comes to getting JSON out of RSS. If for some reason FeedMagick doesn't work for you, or isn't a good fit for your server, check out John Resig's Perl CGI-based RSS to JSON Convertor located here:

```
http://ejohn.org/projects/rss2json/
```

Altering the code from this chapter to use this alternative shouldn't be too onerous a task, if need be. So, keep this service in mind.

Implementing Bookmarks as Comments on Your Site

So, here's the plan for implementation:

- Given a permalink URL to a blog entry or other content item, you can build the URL for a del.icio.us RSS feed containing bookmarks relevant to your content.

- Using an RSS-to-JSON conversion service, you can grab this RSS data and access it from JavaScript — thereby both dodging cross-domain security issues and XML parsing complexity.

- Following the lead of third-party comment services such as HaloScan, you can call upon client-side tricks in JavaScript to integrate and present these bookmarks from others in context alongside your content.

So, with no further ado, Listing 9-14 offers the start of ch09_delicious_comments.js, a JavaScript include that should come in handy to integrate del.icio.us bookmarks into your site alongside the usual comment and trackback fare.

Listing 9-14: ch09_delicious_comments.js (Part 1 of 7)

```
/**
    ch09_delicious_comments.js

    Insert del.icio.us bookmark counts and links for blog
    post permalinks and individual archives.
*/
DeliciousComments = {

    // See: http://decafbad.com/trac/wiki/FeedMagick
    RSS_TO_JSON_URL:
        'http://decafbad.com/2005/12/FeedMagick/www-bin/as-json.php',

    DEL_URL_BASE:     'http://del.icio.us/',
    DEL_ICON_SRC:     'http://decafbad.com/2006/03/delicious.png',
    DEL_ICON_WIDTH:   10,
    DEL_ICON_HEIGHT:  10,
```

Listing 9-14 begins the JavaScript include off with a descriptive comment and the opening lines of a JavaScript object literal assigned to DeliciousComments. In case you're not already familiar with this technique, it's similar to defining a class in Java or a package in Perl: It forms a sort of namespace, within which all the constants and functions defined belong to DeliciousComments and so should not collide with other such things defined elsewhere.

The first constant defined here is RSS_TO_JSON_URL, intended for the location of the as-json.php script from FeedMagick. Although the location provided here points to an installation of the service at decafbad.com, which is operational as of this writing, you should really grab a copy of FeedMagick to install on your own server. That way, if this particular installation goes away, you won't be left out in the cold.

Next, there's DEL_URL_BASE, which provides a configurable URL prefix for all access to del.icio.us. As you'll find in later chapters, this may be useful in case you ever want to switch to using another bookmarking service that offers the same API and data access features as del.icio.us. After this constant comes DEL_ICON_SRC, DEL_ICON_WIDTH, and DEL_ICON_HEIGHT — all of which provide the details for building an icon image later on.

Listing 9-15 provides the details to start initializing this script.

Listing 9-15: ch09_delicious_comments.js (Part 2 of 7)

```
// Initially empty map of ids to posts
_schedule: {},

/**
    On window load, fire off all the scheduled load events.
*/
init: function() {
    for(node_id in this._schedule)
        this._schedule[node_id].load();
},

/**
    Given a destination container node ID, blog post
    permalink, and preference for mini or full display,
    register a comment display for loading.
*/
register: function(node_id, permalink, full_display) {
    var _dc = this;
    this._schedule[node_id] = {
        node_id:      node_id,
        permalink:    permalink,
        full_display: full_display,

        load:   function()     { _dc.loadFeed(this); },
        loaded: function(feed) { _dc.feedLoaded(this, feed); }
    };
},
```

One of the things that a good third-party comments system offers is integration with an existing site through simple tweaks to the site's templates. The code in Listing 9-15 provides the starting point for this sort of integration, with the definitions of the `init()` and `register()` functions in the `DeliciousComments` package.

The `register()` function will be the main integration point for blog and site templates. This will be explained further after the end of this script, but here's an example WordPress template snippet illustrating the use of this function:

```
<div id="delComments-<?php the_id() ?>">
    <script type="text/javascript">
      DeliciousComments.register
         ("delComments-<?php the_ID() ?>", "<?php the_permalink() ?>", true)
    </script>
</div>
```

The parameters needed for the call to `register()` are the following:

- The unique ID for an HTML element into which the script will inject content
- A permalink to a content item or blog post
- A flag selecting which of two display styles will be used

The `register()` function creates a lightweight object to keep track of these three parameters and adds it to `_schedule`, using the HTML element ID as a key.

The `init()` function is called upon the completion of page load as a `window.onload` handler. The goal of `init()` is to iterate through all of the items in `_schedule`, calling the `load()` function on each object found there.

So, the `register()` function allows the page to queue up requests for fetching JSON content while the HTML is still loading into the browser. Once the page has finished loading, `init()` follows through with initiating the requests.

Next, in Listing 9-16, you see the definition of the `loadFeed()` function.

Listing 9-16: ch09_delicious_comments.js (Part 3 of 7)

```
/**
    For a given scheduled post, initiate loading of the per-URL
    del.icio.us feed.
*/
loadFeed: function(post) {

    var cb_ref =
        "DeliciousComments._schedule['"+post.node_id+"'].loaded";

    // See: http://pajhome.org.uk/crypt/md5/md5src.html
```

Listing 9-16 *continued*

```
        var feed_url = this.DEL_URL_BASE+'rss/url/';
        feed_url += hex_md5(post.permalink);

        var script_url  = this.RSS_TO_JSON_URL;
        script_url      += "?in=" + encodeURIComponent(feed_url);
        script_url      += "&callback=" + encodeURIComponent(cb_ref);

        var script_ele  =
            createDOM('script',
                { 'type': 'text/javascript', 'src':script_url });

        document.getElementsByTagName("head")[0].appendChild(script_ele);
    },
```

Each of the objects created in `register()` has a `load()` method. This `load()` method in turn calls the `loadFeed()` function defined in Listing 9-16 with the object itself as the sole parameter. This may sound confusingly circular, but it helps ensure that all the right data gets shuffled to the proper places throughout the asynchronous JSON fetching process.

The first thing `loadFeed()` does is to construct a string reference to the callback function to be called when the JSON feed content has been successfully fetched. Notice that this is the `loaded()` method of the object, referenced by ID in the `_schedule` array. This string is the "padding" in the JSONP call, a string literal that will be treated as a function call wrapped around the data returned from the server.

Next, a feed URL is built, based on the path to the per-URL RSS feeds on del.icio.us and an MD5 hash of the permalink URL for which a fetch of bookmarks is desired. The call to `hex_md5()` isn't built into JavaScript, however — you'll need to grab a copy of Paul Johnston's implementation of MD5 in JavaScript from this page:

```
http://pajhome.org.uk/crypt/md5/md5src.html
```

Simply drop a copy of his `md5.js` into your JavaScript includes directory alongside MochiKit and this script.

Once a reference to the callback function and the feed URL is obtained, it's time to build the URL to the RSS-to-JSON script on the server. This script from the FeedMagick package takes two query parameters:

- `in`: URL to an input RSS feed
- `callback`: String reference to a callback function to call with the returning JSON data

Finally, the `createDOM()` function from MochiKit is used to construct a new `<script>` element based on this script URL. Once this element has been appended to the page's `<head>`

element, the browser runs out and fetches the URL and executes the script — which in turn contains a call to the callback function.

This callback function is the `loaded()` method of an object built in the `register()` function. In another twist of circular references, this object method calls the `feedLoaded()` function defined in Listing 9-17 with a reference to itself and the feed data just successfully fetched.

Listing 9-17: ch09_delicious_comments.js (Part 4 of 7)

```
/**
    Once a feed has loaded, process the feed for the post.
*/
feedLoaded: function(post, feed) {

    // Switch between full or mini display, based on
    // preference at time of scheduling.
    var display_node = (post.full_display) ?
        this.renderFullDisplay(post, feed) :
        this.renderMiniDisplay(post, feed);

    // Insert the display into the parent node.
    appendChildNodes(post.node_id, display_node);

},
```

Again, the `feedLoaded()` function defined in Listing 9-17 is what gets called when a JSON feed request returns successfully with data. As parameters, it accepts a reference to one of the scheduled objects created in `register()`, along with the returned JSON feed data. This method, then, calls either `renderFullDisplay()` or `renderMiniDisplay()` based on the `full_display` property of the object. Both of these functions return an HTML DOM fragment, which is then injected as new content into the appropriate HTML element registered by ID in the `register()` function.

The twists and turns in the journeys made by the little structures created in `register()` should make more sense at this point because they preserve all the context necessary to take this process from beginning to end while everything happens in the disconnected form of asynchronous JSON requests.

Next, in Listing 9-18, comes the definition for the `renderMiniDisplay()` function, the first of a set of functions that renders the JSON data dynamically into HTML content for display in the browser.

Listing 9-18: ch09_delicious_comments.js (Part 5 of 7)

```
/**
    Build a simple bookmark count with icon image and a link
    to all bookmarks for the post.
*/
renderMiniDisplay: function(post, feed) {
    var _dc = this;

    // Compose the URL to bookmarks list for the permalink
    // given for this post.
    var link_url = this.DEL_URL_BASE + "url";
    link_url    += "?url="+encodeURIComponent(post.permalink);

    return SPAN({ 'class':'delCommentCount' },
        A({ 'href': link_url },
            IMG({
                'src':      this.DEL_ICON_SRC,
                'width':    this.DEL_ICON_WIDTH,
                'height':   this.DEL_ICON_HEIGHT
            }),
            ' (' + feed.items.length + ')'
        ),
        ' | '
    );
},
```

The `renderMiniDisplay()` function defined in Listing 9-18 accepts a registered content item's details and feed data, which it uses to build a minimal presentation. This takes the form of a simple icon link that includes a count of bookmarks for the given permalink URL. The DOM construction utility functions from MochiKit are used here to build and return the HTML.

A much more complex example of content creation is offered in the definition of `renderFullDisplay()` in Listing 9-19.

Listing 9-19: ch09_delicious_comments.js (Part 6 of 7)

```
/**
    Build a full list of bookmarks for a given permalinked
    blog post and loaded feed.
*/
renderFullDisplay: function(post, feed) {
    var _dc = this;

    // Compose the URL to bookmarks list for the permalink
```

continued

Listing 9-19 *continued*

```
        // given for this post.
        var link_url = this.DEL_URL_BASE + "url";
        link_url    += "?url="+encodeURIComponent(post.permalink);

        return [
            H3({},
                IMG({ 'src': this.DEL_ICON_SRC }),
                ' ',
                A({'href': link_url},
                    feed.items.length,
                    ' del.icio.us bookmarks for this post'
                )
            ),
            UL({ 'class': 'delComments' },
                map(function(item) {
                    return _dc.renderOneBookmark(item)
                }, feed.items)
            )
        ];
    },
```

In Listing 9-19 is the definition of the `renderFullDisplay()` function, which also accepts the details of a registered content item and bookmark feed data returned from the JSON request. Here, the MochiKit DOM construction utilities are used to build a richer display of the bookmarks found for the permalink URL. An <h3> title contains a count and a link to del.icio.us, under which an HTML list of the bookmarks themselves is constructed.

And, by way of MochiKit's `map()` function, the construction of each bookmark HTML item is farmed out to the `renderOneBookmark()` function, presented in Listing 9-20.

Listing 9-20: ch09_delicious_comments.js (Part 7 of 7)

```
    /**
        Given a bookmark feed item, return rendered HTML.
    */
    renderOneBookmark: function(item) {
        var name = item.dc.creator;
        var tags = item.dc.subject;
        var date = item.dc.date;
        var url  = this.DEL_URL_BASE + name;

        var link = A({ 'href': url }, name, ' @ ', date);
```

Listing 9-20 *continued*

```
        var description = (!item.description) ? '' :
            '"'+item.description+'" ';

        var tag_links = (!tags) ? '' :
            map(function(tag) {
                return [ A({'href':url+'/'+tag}, tag), ' '];
            }, tags.split(' '));

        return LI({ 'class': 'delComment' },
            link, ': ', description, tag_links
        );
    }

}

// Schedule DeliciousComments initialization on window load.
addLoadEvent(function() { DeliciousComments.init() });
```

Each listed bookmark item constructed in Listing 9-20's definition of `renderOneBookmark()` contains a link to the account of the person who has bookmarked the current page, along with the descriptive notes submitted and links to tags used. This provides a pretty compact yet comprehensive display of all the information available for each bookmark found.

Integrating del.icio.us Bookmark Comments with Your Site

To use this finished code on your site, you'll need to do several things:

- Make sure you've acquired and uploaded MochiKit, `md5.js`, and this script into a directory on your Web server for inclusion in your pages.
- Add `<script>` tags into your page headers to include these JavaScript files.
- Alter your blog or page templates to insert calls to `DeliciousComments.register()` in order to load the bookmark data in context.

Once again, you can find MochiKit at its project site located here:

```
www.mochikit.com
```

And, you can find a JavaScript implementation of MD5 here:

```
http://pajhome.org.uk/crypt/md5/md5src.html
```

As for the code from this chapter, as usual you can either type it in yourself or download it from this book's Web site. Once you've gotten these JavaScript files into place on your server, you'll need to tie them into your page template with a set of `<script>` tags like these:

```
<script src="/js/MochiKit/MochiKit.js" type="text/javascript"></script>
<script src="/js/md5.js" type="text/javascript"></script>
<script src="/js/ch09_delicious_comments.js" type="text/javascript"></script>
```

The next step requires you to make alterations to your site's templates. You've already seen this done in this chapter, for adding Bookmark This links to entries in WordPress and Movable Type blogs. The process here is much the same.

So, for example, to include a small icon indicating the number of bookmarks found for a blog post, you'll need to insert code like the following into the `postmetadata` paragraph in `index.php`:

```
<p class="postmetadata">Posted in <?php the_category(', ') ?> | <?php
edit_post_link('Edit', '', ' | '); ?> <span id="delComments-<?php the_id()
?>"></span> <?php comments_popup_link('No Comments &#187;', '1 Comment
&#187;', '% Comments &#187;'); ?></p>

<script type="text/javascript">
    DeliciousComments.register
        ("delComments-<?php the_ID() ?>", "<?php the_permalink() ?>", false)
</script>
```

The important part here is to include both the new `<span>` with an ID of `delComments-<?php the_id() ?>` and the `<script>` tag below it. Notice that the false flag in the `register()` JS function call indicates that the mini display style should be used — this will cause the bookmark count icon for the blog post to appear inline with the rest of the post metadata elements.

Moving along, you can use the full display style to integrate a list of bookmarks on your comments page. In the default WordPress theme, you can find this in the `comments.php` template. Look for the line that reads "You can start editing here," and paste in the following HTML:

```
<div id="delFullComments-<?php the_id() ?>">
    <script type="text/javascript">
      DeliciousComments.register
        ("delFullComments-<?php the_ID() ?>", "<?php the_permalink() ?>", true)
    </script>
</div>
```

Notice that this code looks a lot like the template change made for including the bookmark count icon — only this time, the content will be injected into a standalone `<div>` tag and the display style parameter is set to `true`. This will cause the fully rendered bookmark list to be inserted here.

For Movable Type, the preceding code snippets can be used with little alteration. In WordPress, `<?php the_ID() ?>` is used to insert a unique ID for the blog post — but, in Movable Type, you'll use `<$MTEntryID$>`. And, where WordPress uses `<?php the_permalink()?>` to supply the blog post's permalink URL, you'll use `<$MTEntryPermalink$>` for Movable Type. So, for example, to insert a list of bookmarks for a post in a comments page in Movable Type, try the following template code:

```
<div id="delFullComments-<$MTEntryID$>">
    <script type="text/javascript">
        DeliciousComments.register
            ("delFullComments-<$MTEntryID$>", "<$MTEntryPermalink$>", true)
    </script>
</div>
```

Once you've got everything correctly configured, you should be able to see bookmark count icons appearing next to your blog entries, as shown in Figure 9-18. And then, when you pay a visit to one of your entries, you should see a detailed list of bookmarks found for the post in Figure 9-19.

FIGURE 9-18: Bookmark count icons included in post metadata in WordPress

FIGURE 9-19: Bookmarks listed as comments on a WordPress blog entry

The nice part about the way this script works is that you should be able to use it with just a few small tweaks for whatever blogging package or content management system you're using on your site. Also, because the HTML produced by this code comes with CSS class names and IDs attached, you should be able to style these bookmark displays in whatever way you see fit. And finally, because all the HTML rendering parts are broken out into separate functions, you can even further customize this script by redefining these in a separate JS include overriding the default rendering.

Summary

This chapter has offered a collection of ways to use del.icio.us bookmarks with your blog and content, to varying degrees of integration and contextual ties between content and bookmarks. From simple Bookmark This buttons up to treating bookmarks from others as a sort of comment system, these techniques can further tie your content and bookmarks together.

In the next part of the book, however, things take a different turn as you explore bookmarking solutions beyond del.icio.us — starting with a look at a few of the open source Web bookmarking packages.

Beyond del.icio.us

Exploring Open Source Alternatives

As a service, del.icio.us is a great way to share and tag bookmarks. And, through the data feeds and API operations made available, it's hard to think of how del.icio.us could be more open or give you better access to your account's data. But sometimes, the use of a third-party service can be a stumbling block. In this chapter, you are introduced to a few of the open source projects under development that offer similar features as del.icio.us or attempt to clone the service outright.

Why Use an Open Source Alternative?

With all of the avenues for access made available by del.icio.us, it might seem silly to want to run your own clone of the service. As you've seen throughout this book, there's really no effort made by the operators of del.icio.us to lock you into the service or otherwise restrict your use beyond concerns of resource limitations. On the contrary, you can make a complete backup of your data at any point, and the del.icio.us API provides many options for managing bookmark collections with third-party tools.

However, the fact remains that del.icio.us is a service whose operation is out of your control. Although it may be highly unlikely, del.icio.us could disappear one day, or change directions in development in a way that introduces restrictions that you don't want to deal with. Also, for some situations, the openness of del.icio.us can be a drawback — such as for use as a private research tool on a company's intranet.

And then, even with how remote the preceding situations may be, there's the plain desire for tinkerers to get under the hood and play with things themselves. Because the source code of del.icio.us itself is not available, this means that the wheel needs to be reinvented and so enquiring tinkerers start from scratch. And, it's important to note that some del.icio.us-like projects have begun as independent inventions, some long before del.icio.us itself came upon the scene. So, because everyone has his or her own ideas on how things should be done, many efforts are in progress — some sticking close to the design notions of del.icio.us and others diverging to pursue the developers' own ideas for improvement.

Checking Out Scuttle for Bookmark Sharing

Scuttle is a Web-based social bookmarks manager written in PHP. As a clone, it offers quite a few of the features of del.icio.us — including user accounts, bookmark posting and tagging, search, RSS feeds, and a pretty full-featured work-alike API. You can see a public installation of this project here:

```
http://scuttle.org
```

And, if you'd like to download and install a copy of Scuttle for yourself, you can find it available as a GNU-licensed open source project on SourceForge:

```
http://sourceforge.net/projects/scuttle/
```

As of this writing, there's quite a bit of difference between the latest release version of this project (v0.5.1) and the code available from the project's CVS repository. The public installation of Scuttle is likely to resemble the CVS code, and it looks like there's a lot of development going on with this project. So, the version presented in this chapter was installed fresh from CVS, in the hopes that what you see here will be closer to the release version available when this book hits the shelves. You can find details on how to acquire this code from the project pages here:

```
http://sourceforge.net/cvs/?group_id=134378
```

Installing Scuttle

The installation process for Scuttle is fairly painless. It's not quite as easy to get running as some PHP apps that come equipped with guided installation wizards — but it does come with all the dependencies it requires. Of course, you will still need a PHP-enabled Web server and a MySQL database. There's code in place to support other databases' packages, but you'll need to set those up by hand — and it sounds like this support is early in its development.

At any rate, for MySQL, Scuttle comes with a `tables.sql` file containing a schema you can use to prepare the database. For example, here are commands you might use for setting things up from a UNIX shell:

```
$ mysqladmin -uroot -p create scuttle
$ mysql -uroot -p scuttle < tables.sql
$ mysql -uroot -p -e 'grant all privileges on scuttle.* to \
        scuttleuser@localhost identified by "scuttlepass"'
```

Your mileage may vary, however, if your access to MySQL on your Web server is managed through a Web-based console. The tool provided by your Web host may have a way to import SQL dumps and configure accounts like this. On the other hand, you may not need or be able to configure a new account on new databases, and may simply use the single login used by your hosting account and import the new tables. For what it's worth, the names of all tables used by Scuttle are prefixed by `sc`, so this may help in cohabitating with other shared database tables.

Configuration also requires that you edit a single PHP include file to supply your MySQL authentication details, but that's the bulk of what's needed to install Scuttle. Here's what the modified database configuration variables might look like, with regard to the preceding MySQL setup:

```
$dbhost  = '127.0.0.1';
$dbport  = '3306';
$dbuname = 'scuttleuser';
$dbpass  = 'scuttlepass';
$dbname  = 'scuttle';
$dbtype  = 'mysql';
```

Once you've uploaded the Scuttle PHP code to your Web server, prepared the MySQL database, and modified the configuration details accordingly, you can visit the index page and fire things up (see Figure 10-1).

FIGURE 10-1: Scuttle recent bookmarks page

Registering for a Scuttle Account

Upon initial installation, your copy of Scuttle won't yet contain any bookmarks. You're likely to first see a message telling you as much, rather than precisely what's shown in Figure 10-1. So, to start adding bookmarks to your Scuttle installation, you'll first need to sign up for an account. This process is much the same as with del.icio.us. First, you need to click the Register link in the top page header. This will take you to the page shown in Figure 10-2. Fill out your details and create an account, after which you can click the Log In button in the page header and supply your authentication details on the page presented in Figure 10-3.

FIGURE 10-2: Registering for a Scuttle account

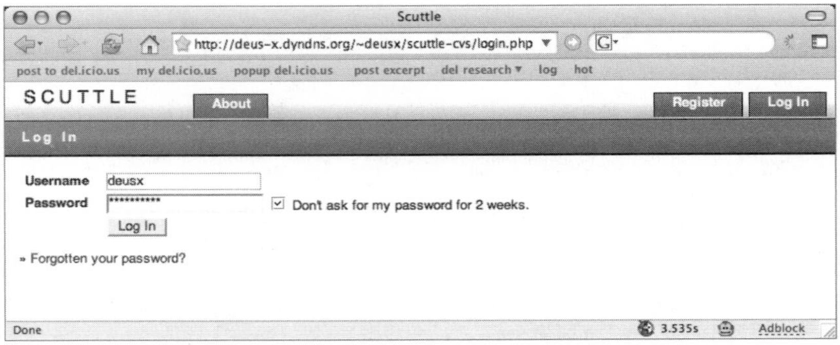

FIGURE 10-3: Logging in to Scuttle

Adding Bookmarks in Scuttle

Once logged in after registering, you are taken to your currently empty bookmark collection. From here, click the Add a Bookmark header button that has appeared in response to your logged-in state. Here, you can enter a URL, title, description, and tags to compose this bookmark (see Figure 10-4).

One neat feature that Scuttle's bookmark posting page has over del.icio.us is that, once you've entered a URL, the system uses Ajax to execute a PHP script on the server that automatically finds the title of an HTML page at that address. If you don't type anything in the title field, a "barber pole" animation fills the field as the system attempts to find the title for you. This page diverges from del.icio.us, however, in that (as of this writing) tags are *comma-separated* rather than space-separated — this can put a bit of a crimp in your style if you're not expecting it.

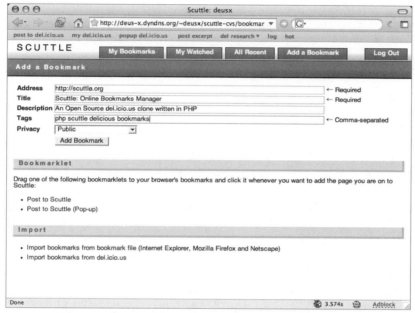

FIGURE 10-4: Adding a new bookmark to Scuttle

Importing Bookmarks from del.icio.us

Also available from this page is a pair of bookmarklets to help you in posting to your collection, as well as some import options. If you ran the programs from Chapter 8 to back up your del.icio.us bookmarks, then you've got some XML available that Scuttle can use to import bookmarks into your account. If you click the "Import bookmarks from del.icio.us" link, you'll see the page in Figure 10-5.

You can use this form to bulk upload your backed up bookmarks — provided that your export is under 1MB. You may want to try importing just a day's worth of bookmarks or so — which the backup script from Chapter 8 can also provide — to see how things work. Just so you're forewarned: As to be expected, my own collection of almost 7,000 bookmarks didn't go down easily as a single import.

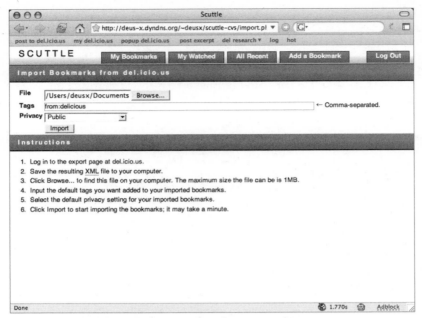

FIGURE 10-5: Importing del.icio.us bookmarks into Scuttle

Browsing and Searching Bookmarks in Scuttle

After you've gotten some bookmarks into your account, you can visit your collection (as shown in Figure 10-6) at any time by clicking the My Bookmarks button in the page header. There's another touch of Ajax magic here, too, when you delete bookmarks: After being asked to confirm the deletion, the bookmark turns gray and then shortly vanishes from the page after the server has deleted it in response to an in-page request.

You can also manage a set of watched bookmark subscriptions, not unlike the inbox feature del.icio.us offers. If you're just playing with Scuttle on a machine of your own and have only a single account, this won't do much for you — but when you view the bookmarks belonging to an individual user, an Add to Watchlist link appears that allows you to add their bookmarks to your subscriptions.

Another interesting addition beyond del.icio.us features is that Scuttle bookmarks allow for three levels of privacy: public, visible to watchlist members, and private. So, the watchlist isn't just a simple inbox, it's more like a two-way buddy list.

As you browse around bookmark listings, you'll find that much of the slicing by tags and users is carried over from del.icio.us, as are some of the related tags (see Figure 10-7). A cloud of popular tags is also available for your perusal, as shown in Figure 10-8. There are RSS feeds associated with just about every bookmark listing, and you can perform full text searches on all bookmarks, your bookmarks, or those of users on your watchlist.

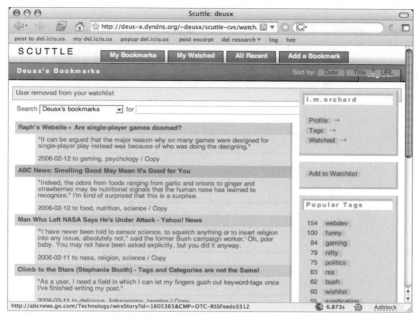

FIGURE 10-6: Viewing a single user's Scuttle bookmarks

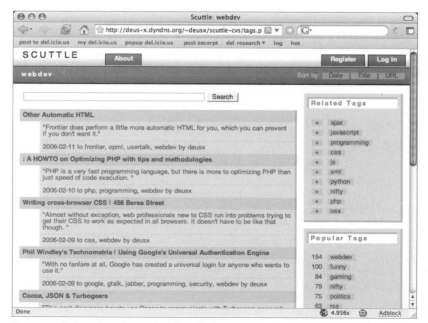

FIGURE 10-7: Viewing Scuttle bookmarks by tag

FIGURE 10-8: Popular tags in a cloud in Scuttle

About the Scuttle API

Like del.icio.us, Scuttle also offers a plain old XML–style API. Indeed, Scuttle attempts to closely follow the del.icio.us API with methods including the following as of this writing:

- `posts/get`
- `posts/all`
- `posts/delete`
- `posts/recent`
- `posts/all`
- `posts/update`
- `posts/dates`
- `tags/get`
- `tags/rename`

These methods are accessible via HTTP GET with Basic Authentication and all follow the same data formats and parameter conventions as you saw in Chapter 4. There is one caveat to this compatibility, however: To match the same URLs that del.icio.us uses, with the exception of an API URL prefix, your Apache Web server will need to have `mod_rewrite` enabled.

If you don't have this feature of Apache available, or aren't using Apache as your Web server, you'll need to fall back to using the PHP scripts implementing the API directly. Thus, `api/posts/get` becomes `api/posts_get.php` and you'll need to adjust your programs accordingly. If you've got mod_rewrite, you'll find that any of your scripts limited to the above list of API methods should work fine with Scuttle without modification.

If you'd like to read more about the Scuttle API, check out the Scuttle Wiki page on the subject located here:

```
http://scuttle.org/wiki/doku.php?id=scuttle_api
```

Bookmarks and Browser Integration with SiteBar

SiteBar is a PHP Web application that's available as open source, but also offered as a hosted service with various free and for-pay options. You can find all the details on SiteBar and sign up to give it a try at this URL:

```
http://sitebar.org/
```

While SiteBar is a bookmarks manager, it's not a del.icio.us clone as such. Instead, it appears more suited as a repository for personal bookmarks — or perhaps for use as an intranet research tool in small groups. SiteBar is less about sharing bookmarks socially, and more focused on organizing bookmarks with a Web-based service.

There aren't really del.icio.us-style tagging or socially driven features offered by SiteBar, nor is a Web API exposed. However, you'll find that SiteBar supports quite a list of formats for importing and exporting bookmark from browsers, RSS and Atom feeds, and OPML outlines to name a few.

In addition, SiteBar offers many avenues for browser integration via plug-ins and sidebars, as well as options for embedding it in Web sites and applications. Although the user interface for SiteBar is Web-based, it closely resembles desktop applications through the use of Dynamic HTML elements and contextual menus. You can manage user accounts and security access controls, restricting folders where users can view and submit bookmarks.

Installing and Configuring SiteBar

To install SiteBar, you'll need access to a Web server with a MySQL database and PHP installed. You'll also need to download the source to SiteBar, found here:

```
http://sitebar.org/downloads.php
```

You can find an installation guide linked from the same page, but the process is fairly straightforward. After downloading a tarball or zip archive of the SiteBar source, expand it and upload the contents to your Web server. Once the upload is complete, you can visit the index.php page found in the package directory, which will present you with an initial database setup wizard page (see Figure 10-9).

FIGURE 10-9: SiteBar database configuration wizard

You'll need to know the authentication details for your MySQL database, such as user name and password, as well as a database name. If you're on a shared account with just a single login and database, you can just use these details — the names of all tables used by SiteBar are prefixed with sitebar, so this installation shouldn't clobber any other apps you've got sharing the database.

Once you've filled out the database details, you can click the Check Settings button to ensure that SiteBar can connect to the database. Once that's working properly, a click of the Create Database button will ensure that the SiteBar database and tables are all created if necessary.

Finally, your configuration settings need to be saved to the Web server. You have two options for this: Clicking Write to File will attempt to write the configuration settings to the file system directly. To do this, your Web server will need to have write permission to the inc folder in the SiteBar directory. If this is undesirable or not possible, you can opt to click Download Settings, which will allow you to grab a copy of the configuration settings file and upload it into the inc directory by hand.

After you've got the configuration file updated and in place, you'll be able to visit the index page again. You're almost but not quite done with the installation process. The final step is to click the Setup link from `index.php`. This presents you with the page in Figure 10-10 — here you can create an administrator account and password for yourself, as well as fill out a few details on the Web server where this instance of SiteBar will run.

Then, finally, with the database configuration and initial setup completed, you can visit the index page again and be rewarded with the blank bookmarking slate shown in Figure 10-11.

FIGURE 10-10: Post-installation setup in SiteBar

FIGURE 10-11: Initial view of configured and installed SiteBar instance

Managing Bookmarks and Folders in SiteBar

One thing to notice from all of the screenshots of SiteBar presented so far in this chapter is that this is really meant to be a browsing companion. All but a few pages in this application are presented in a very narrow template — a site bar, if you will. This is so that SiteBar can be included in a frameset on a Web site, or even in a browser sidebar. SiteBar is meant to be an accessory tool, not the main attraction.

As a tool, SiteBar's Dynamic HTML features attempt to mimic some conventions of desktop applications. For example, try right-clicking (on Windows) or Control-clicking (on Mac) on one of the main initial groups in the page — such as Admin's Bookmarks. This will call up a contextual menu, as shown in Figure 10-12. From here, you can begin the process of managing folders and bookmarks.

FIGURE 10-12: Contextual
menu on a folder in SiteBar

Click Add Folder, and you'll be given a form like the one in Figure 10-13. Here, you can supply the details to create a new subfolder in which to group and organize bookmarks. Figure 10-14 shows you how things look with a freshly created folder.

FIGURE 10-13: Adding a
new folder in SiteBar

FIGURE 10-14: New folder
added in SiteBar

Next, try adding a bookmark to a folder via the Add Link item in the contextual menu. This will take you to the form in Figure 10-15, in which you can supply your own details for the bookmark — or, if you click Retrieve Link Information, SiteBar will run out and try grabbing details from a supplied URL automatically.

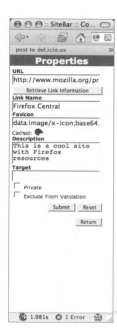

FIGURE 10-15: Adding a bookmark to a folder in SiteBar

After you've added a bookmark, try checking out properties on the folder you just added. This will give you the options displayed in Figure 10-16, including actions such as importing and exporting bookmarks and managing security for the folder. If you click the Security button, this will in turn take you to the form shown in Figure 10-17, where you can set fairly fine-grained access controls on groups of users and their ability to manage and see links contained in this folder.

With these controls, you can set up lots of rich combinations of users and groups with just about any level of access to bookmarks stored in SiteBar.

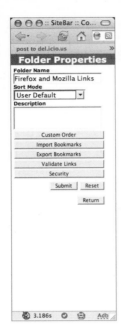

FIGURE 10-16: Editing
folder properties in
SiteBar

FIGURE 10-17:
Managing security
settings on a folder
in SiteBar

Importing and Exporting Bookmarks with SiteBar

Along with managing folders and bookmarks on an individual level in SiteBar, you can also reach for a wide array of import and export options. Although at present, SiteBar doesn't support the XML format offered by del.icio.us, you can use the bookmark export formats available from most Web browsers, as well as from RSS feeds and OPML (Outline Processor Markup Language) outlines.

For example, if you want to get your Firefox bookmarks into SiteBar, you can select the Manage Bookmarks option from the Bookmarks menu and use the File/Export option from there. Firefox produces an HTML-based format, which SiteBar readily accepts. From either a contextual menu on the main SiteBar view, or using the Import Bookmarks button, as shown previously in Figure 10-16, you can pull up the form in Figure 10-18. Here, you can select a bookmark export file from your local filesystem and upload it for SiteBar to parse and import.

Again, SiteBar will accept input from a number of formats, and offers the ability to automatically detect the format of the data you're uploading. Still, if things aren't quite working, you can select an import format directly from the pull-down option menu in the form. Upon submitting a set of bookmarks for import, you should see them appear in the collection if all goes well (see Figure 10-19).

To take things full circle, SiteBar supports a long list of export formats to get your bookmarks back out of the system once you've amassed a collection. The export feature can be invoked from the contextual menu of any folder, as well as the Export Bookmarks button in the folder properties form. This form is depicted in Figure 10-20. As you can see, there's a drop-down menu you can use to select a desired output format, as well as to specify sort order and a handful of other options.

FIGURE 10-18:
Importing bookmarks
in SiteBar

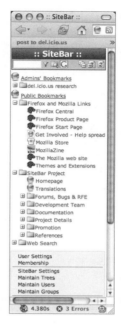

FIGURE 10-19:
Bookmarks imported
in SiteBar

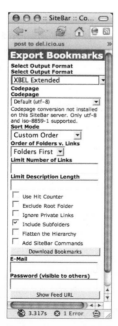

FIGURE 10-20: Exporting
bookmarks from SiteBar

Browsing Bookmarks and Feeds in SiteBar

Although most of your interaction with SiteBar takes place within a narrow, tool-oriented user interface, there are a few full-page summary views you can access.

One of the options in the contextual menus on folders is Browse Folder — upon clicking this, you break out of the tool interface and see a directory listing like the one shown in Figure 10-21. Here, you can get a more perusal-friendly Web directory of your bookmarks. It's a read-only view, but you can more easily see details such as the time when a link was added and any notes that have been added in the link properties.

FIGURE 10-21: Viewing a directory listing in SiteBar

Another feature that SiteBar offers is a sort of link news portal that's made available via the Show Link News option found in contextual menus, as well as in a link toward the bottom of the main tool view. If you click this, you'll be presented with the full-page view shown in Figure 10-22. Here, you can find various reports of link visit popularity, as well as recent bookmark addition and modification behavior. Also notice that each one of these categories includes a link to an RSS feed — you can subscribe to any of these to keep up-to-date on SiteBar activity.

FIGURE 10-22: Viewing link news from SiteBar

Web Browser Integration with SiteBar

Here's where the thin user interface of SiteBar comes in handy: If you click the Open Integrator link in the main tool view, you will see a menu of options (see Figure 10-23) for integrating SiteBar into your daily browsing habits. You'll find links to instructions to embed SiteBar as a persistent utility sidebar in your favorite browser, as well as a set of bookmarklets to quickly add links to your SiteBar instance while you're out and about on the Web. You'll also be able to find a few tools for integrating SiteBar into other Web pages, including some instructions on embedding hierarchical menus in PHP pages.

Although SiteBar doesn't offer quite the same feature set for bookmark management as del.icio.us, it does offer a wide array of import and export features, user and group management options, and browser integration opportunities that can make it a decent alternative for personal link capturing or group research facilitation.

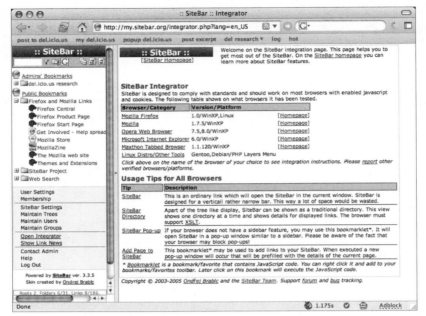

FIGURE 10-23: The SiteBar integrator page

Keeping Bookmarks and Snapshots with Insipid

Insipid is an open source del.icio.us clone written in Perl by Luke Reeves. As a clone, Insipid is a pretty lightweight single-user bookmark manager: It doesn't offer an API or replicate many of the features of del.icio.us beyond the basics — but in return, Insipid can be installed with few prerequisites beyond a MySQL or PostgreSQL database and a Web server on which you can run Perl CGI scripts.

You can find the Insipid project page here:

```
www.neuro-tech.net/insipid/
```

If you'd like to see an instance of Insipid in action, check out the author's bookmark collection here:

```
www.neuro-tech.net/Luke/bookmarks
```

Installing Insipid

As of this writing, the latest version of Insipid is available here:

```
www.neuro-tech.net/insipid/insipid-0.9.17.tar.gz
```

Download this archive and unpack it — you'll find everything you need to install this application under the `insipid` directory extracted from the package. Move or copy this directory over to your Web server in a location where CGI scripts can be run. There's a README file in this directory that you should check out for the latest instructions, but there's not much to the process.

You will need to have access to either a MySQL or PostgreSQL database server, and ensure that the appropriate Perl DBI modules are installed. Your server may already have these in place, but you may need to call upon CPAN (see Chapter 5) to install them yourself like so:

```
$ cpan DBI DBD::mysql
```

In addition, this software requires the XML::Writer module, available here:

```
http://search.cpan.org/~josephw/XML-Writer-0.600/
```

You can download the module and install it by hand, or use CPAN to install it automatically:

```
$ cpan XML::Writer
```

Insipid is configured by modifying the `insipid-config.cgi`, wherein you'll need to specify the database type, database authentication details, the Web path to the installed files, as well as a user name and password to use in securing your bookmarks. For example, here's what my `insipid-config.cgi` looks like:

```
dbname = insipid
dbuser = insipidusr
dbpass = insipidpass
dbtype = mysql
pagepath = /~deusx/insipid
username = deusx
userpass = mypasswd
```

And, that's about it — make sure you can access `insipid.cgi` as a CGI script and navigate to it from your browser. Upon first execution, Insipid will attempt to connect to the database and set up all of its own tables and initial set of data. You should be rewarded with a page somewhat like Figure 10-24, albeit devoid of bookmarks at first.

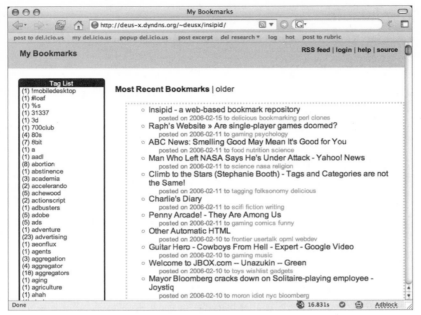

FIGURE 10-24: Insipid recent bookmarks page

Importing Bookmarks into Insipid

Once you've got Insipid up and running, you can import bookmarks from your del.icio.us account into the database. You'll first need to log in to Insipid via the link in the top navigation. Use the name and password you provided in `insipid-config.cgi`. After login, you should see a new set of links in the top navigation, including "import". Click this, and you should see a form like the one in Figure 10-25.

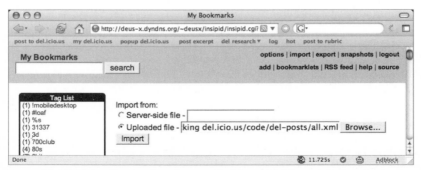

FIGURE 10-25: Uploading bookmarks exported from del.icio.us into Insipid

From here, you can supply an export from del.icio.us to dump into the database. Again, you can use the programs from Chapter 8 to acquire an XML export of your del.icio.us bookmarks. The import process will take a few minutes, but shouldn't require any further manual intervention. As opposed to the import process with Scuttle, this one appeared to handle very large bookmark imports without much incident.

Managing Bookmarks and Snapshots in Insipid

Using Insipid to manage bookmarks is simple and straightforward, once you've logged in. To manage existing bookmarks, you should find "delete" and "edit" links beside each (see Figure 10-26). To post new bookmarks, you can click the "add" link or use bookmarklets — both of which are made available in the top navigation links. Check out Figure 10-27 for an example of Insipid's bookmark posting form.

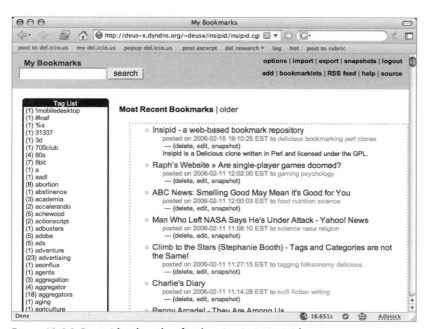

FIGURE 10-26: Recent bookmarks after logging in to Insipid

An interesting feature offered by Insipid that's somewhat unique among del.icio.us clones is the ability to take snapshots of the pages you've bookmarked. When you click a "snapshot" link next to one of your bookmarks, Insipid downloads a local copy of the page and associated assets. This will subsequently reveal a "view snapshot" link next to bookmarks with available snapshots, and you can manage the set of local snapshots with the "snapshots" link in the top navigation (see Figure 10-28).

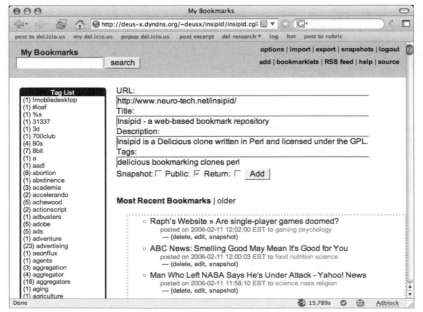

FIGURE 10-27: Posting a bookmark with Insipid

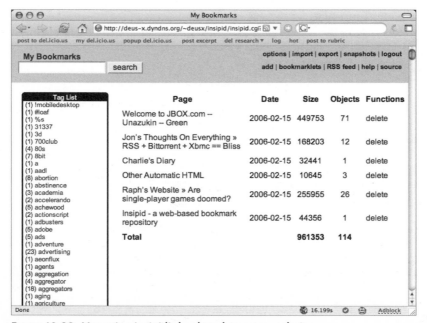

FIGURE 10-28: Managing Insipid's bookmark page snapshots

And, to wrap up, although Insipid doesn't offer an API like that of del.icio.us, it does offer XML export and RSS feeds. You can find the export facility in the top navigation, along with a link to the current view's RSS feed. The RSS feeds offered by Insipid can also be filtered by tag, and you can find tag-specific feeds linked into the current page header, available for autodiscovery in browsers such as Firefox.

Using Rubric for Notes and Bookmarks

Rubric, written by Ricardo Signes, is described on its project page as "a notes and bookmarks manager with tagging." This Web application is written in Perl and is available as open source from the CPAN here:

```
http://search.cpan.org/~rjbs/Rubric/
```

In contrast to Scuttle, Rubric is not a comprehensive clone of the services and API methods offered by del.icio.us. On the contrary, although it draws much inspiration from del.icio.us in terms of tagging and bookmarking features, Rubric strikes off on its own a bit by adding some simple note-taking or blogging features and its own API implementation. You can find Rubric's author using the software to power his own blog and bookmarks here:

```
http://rjbs.manxome.org/rubric/
```

It's also interesting to note that Rubric has been used as the foundation for a del.icio.us competitor named de.lirio.us, located here:

```
http://de.lirio.us/
```

You can check these two sites out to get a bit of a feel for how this tool looks and feels before you try installing it. Rubric is in a usable but rough state, but it's still worth taking a look.

Installing Rubric

If you've decided you'd like to take Rubric a spin, be forewarned that the in-development state of this project means that it assumes a modicum of familiarity with Perl and some hands-on installation work, preferably from a UNIX command-line shell. And, like many projects implemented in Perl, Rubric comes with a list of module prerequisites that need installation before you're up and running. You can get a sense of this list of requirements at the following URL:

```
http://search.cpan.org/src/RJBS/Rubric-0.13_02/Makefile.PL
```

This isn't really a problem, however, if you're familiar with Perl and how to install modules via the Comprehensive Perl Archive Network (or CPAN). The CPAN tools can easily chase down and install all of the needed dependencies without much handholding. And, if you've already been in the thick of Web development with Perl, it's quite likely that you've also already installed the bulk of the modules demanded by Rubric.

So, given these caveats, if you're still ready to give it a shot you can use CPAN to install Rubric and all of its dependencies on a UNIX shell like so:

```
$ cpan Rubric
```

If you've already configured CPAN in your installation of Perl, this command should happily run off and start installing all the necessary parts including the most recent release of Rubric. Note that you may need root or administrator access — or the use of the `sudo` command — in order to install via CPAN.

In addition, if you're feeling adventurous, you can install an even newer developer release with this CPAN invocation:

```
$ cpan R/RJ/RJBS/Rubric-0.13_02.tar.gz
```

This is the newest version as of this writing and is the version the rest of this chapter will discuss, but you may want to double check for the latest on CPAN. You can also install Rubric manually by downloading its archive package from the project page listed previously, but going the automatic route should give you fewer headaches.

Creating and Configuring a Rubric Instance

One of the easiest ways to get an instance of Rubric up and running is by way of a CGI script. There's a README file that accompanies Rubric, although you can read the latest version of the instructions here:

```
http://search.cpan.org/dist/Rubric/README
```

The modules behind Rubric normally get installed globally alongside the rest of the Perl modules on your system, but the Rubric package comes along with a CGI script that ties everything together. If you installed Rubric by hand, this script was unpacked from the archive along with everything else. Otherwise, you'll need to check your local CPAN build directories for the unpacked archive directory (i.e. `$HOME/.cpan/build/Rubric-0.13_02`).

Once you've found the place where the Rubric archive was unpacked, create a directory on your Web server where the execution of CGI scripts is allowed. Copy the following from the Rubric archive into this directory on your Web server:

- `rubric.cgi`
- `css/rubric.css`
- `etc/rubric.yml`
- `templates/`

Note that all of the files starting with `rubric` must end up at the same directory level, but you'll want to copy the directory `templates` itself. So, for instance, this is how a directory listing looks after copying the files:

```
$ ls
rubric.css      rubric.yml      rubric.cgi      templates/
```

Once these files are in place, you can edit `rubric.yml` to configure the instance. For example, my installation's configuration looks like this:

```
dsn: |-
  dbi:SQLite:dbname=rubric.db
uri_root: |-
  http://deus-x.dyndns.org/~deusx/rubric/rubric.cgi
css_href: |-
  /~deusx/rubric/rubric.css
template_path: |-
  /Users/deusx/Sites/rubric/templates
```

The `uri_root`, `css_href`, and `template_path` settings will need alterations to suit the locations of files you've copied to your Web server. After tweaking the configuration file, the next step is to prepare the SQLite database for use by Rubric. You can do this with the following command, while in the same directory as your modified `rubric.yml` file:

```
$ perl -MRubric::DBI::Setup -e'Rubric::DBI::Setup->setup_tables'
```

Alternately, you may find a script named `makedb.pl` under the `bin` directory of the unpacked Rubric archive — you can use this instead to do the same thing, if it's available:

```
$ perl makedb.pl
```

Once you've created the blank database, you can then create a new user account for yourself with the `adduser.pl` script, also under the `bin` directory in the package:

```
$ perl adduser.pl rubric_username rubric_password your@email.com
```

Importing del.icio.us Bookmarks into Rubric

Although your new Rubric instance should be ready for use after you finish the configuration, you might want to preload it with bookmarks imported from your del.icio.us account. At this writing, however, there is no facility within Rubric to import bookmarks via a browser. Instead, you'll need to use a command-line tool to bulk load bookmarks into the SQLite database for use by Rubric.

To do this, you need to install a del.icio.us backup script written by Rubric's author, located here:

```
http://search.cpan.org/~rjbs/delicious-backup-0.01/
```

This script can also be installed via CPAN with an invocation like the following:

```
$ cpan R/RJ/RJBS/delicious-backup-0.01.tar.gz
```

You'll probably want to double check that this is the latest version of the backup script, but the preceding command should get the tool installed for you. After getting the backup script installed, you'll need to supply your del.icio.us user name and password in a configuration file named `.delicious` in your home directory. The contents of `.delicious` should look like this:

```
user: yourusername
pswd: yourpassword
```

The next step is to actually use this script to download a copy of your del.icio.us bookmarks in YAML (Yet Another Markup Language) format, like so:

```
$ /usr/bin/delbackup -y > bookmarks.yml
```

This process may take some time, as the `delbackup` script uses the del.icio.us API to pull down your bookmark collection as a YAML export. Once it's done, however, you can dump the data into the Rubric database with a script found under the bin directory of the unpacked Rubric archive:

```
$ perl load_yml.pl rubric_username < bookmarks.yml
```

Note that this command uses the same `rubric_username` supplied to the `adduser.pl` script above. This will import your del.icio.us bookmarks into your Rubric account.

Managing Bookmarks with Rubric

Finally, after installation and configuration are complete, you should be able to visit your new Rubric instance in a browser and be rewarded with a view like Figure 10-29. From this page, you can see most of the basic features of Rubric: bookmarks, notes, tags, and search. You can also register for an account, as shown in Figure 10-30 — although you should already have an account created thanks to the `adduser.pl` script mentioned earlier. You can log in to your account with the top navigation link, which presents you with the login form as shown in Figure 10-31.

Once logged in, you can post a new bookmark or note using the "new entry" link in the top navigation. You can see the entry form in Figure 10-32. This is where Rubric's slightly different focus comes into play: Notice that along with a description field for the bookmark entry, there's also a much larger body text field.

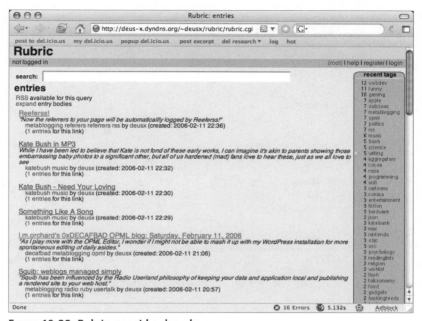

FIGURE 10-29: Rubric recent bookmarks page

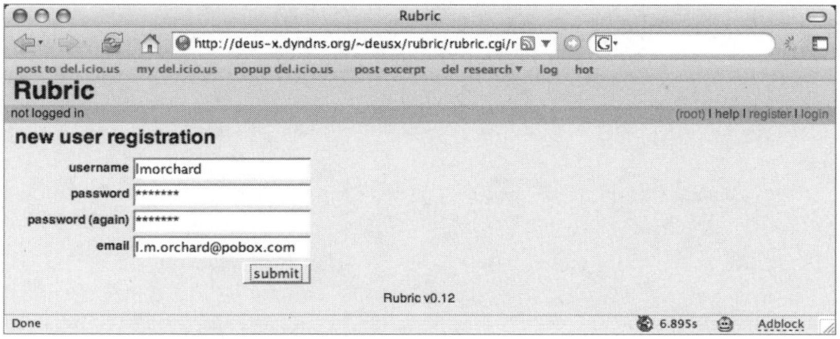

FIGURE 10-30: Registering for a Rubric account

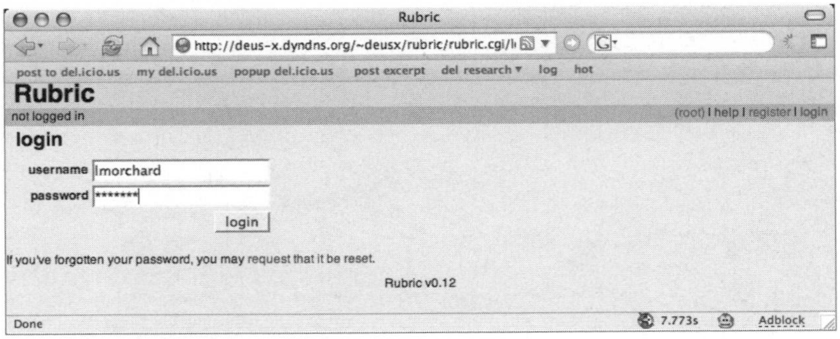

FIGURE 10-31: Logging in to Rubric

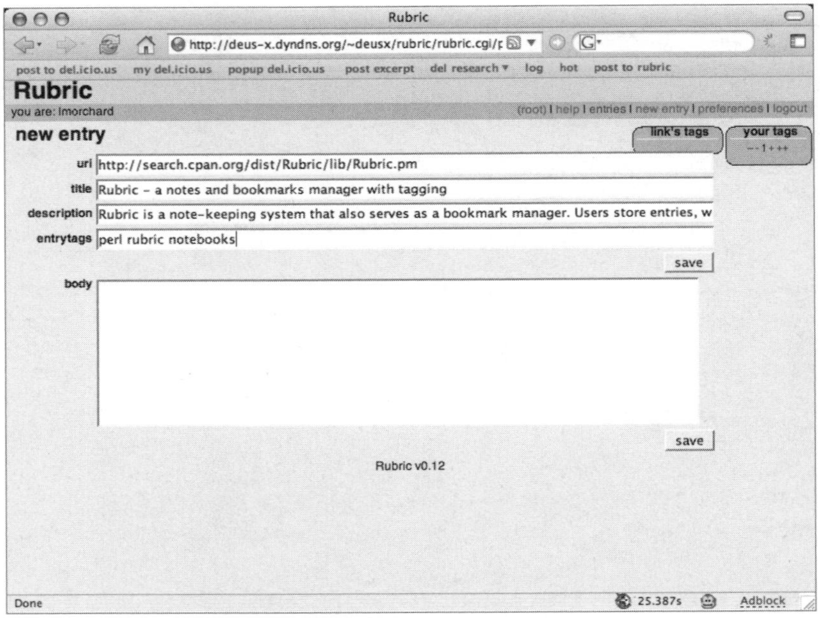

FIGURE 10-32: Adding a new bookmark to Rubric

Along with keeping and sharing bookmarks, Rubric can be used as a rudimentary blogging system — and this text field reflects that aspect of the system because you can compose much longer bits of writing here than you can on del.icio.us. This is a feature that appears to be under active development, including effort applied to introducing automatic text formatting conveniences offered by other blogging packages.

About the Rubric API and RSS Feeds

Rubric offers an API and RSS feeds, but does not attempt to clone the equivalents at del.icio.us. Instead, Rubric treats these more as output template variations on the same methods allowed via the Web browser user interface. Thus, for example, you can view the latest entries in a browser at a URL like this:

```
http://rjbs.manxome.org/rubric/entries
```

If you want this same data in RSS format, you can add a format parameter:

```
http://rjbs.manxome.org/rubric/entries?format=rss
```

There's also the start of an API for Rubric, so if you'd like to see the most recent entries in Rubric API XML format, try this:

```
http://rjbs.manxome.org/rubric/entries?format=api
```

As of this writing, the API is in its early stages and offers just read-only access to bookmarks. But because Rubric is under active development, this story may change by the time you check out the project.

Summary

This chapter introduced you to a few of the available open source alternatives to del.icio.us. These are by no means an exhaustive set of packages you can find for download, but they are fairly representative of what's out there. You could use one of these packages to manage private bookmarks on a server of your own, yet still get the benefits of a Web-based application. Similarly, you could install an open source bookmark manager on a company intranet behind a firewall to facilitate group research.

In the next chapter, you look at some of the entries in the growing list of sites competing with del.icio.us in the social bookmarking space. Although there are a few exceptions, most of these sites are not open source but do offer free access to their services and varying degrees of similarity with the features of del.icio.us.

Checking Out
the Competition

The star of this book is, of course, del.icio.us. But, as you may well know, del.icio.us isn't the only game in town with respect to social bookmarking. In fact, del.icio.us wasn't even the first site to offer bookmark-sharing services, and it certainly won't be the last. In this chapter, you get an introduction to a few of the competitors in the social bookmarking scene.

Advanced Search and Filtering with Simpy

Simpy is a straightforward social bookmarking site — much like del.icio.us, but with the addition of freeform note-taking and advanced search features. You can see a screenshot of the Simpy home page with recent links in Figure 11-1, and visit this site yourself here:

```
www.simpy.com/
```

With Simpy, you get a full set of tools to manage and share bookmarks annotated with title, notes, and tags. These tools include bookmarklets to post while you browse, RSS and Atom feeds to subscribe to updates by person and tag, and a custom REST-based API for third-party applications. So far, these features make Simpy look like an unassuming del.icio.us alternative.

However, in addition, you can choose to make your bookmarks public or private, and even send email notifications to friends when you post a new link. Simpy offers the ability to export bookmarks and import data from del.icio.us and most Web browsers. You can leave out URLs entirely and manage tagged text notes — shopping lists, quotations, To Do items, whatever. Simpy also monitors the health of your bookmarks, checking for dead links and following redirects. In addition, the text of pages is downloaded and indexed along with your notes and tags.

FIGURE 11-1: Simpy home page

One of the places where Simpy really shines, however, is in advanced search queries. You can perform searches for text specified in the title, nickname, and tags metadata fields — as well as focusing on terms within notes and the full text of the bookmarked pages. These field-specific search terms can be mixed together and combined with wildcard matches. And, you can enrich your queries with Boolean operators such as AND, OR, and NOT. Read more about Simpy search capabilities here:

```
www.simpy.com/simpy/FAQ.do#search
```

It's interesting to note that you can get search results in syndication feed form, as described here:

```
www.simpy.com/simpy/service/feed/
```

On the social side of things, Simpy provides the ability to form groups of users by invitation for sharing bookmarks by topic or interest — this is in addition to the ability to query bookmarks by tag. And, in a cross between a search and an inbox feature, you can build Topics from persistent search filters and user bookmark subscriptions. Of course, bookmarks found via group or filtered via topic can be requested in RSS form and monitored for updates from a news aggregator.

Bookmarking in Eclectic Style with Feed Me Links

Feed Me Links is a social bookmarking site whose existence actually predates del.icio.us by several years, as it first launched for public use in 2002. Check it out in Figure 11-2, and here on the Web at this URL:

```
http://feedmelinks.com/
```

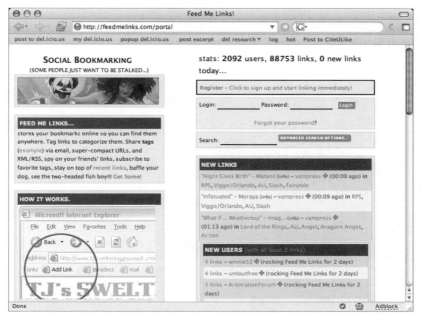

FIGURE 11-2: Feed Me Links home page

At Feed Me Links, you'll find a wide array of bookmarklets, sidebars, browser plug-ins, and search add-ons available to assist in integrating it into your bookmarking and search habits. RSS feeds are available for every user and tag, and there are a number of ways to get data out of the system in XML form and as a stylish Flash-based sidebar (see Figure 11-3). Feed Me Links places an emphasis on the social, including the ability to upload a personal icon and build a contact list of your "peeps" (see Figure 11-4). You can also further annotate others' bookmarks with comments of your own. Feed Me Links has a measure of eclectic visual style and history behind it, which makes it a bit more engaging than the plain stylings on display at del.icio.us.

FIGURE 11-3: Flash-based
sidebar for Feed Me Links

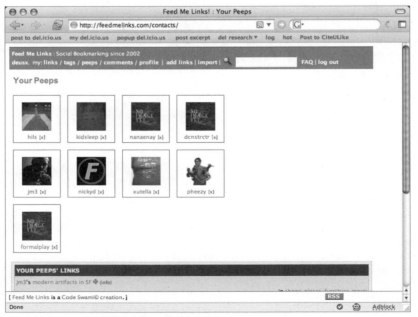

FIGURE 11-4: Contacts list in Feed Me Links

The primary author of Feed Me Links, John Manoogian III, has recently made the jump to open source with this site. Installation instructions weren't included for this project in the previous chapter, but this project is worth checking out as it progresses further. To do so, pay a visit to the project's home on SourceForge:

```
http://sourceforge.net/projects/feed-me-links/
```

Humane Bookmarking with Ma.gnolia

Ma.gnolia is a social bookmarking site with an extra emphasis on the social and visual design aspects, available here:

```
http://ma.gnolia.com/
```

As you can see in Figure 11-5, there's an effort toward improved visual design and aesthetics as key features, with nods toward eye pleasing qualities and usability. Including the ability to attach a title, description, and tags on each link, Ma.gnolia supports the standard set of bookmarking features shown in Figure 11-6.

FIGURE 11-5: The Ma.gnolia home page

FIGURE 11-6: Personal bookmarks at Ma.gnolia

Beyond these, there are also more specifically social features — with groups (see Figure 11-7) and a contact list (see Figure 11-8) instead of del.icio.us-style inbox subscriptions. To put a spotlight on individual users, there's also a section for Featured Linkers, which has included a few linkers with some measure of celebrity outside of alpha-geek circles — such as Ira Glass of NPR fame, and the well-known cooking ace Alton Brown. These touches help push Ma.gnolia out of the sometimes stark and sterile utility niche del.icio.us serves.

Additionally, Ma.gnolia offers the ability to mark individual bookmarks as private and assigns a one- to five-star rating. Thumbnail images and cached versions of bookmarked pages are made available as well. It's also interesting to note that Magnolia provides semi-pronounceable short URLs for bookmarks. For example:

```
http://ma.gnolia.com/bookmarks/scowon/dispatch
http://ma.gnolia.com/bookmarks/netostu/dispatch
```

On the other hand, although this site does not yet offer a Web-based API, there is limited support for linkrolls based on JavaScript includes. Opportunities for automated access and integration in third-party applications are limited as of this writing. However, all in all, Ma.gnolia aims for a more humane social networking experience as opposed to a utilitarian service. Everything from visual design down to URL design reflects this goal.

FIGURE 11-7: Groups at Ma.gnolia

FIGURE 11-8: Contacts and People at Ma.gnolia

Casting Shadow Pages and Bookmarks on Shadows

Shadows is a social bookmarking site whose services are centered on the concept of a Shadow Page, where users can contribute extended discussion and feedback about a bookmarked URL. You can check Shadows out here:

    www.shadows.com/

As a social bookmarking site, Shadows supports the standard basic features for posting and searching bookmarks with descriptive notes and tags. This site also provides the ability to attach a one- to five-star rating to postings. And to make habitual usage easier, you can grab a pair of bookmarklets or download a toolbar for Firefox and Internet Explorer browsers.

In terms of data access, Shadows offers RSS and Atom feeds for most page views — and it appears that these feeds even feature Shadows-specific extensions to include privacy and ratings data along with each bookmark feed item. Additionally, there's a clone of the del.icio.us API that closely follows the original, such that it shouldn't be very difficult to adapt third-party tools for use with Shadows. You can read about the API here:

    www.shadows.com/features/site/help/api.htm

Shadows also supports a bit more of the social side of bookmarking, with richer personal profile pages than del.icio.us (see Figure 11-9), as well as topical user groups you can join (see Figure 11-10).

FIGURE 11-9: A Shadows personal profile

FIGURE 11-10: One of the topical groups on Shadows

The main attraction of Shadows, however, is the Shadow Page — you can see one of these in Figure 11-11. Beyond the simple view on bookmarks by URL that del.icio.us offers, a Shadow Page provides a thumbnail of the page, per-URL and per-domain discussion forums, and a summary of others' bookmarks and ratings. Shadow Pages are a bit like miniature portals, offering a bit more depth to the community's bookmarks and tags devoted to individual links.

Uncovering the Latest News with digg

digg could be more accurately described as competition for popular news sites than for del.icio.us, but it does offer many features in common with social bookmarking services. You can see a snapshot of the digg home page in Figure 11-12, and visit the site yourself at this address:

```
http://digg.com
```

FIGURE 11-11: A Shadow Page on Shadows

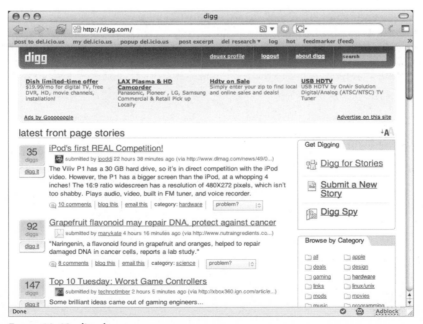

FIGURE 11-12: digg home page

Most social bookmarking sites center on a personal collection of bookmarks, with varying degrees of sharing and social features. digg, on the other hand, is all about sharing links with others for commentary and collaborative promotion. Although it is possible to filter by user on digg (see Figure 11-13), this site is definitely more about collaborative filtering than individual utility. And although there is some personal reward to sharing bookmarks on other sites, digg structures itself around providing reputation-based incentive for sharing the most interesting news through the use of scoreboards (see Figure 11-14) and badges displaying the number of "diggs" of approval a particular posting has received.

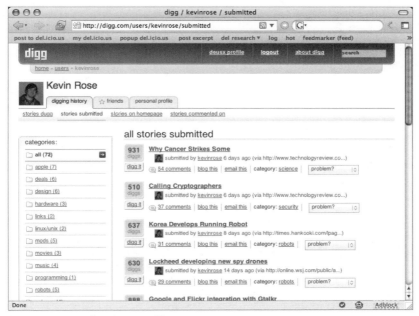

FIGURE 11-13: A digg user profile

Because digg is more about the intentional promotion of interesting items from around the Web, you won't necessarily find an official bookmarklet for super-fast posting or an import/export facility for your bookmarks. digg requires more attention and personal involvement — the idea being that people are actively attempting to supply useful and interesting stories to the community. The utility in digg is less about sharing a collection, and more in sharing attention.

An API for third-party applications may be under development — but because the site itself is meant to be a focal point and not a generic utility, this API will likely look a bit different from the one offered by del.icio.us. With respect to data feeds available from digg, you can find RSS feeds for any category or user's postings, as well as build JavaScript includes to include digg headlines on your own site.

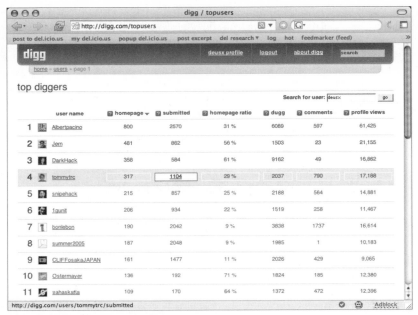

FIGURE 11-14: digg Top Users scoreboard

Combining Feeds and Bookmarks with Feedmarker

Feedmarker is a combination RSS/Atom feed reader and bookmarking service. You can visit the home page shown in Figure 11-15 at this URL:

```
www.feedmarker.com
```

Rather than specializing in visual aesthetics or social connectivity, Feedmarker augments shared bookmarking with subscriptions to RSS and Atom feeds. You can use a pair of bookmarklets to add the current pages to your collection, as well as to auto-discover and subscribe to a syndication feed associated with the current page. You can annotate bookmarks and feed subscriptions with a title, tags, and notes. Feed subscriptions, however, allow access to the latest updated items from feeds — you can drill down into the item content as shown in Figure 11-16. In a sense, these feed subscriptions on Feedmarker are akin to the Live Bookmarks in Firefox mentioned earlier in this book.

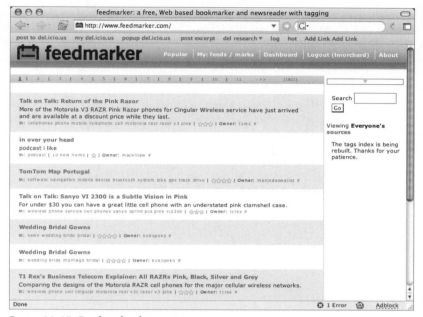

FIGURE 11-15: Feedmarker home page

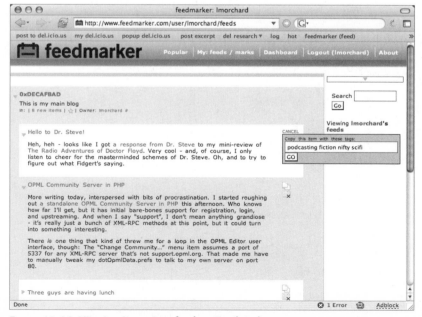

FIGURE 11-16: Viewing items in a feed on Feedmarker

What's interesting to note about this bookmarking/feed reader integration, however, is that you can route feed items right into your bookmark collection as you read. With each feed item, there's an Ajax-powered "copy" icon that, when clicked, will prompt you for a choice of tags and then add the current feed item into your collection without disrupting the page. This allows for a nice all-in-one workflow between sifting through updates on your favorite sites and capturing items of interest worth sharing or reading later.

With respect to data access, there's a nice combined feed of items received from subscribed feeds, as well as a JavaScript include of the same data. You can use this feed in an aggregator to get everything in one shot from Feedmarker, or build a sidebar for your site from the JS data. There does not, however, appear to be an API for Feedmarker at present.

Managing Your Special URLs with Spurl

Spurl offers social bookmarking with a few extra organization features. The Spurl home page is shown in Figure 11-17. You can visit it yourself at the following address:

```
http://spurl.net/
```

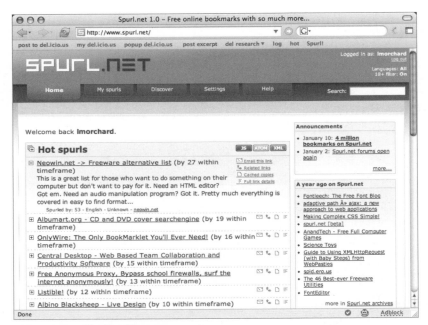

FIGURE 11-17: The Spurl home page

According to the FAQ pages, Spurl stands for "special url" — used both as a noun for book-marks and as a verb for the act of bookmarking. And, like most other social bookmarking sites, Spurl offers the ability to post links annotated with tags and extended description (see Figure 11-18).

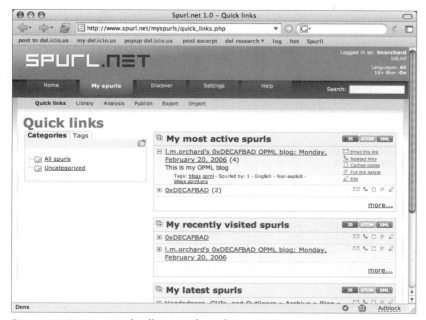

FIGURE 11-18: A personal collection of Spurls

However, once you've submitted a bookmark to the site, you can perform full-text searches on your own collection and others'. Spurl caches local copies of bookmarked pages, facilitating both search and later retrieval if or when the bookmarked resource disappears from the Web — thus helping defeat "linkrot." In Figure 11-19, you can see how a cached page is presented. Spurl includes a frame at the top of the page indicating that you are indeed viewing a cached copy, as well as a selection box to choose among several potential snapshots taken over time.

Like the SiteBar application mentioned in Chapter 10, Spurl offers a sidebar for browser inte-gration (see Figure 11-20). You can use this sidebar to keep your bookmark collection close at hand, as well as to navigate folders of bookmarks you can manage from within your account. And, that's another key feature of Spurl: Along with tags, you can arrange your bookmarks into a hierarchical folder of categories — thus getting the best of both worlds, in case you're not entirely sold on the idea of tags as the ultimate in bookmark organization.

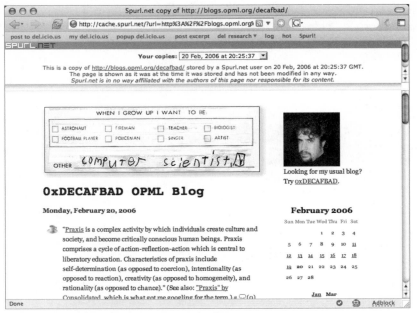

FIGURE 11-19: Viewing a page cached by Spurl

FIGURE 11-20:
The Spurl sidebar

One last set of features worth mentioning is that just about every list of bookmarks on Spurl is also offered in JavaScript include, RSS, and Atom feed formats. There's also an API available, but as of this writing the FAQ pages instruct third-party developers to contact the operators of Spurl directly for details and documentation on how to access it.

Selective Bookmark Sharing with Jots

Jots is a bookmarking service that shares many features with del.icio.us. You can visit the Jots home page, shown in Figure 11-21, at this URL:

```
www.jots.com/
```

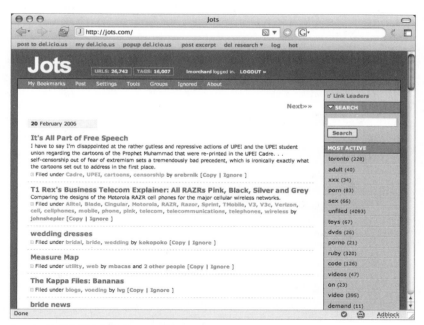

FIGURE 11-21: The Jots home page

Jots features a simple user interface for posting tagged and annotated bookmarks, as well as offering tag-based navigation and search. You can also find RSS feeds for nearly every page view on the site. Bookmarklets for use during your daily browsing habits are available under the Tools section, as is a daily blog post feature similar to the one presented for del.icio.us back in Chapter 8.

However, one feature where Jots diverges from del.icio.us — and most other social bookmarking sites — is in its implementation of groups. While some bookmarking sites offer groups as a way for people to share topical bookmarks, groups on Jots is more of a selective privacy feature: You can create a named group and assign users to it (see Figure 11-22). This group's name can then be prefixed with an @ character and used as a "privileged tag" — thus collegebuddies becomes @collegebuddies.

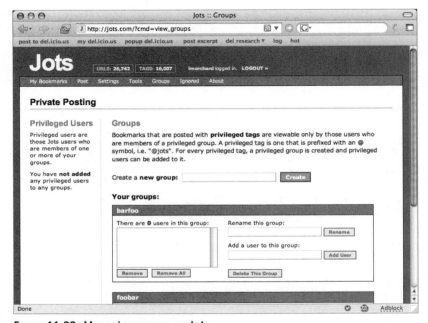

FIGURE 11-22: Managing groups on Jots

Any bookmarks to which you attach a privileged tag are then visible only to users you've added to the associated group. This is, in a way, the inverse of how most social networking sites handle groups — rather than allowing anyone to join the group, you're in charge of the group membership for your own privileged tags.

Another area where Jots differs from del.icio.us is in its API. Rather than cloning the HTTP-and-XML API offered by del.icio.us, Jots exposes an API via XML-RPC. The Jots API offers methods to create, delete, and edit bookmarks — as well as a number of methods to manage groups and group members. You can read about the Jots API methods here:

```
http://jots.com/pages/xmlrpc_api.html
```

Bookmarking for Scientists with Connotea

Connotea offers a shared bookmarking service mainly targeted toward academics and scientists. A screenshot of recent links posted is offered in Figure 11-23, and the site itself is located here:

```
www.connotea.org/
```

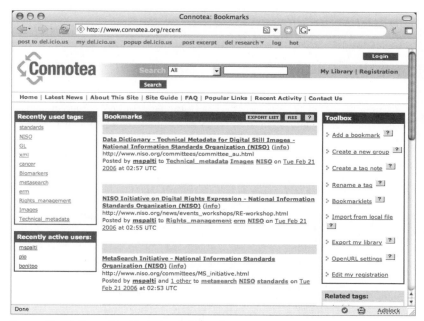

FIGURE 11-23: Recent bookmarks at Connotea

As with del.icio.us, you can register for an account with Connotea and post annotated bookmarks directly or via a set of available bookmarklets. However, in using Connotea, along with URLs from the Web at large, you can also bookmark articles from scientific journals — such as *Nature* — which offer Digital Object Identifiers (or DOIs; see www.doi.org).

Connotea attempts to resolve bookmarked DOIs to automatically uncover bibliographic information, such as the author and publication in which the resource may be found (see Figure 11-24). Additionally, if you happen to have access to a library that supports OpenURL access to its card catalog, Connotea can directly connect you to a copy of a bookmarked publication residing in your local library stacks. You can read more about these features in the Connotea guide, located here:

```
www.connotea.org/guide
```

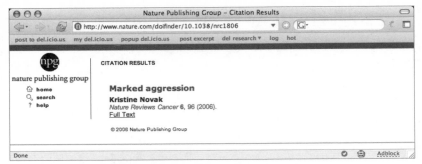

FIGURE 11-24: Chasing down a DOI reference from Connotea

Connotea is also available as open source software. Because it's a bit of a special-interest bookmarking service and takes a bit or work to get up and running, Connotea wasn't included in Chapter 10. But, should you want to check it out, you can find details and instructions for installation here:

```
www.connotea.org/code
```

Capturing Bibliographic Citations with CiteULike

CiteULike is another bookmarking service for academics and scientists — perhaps more properly competition for Connotea than del.icio.us. Where Connotea offers a bit of support for collecting bibliographic data, assembling collections of academic papers and publications is the main goal at CiteULike. The CiteULike home page is shown in Figure 11-25, which you can visit at the following URL:

```
www.citeulike.org/
```

Although you can use CiteULike to manage bookmarks in general, the main attraction of this service is its support for the automated extraction of bibliographic information from resources found at over two-dozen publications and archives of scholarly papers. You can find a handy bookmarklet to assist in posting bookmarks, along with a list of supported sites and publications, located at this address:

```
www.citeulike.org/post
```

As you can see in Figure 11-26, CiteULike allows users to post bookmarks annotated with title and tags. However, CiteULike goes even further by automatically digging up the names of authors, cover art, and more. Visiting a bookmarked resource on CiteULike, you'll find that the service can capture the text of book and article abstracts, as well as versions of the resource in multiple languages.

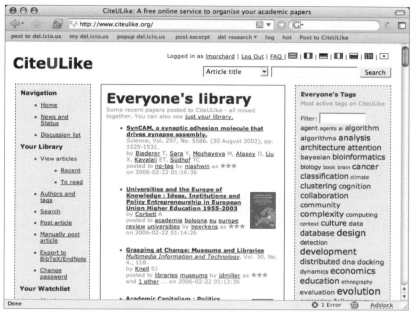

FIGURE 11-25: CiteULike home page

FIGURE 11-26: Annotated publications bookmarked at CiteULike

CiteULike is not entirely open source as Connotea is. However, Richard Cameron — the operator of CiteULike — invites users to contribute to its development by authoring new plug-ins to extract bookmark data from more sites and archives of publications. You can find more details on this request by reading the site's FAQ pages, found here:

```
www.citeulike.org/faq/all.adp
```

Summary

This chapter provided an introduction to some of the competition for del.icio.us and what features make each site a unique offering. This is far from a comprehensive set of del.icio.us alternatives you'll find out there, but from these you should be able to get a pretty good idea of how others are trying to follow or improve upon the standard social bookmarking features supported by del.icio.us — and how some are working to break the mold.

Site URLs, Feeds, and API Methods Reference

Throughout the pages of this book, you can learn about the browser-accessible URLs, open API methods, and data feeds made available by del.icio.us. However, when you get down to playing around with some hacks of your own, it's more useful to have everything in a distilled form — rather than flipping back and forth through the whole book.

With that in mind, my intent in this appendix is to present a quick reference to many of the URLs and formats introduced throughout the book. Here, you'll find a lot of material repeated from earlier chapters, but in a more condensed form. Once you've gotten the hang of how things work, I hope this part of the book can offer quick reminders while you tinker with your own del.icio.us mashups and applications. (Note that placeholder text in URLs is indicated by italic.)

Browser-Viewable Public URLs

While perhaps not an API per se, the structure of browser-accessible URLs making up the del.icio.us user interface form very regular and easy-to-template patterns. This makes it easy to automate navigation to various parts of del.icio.us through things such as hyperlinks, bookmarklets, and Greasemonkey user scripts.

The following is an annotated list of URLs available at del.icio.us that you can access without first needing to log in to a user account:

- `http://del.icio.us/`

  - This is, of course, the del.icio.us home page.

- `http://del.icio.us/help`

  - You can visit this URL to check out the documentation and help available at del.icio.us.

- `http://del.icio.us/popular`
  - This is the address of a page presenting the day's most popular bookmarks.
- `http://del.icio.us/popular?new`
  - Appending the `?new` parameter filters the popular view for only those bookmarks posted fresh today.
- `http://del.icio.us/popular/TAG`
  - The popular bookmarks page can be filtered by tag, specified by the value of the placeholder `TAG`.
- `http://del.icio.us/tag/`
  - A cloud presentation of the top tags used on del.icio.us is available at this URL.
- `http://del.icio.us/tag/TAG`
  - By replacing the placeholder `TAG`, you can get a view of the latest bookmarks to which that tag has been attached.
- `http://del.icio.us/tag/TAG1+TAG2+...+TAGn`
  - The view of bookmarks by tag can be extended to viewing the intersection of any number of +-separated values for `TAG1..TAGn` placeholders.
- `http://del.icio.us/url?url=URL`
  - By supplying the URL-encoded form of a link as the `URL` placeholder value, you can view a detail page listing the history of users who have bookmarked it as well as their respective submitted descriptions.
- `http://del.icio.us/url/MD5`
  - The previous URL is basically a convenient alternate for this one. Here, instead of passing a doubly encoded URL in a parameter, the MD5 hash of a URL is employed as part of the path. Note that the previous URL actually results in a redirect to this URL.
- `http://del.icio.us/url/MD5?related=1`
  - By appending a related parameter onto the previous URL, you can cause del.icio.us to make recommendations about other possibly related bookmarks for further browsing.
- `http://del.icio.us/USER`
  - Visit a single user's bookmark collection by supplying the user's name for the `USER` placeholder in this URL.
- `http://del.icio.us/USER/TAG`
  - The view of a user's bookmarks can be filtered by the tag in place of `TAG`.

- `http://del.icio.us/`*`USER`*`/`*`TAG1`*`+`*`TAG2`*`+...+`*`TAGn`*

  - As in the case for tags in general, multiple +-separated tags may be supplied to filter a user's bookmarks on the intersection of tags.

- `http://del.icio.us/inbox/`*`USER`*

  - The aggregated bookmarks from a user's inbox subscriptions are viewable at this URL. Note that the inbox feature is not a private one.

Browser-Viewable Private URLs

Once a user has logged in, there's an expanded set of URLs available. These include the means to post new bookmarks, as well as pages to manage account settings.

The following is a list of annotated URLs that are available to a user only after login:

- `http://del.icio.us/logout`

  - Visiting this URL causes the current user to end his or her login session.

- `http://del.icio.us/post/`

  - Send a user to this page to get the first stage of the generic bookmark posting form.

- `http://del.icio.us/post?url=`*`URL`*`&` `description=`*`DESCRIPTION`*`&notes=`*`NOTES`*

  - By filling in the placeholders in this URL with a bookmark link, short description, and more verbose notes, you can send a user to a bookmarking form pre-populated with this data. Note that although the URL field is required, the other two are optional.

- `http://del.icio.us/post?url=`*`URL`* `&title=`*`TITLE`*`&extended=`*`EXTENDED`*

  - This URL appears to be a variant of the previous one, where the `title` parameter is a synonym for `description`, and `extended` is treated the same as `notes`. In addition, as discussed in Chapter 2, using the `title` synonym in lieu of `description` appears to short-circuit automated bookmarklet posting.

- `http://del.icio.us/post?noui=1&jump=doclose|no`

  - These are optional parameters that can be appended to either of the previous URLs.

  - If `noui` is set to any value (1 or 0), then none of the JavaScript-driven tag recommendation machinery will be supplied — thus providing a simpler bookmark posting form.

  - If `jump` is set to `doclose`, the browser window (presumably a popup) will close at the end of posting the bookmark.

- If `jump` is set to `no`, del.icio.us will return to the user's collection of bookmarks.

- If `jump` is not supplied at all, del.icio.us will redirect the user to the URL just bookmarked as the final step. This all provides a bit of choice in driving bookmarking workflow.

- `http://del.icio.us/for/USER`

  - Any bookmarks tagged with `for:USER` can be privately viewed at this address.

- `http://del.icio.us/settings/USER/antisocial`

  - Settings for ignoring individual users and tags on the front page and the previous URL can be managed here.

- `http://del.icio.us/settings/USER/profile`

  - From this page, a user can manage his or her personal profile information and change passwords.

- `http://del.icio.us/settings/USER/tags`

  - You can rename and delete tags applied to all bookmarks in your collection at this URL, facilitating tag gardening over time.

- `http://del.icio.us/settings/USER/import`

  - As of this writing, this feature is being rebuilt — but this is where you'll be able to import bookmarks from your browser and potentially other bookmarking services.

- `http://del.icio.us/settings/USER/export`

  - If you'd like to back up your bookmarks or move to another service, you can use this page to download a copy of your collection in XML.

- `http://del.icio.us/settings/USER/inbox`

  - Although the aggregate results of a user's inbox are public, the subscriptions in an inbox are privately managed at this page.

- `http://del.icio.us/settings/USER/bundle`

  - This settings page facilitates the creation and management of tag bundles for a user.

- `http://del.icio.us/settings/USER/daily`

  - As discussed in Chapter 8, this page allows users to schedule daily blog posting jobs from del.icio.us via the Blogger API supported by many blog software packages.

- `http://del.icio.us/settings/USER/license`

  - From this settings page, you can choose a license under which bookmarks are offered in RSS feeds. Choices include options ranging from all rights reserved, to a number of Creative Commons licenses.

RSS Feeds

Most of the browser-viewable URLs available for public access have equivalent URLs that yield alternate RSS feeds. As a rule of thumb, if you drop /rss into the URL just after the del.icio.us, you're likely to get what you're after. Be warned, however, that your software shouldn't poll any of these feeds more than twice an hour — not only does del.icio.us not make useful updates to them more often than that, but you might also find yourself throttled or blocked from accessing the feeds altogether.

So, for quick reference, here's an annotated list of some RSS-producing URLs you can access at del.icio.us:

- http://del.icio.us/rss/

  - This is a firehose feed of all bookmarks posted to del.icio.us.

- http://del.icio.us/rss/popular

  - In this feed, you find items drawn from the day's most popular posted bookmarks.

- http://del.icio.us/rss/tag/*TAG*

  - You can filter the firehose of del.icio.us postings down to a single tag with this RSS feed URL. Just supply the desired tag for the *TAG* placeholder. However, as of this writing, attempting to supply multiple tags as an intersection doesn't seem to work for RSS feed URLs.

- http://del.icio.us/rss/*USER*

  - If you'd like to subscribe to a single user's bookmarks as they're posted, this is the feed to use. Be sure to replace the placeholder *USER* with the desired user name.

- http://del.icio.us/rss/*USER*/*TAG*

  - To restrict items returned in the RSS feed to a single tag from a user's collection, use this URL.

- http://del.icio.us/rss/*USER*/*TAG1*+*TAG2*+...+*TAGn*

  - Multiple tags can be supplied to request a tag intersection as a filter for a user's bookmarks. This feed URL construction appears to work, despite the general tag query case not supporting it.

- http://del.icio.us/rss/url?url=*URL*

  - By supplying a doubly encoded URL for the *URL* placeholder, you can track bookmarking activity as it occurs on a single Web page.

- http://del.icio.us/rss/url/*MD5*

  - If you've got access to MD5 hashing routines, this might be a simpler option than the previous per-URL feed option. This form of RSS feed URL was used in Chapter 9 to build the JavaScript-based del.icio.us comments system.

- `http://del.icio.us/rss/for/USER?private=PRIVATE`

  - This feed URL can provide you with a feed of bookmarks posted for your attention using the `for:` tag prefix. However, there's no documented way to programmatically produce the correct value for *PRIVATE* — you'll need to log into del.icio.us and visit the following page to find this feed: `http://del.icio.us/for/deusx`.

JSON Feeds

Another alternate form in which bookmarks may be queried from del.icio.us are JSON feeds. Essentially, these are bookmark posts expressed as valid but simplified JavaScript data structures. The most basic use of these feeds is in the construction of client-side JavaScript includes, used in displaying links in blog sidebars and such. You can find more advanced examples of JSON use in Chapter 9.

This is a relatively new feature, however, and as of this writing you can really get JSON feeds for bookmarks only of single users and a user's tags. The following are URLs available for use in fetching JSON feeds:

- `http://del.icio.us/feeds/json/USER`

  - At this URL, you can find JSON-encoded recent bookmarks for a single user.

- `http://del.icio.us/feeds/json/USER/TAG`

  - By appending a tag, you can filter the JSON-encoded bookmarks to a single tag from a user's recent postings.

- `http://del.icio.us/feeds/json/USER/TAG1+TAG2+...+TAGn`

  - Multiple tags may be used as part of the JSON query to perform a tag intersection filter on a user's recent bookmarks.

- `http://del.icio.us/feeds/json/USER?count=COUNT`

  - The default number of bookmarks returned by a JSON request is 15. This optional `count` parameter allows you to specify a new count, between 1 and 100.

- `http://del.icio.us/feeds/json/USER?raw=1`

  - Typically, the JSON data returned by del.icio.us comes constructed as the definition of a data structure assigned to the variable `Delicious.posts`. Supplying the optional parameter `raw` will cause just the data structure itself to be returned, detached from any other JavaScript code. This can be useful for programs that may be able to parse JSON, but not full JavaScript code.

- `http://del.icio.us/feeds/json/USER?callback=CALLBACK`

  - By supplying a value for the optional parameter `callback`, the raw form of the JSON data will be wrapped in a call to the named function. This is a technique known as JSONP, which provides a way to trigger processing code upon a successful dynamic fetch of JSON data.

Listing A-1 offers a reminder of what JSON data returned from del.icio.us looks like.

Listing A-1: Sample JSON feed from del.icio.us

```
if(typeof(Delicious) == 'undefined') Delicious = {};
Delicious.posts = [

    {"u":"http://support.opml.org/2006/02/01#a671",
     "n":"\"How to install your own server\"",
     "d":"OPML Editor support: OPML Community Server Howto",
     "t":["frontier","opml","webdev"]},

    {"u":"http://rentzsch.com/suck/stopStopStopHurtingTheInternet",
     "n":"\"My God, they've made metal look good.\" ...",
     "d":"rentzsch.com: Stop Stop Stop Hurting the Internet",
     "t":["msft","msie","vista","gui","safari","apple","webdev"]}

]
```

Note that the data shown in Listing A-1 has been reformatted to be just a little easier to visually inspect. In reality, JSON data returned from del.icio.us has little or no extraneous line breaks or white space included. This data is composed as JavaScript, defining the variable `Delicious.posts` as a list of objects. Each of these objects contains a set of properties:

- u — URL
- n — Title or name
- d — Description
- t — List of tags attached

In addition, Listing A-2 shows what changes when the optional `raw` parameter is included in the query.

Listing A-2: Sample raw JSON feed from del.icio.us

```
[
    {"u":"http://support.opml.org/2006/02/01#a671",
     "n":"\"How to install your own server\"",
     "d":"OPML Editor support: OPML Community Server Howto",
     "t":["frontier","opml","webdev"]},

    {"u":"http://rentzsch.com/suck/stopStopStopHurtingTheInternet",
```

continued

Listing A-2 *continued*

```
    "n":"\"My God, they've made metal look good.\" ...",
    "d":"rentzsch.com: Stop Stop Stop Hurting the Internet",
    "t":["msft","msie","vista","gui","safari","apple","webdev"]}
]
```

Note that Listing A-2 is raw JSON data, without any additional JavaScript code. And, just for the sake of completeness, Listing A-3 offers an example of the result of a query using the `callback` parameter.

Listing A-3: Sample raw JSON feed with callback from del.icio.us

```
FooBar.process_bookmarks([
    {"u":"http://support.opml.org/2006/02/01#a671",
     "n":"\"How to install your own server\"",
     "d":"OPML Editor support: OPML Community Server Howto",
     "t":["frontier","opml","webdev"]},

    {"u":"http://rentzsch.com/suck/stopStopStopHurtingTheInternet",
     "n":"\"My God, they've made metal look good.\" ...",
     "d":"rentzsch.com: Stop Stop Stop Hurting the Internet",
     "t":["msft","msie","vista","gui","safari","apple","webdev"]}
])
```

Listing A-3 shows the results of a JSON query made with a `callback` parameter value of `FooBar.process_bookmarks`. If you had defined a JavaScript package named `FooBar`, containing a function `process_bookmarks`, this function would be called upon the successful fetch and execution of this JSON code. You can see this technique in use in Chapter 9 during the display of related del.icio.us links.

File Type and Media Tags

When certain kinds of file URLs are bookmarked at del.icio.us — particularly those identified by extension as being certain kinds of media files or documents — a set of special system tags is automatically applied.

Note that these tags have special meaning in the context of RSS feeds. When an RSS feed is queried from one of these tags, the format changes to an RSS 2.0 feed with `<enclosure>` tags. In essence, this turns the feed into a podcast or video cast feed compatible with podcast tuners.

This concept was explained in detail in Chapter 6, but the table mapping extensions to tags is reproduced in Table A-1 for quick reference.

Table A-1   File Extensions Mapped to File Type and Media Tags

File Extension	File Type Tag	Media Tag
.mp3	system:filetype:mp3	system:media:audio
.wav	system:filetype:wav	system:media:audio
.mpg	system:filetype:mpg	system:media:video
.mpeg	system:filetype:mpeg	system:media:video
.avi	system:filetype:avi	system:media:video
.wmv	system:filetype:wmv	system:media:video
.mov	system:filetype:mov	system:media:video
.tiff	system:filetype:jpg	system:media:image
.jpeg	system:filetype:jpeg	system:media:image
.gif	system:filetype:gif	system:media:image
.tiff	system:filetype:png	system:media:image

HTTP API Methods and XML Response Formats

The API based on HTTP GET and XML offered by del.icio.us was explored in depth in Chapter 4, and made appearances throughout the rest of the book. This is one of the most interesting facets of del.icio.us for developers and tinkerers, so this section of the appendix collects descriptions of methods offered by the API, as well as summaries of the XML data produced by each.

You can read the latest documentation on the API at the following URL:

```
http://del.icio.us/help/api/
```

As with all areas of del.icio.us, this API is under constant development, so be sure to consult this page for up-to-date information.

Using the HTTP API Methods

A few things to remember in general when using the del.icio.us API, rephrased from the previously mentioned documentation:

- All methods require HTTP authentication, with the user name and password being that of a registered del.icio.us user account.

- Although at present, the URLs to all API methods begin with the same common base (e.g., `http://del.icio.us/api`), you should be sure to parameterize this base URL in your programs. For some time now, there have been stated plans to move the API to a new base URL and/or release future versions of the API at different base URLs.

- Wait at least 1 second between successive calls to the API. Performing more frequent calls to the API may result in your program's access being throttled — resulting in HTTP 503 Service Unavailable errors — or your IP address banned from API use altogether. Ideally, a wrapper library for your favorite programming environment will take care of this requirement.

- And, speaking of getting throttled or banned: If you're making direct calls to the API — while building an API wrapper of your own, for instance — be sure to supply a unique value for the User-Agent header sent with requests. This will allow the servers at del.icio.us to identify requests made by your code and differentiate it from others, which may help keep your application from getting caught in a blanket ban or throttle.

- Never post bookmarks to a user's collection or add tags or notes without their permission. This is a requirement to use the API, and is just being polite to the user. Adding tags or note text that identifies the use of your software is just plain rude and considered an abuse of the API.

Managing Bookmark Posts

The majority of the methods exposed by the del.icio.us API are useful for searching, fetching, and managing bookmarks.

Retrieving Bookmark Data by Tag, Date, and URL

```
http://del.icio.us/api/posts/get?tag=TAG&dt=DATE&url=URL
```

Description

Use this method to fetch bookmarks matching given parameters — defaulting to the last recent date when bookmarks were posted if no parameters are found.

Parameters

- `tag=TAG` (optional): Tag by which to filter bookmarks retrieved.

- `dt=DATE` (optional): Date by which to filter bookmarks, specified as a profile of the ISO8601 date format (e.g., `2006-03-15T13:10:00Z`).

- `url=URL` (optional): When supplied, available bookmark data for a single URL is returned.

Response XML

```
<?xml version='1.0' standalone='yes'?>
<posts dt="2006-03-15" tag="" user="deusx">

   <post href="http://blog.deconcept.com/2006/03/13/modern-
approach-flash-seo/"
         description="deconcept - A modern approach to Flash SEO"
```

```
       extended="&quot;You start with your HTML (your
content)...&quot;"
       hash="bfa6de80d06e5fbddbb3f96b4ea726b0"
       others="69"
       tag="css flash javascript seo webdev xhtml"
       time="2006-03-15T12:23:16Z" />

</posts>
```

Note that this sample XML data has been reformatted slightly for readability.

This is the general format for bookmark data returned from API methods: a document element `<posts>` containing many `<post>` elements. Attributes on the `<posts>` tag reflect parameters supplied with the request (e.g., dt, tag, and user). As for the `<post>` tags, they offer data in a number of attributes, including the following:

- href: The bookmarked URL
- description: A short description supplied for the bookmark
- extended: Longer notes attached posted with the bookmark
- hash: An MD5 hash of the bookmark URL
- others: A count of other users who have bookmarked this URL
- tag: Space-separated list of tags attached to this bookmark
- time: ISO8601 timestamp indicating when this bookmark was posted

Retrieving Recently Posted Bookmarks

```
http://del.icio.us/api/posts/recent?tag=TAG&count=COUNT
```

Description
Rather than retrieving a full day's worth of bookmarks, this method can be used to fetch a specified count of bookmarks regardless of date.

Parameters
- tag=TAG (optional): Tag by which to filter recent bookmarks
- count=COUNT (optional): Number of bookmarks to return, with a default of 15 and a maximum value of 100

Response XML
```
<?xml version='1.0' standalone='yes'?>
<posts tag="" user="deusx">

  <post href="http://blog.modernmechanix.com/2006/03/13/ascii-art-
1948/"
```

```
            description="Modern Mechanix - ASCII Art - 1948"
            extended="&quot;WHILE purely entertaining,
doodling...&quot;"
            hash="2115fcc36b029a7f3028968184c326ff"
            tag="retro asciiart"
            time="2006-03-14T12:11:09Z" />

</posts>
```

Bookmarks returned by this method follow the same XML format as other methods, with the same essential attributes.

Fetching All Bookmarks

```
http://del.icio.us/api/posts/all?tag=TAG
```

Description

This method can be used to fetch data for all bookmarks. Because this method is very resource intensive and can potentially return a great deal of data, it should be used very rarely. For instance, your application could use it upon its first run or for occasional complete backups. Otherwise, more specific bookmark fetches should be used.

Parameters

- tag=TAG (optional): Filter all tags fetched by the TAG you supply.

Response XML

```
<?xml version='1.0' standalone='yes'?>
<posts update="2006-03-15T12:23:16Z" user="deusx">

  <post
href="http://blogcritics.org/archives/2005/10/24/045230.php"
        description="Blogcritics.org: CD Review: The Pogues"
        extended="&quot;For those who don't know any
better,...&quot;"
        hash="acb505259a172540a86a06dc284d27a3"
        tag="music pogues 80s"
        time="2005-10-24T14:09:05Z" />

</posts>
```

Bookmarks returned by this method follow the same XML format as other methods, with the same essential attributes.

Checking the Time of the Last Posted Bookmark

```
http://del.icio.us/api/posts/update
```

Description

This method returns the date of the most recently posted bookmark. The API documentation advises making a call to this method before attempting a fetch of all bookmarks, to be sure that there've been new bookmarks since the previous fetch.

Parameters

- None.

Response XML

```
<?xml version='1.0' standalone='yes'?>
<update time="2006-03-15T12:23:16Z" />
```

The XML format returned by this method is very simple: a single `<update>` element with a `time` attribute containing an ISO8601 timestamp of the last recent bookmark posted.

Fetching a List of Dates with Available Bookmarks

```
http://del.icio.us/api/posts/dates?tag=TAG
```

Description

Some methods accept timestamp values for filtering, which can be constructed at runtime in your programs. However, by using this method, you can fetch a sort of timestamp "table of contents" for all bookmarks or individual tags.

Parameters

- `tag` (optional): Filter dates list for a given tag

Response XML

```
<?xml version='1.0' standalone='yes'?>
<dates tag="" user="deusx">
  <date count="16" date="2006-03-15" />
  <date count="15" date="2006-03-14" />
  <date count="27" date="2006-03-13" />
...
  <date count="7" date="2003-09-15" />
</dates>
```

This format consists of a `<dates>` document element containing a number of `<date>` elements. The `<dates>` element lists attributes reflecting the API query parameters, while each `<date>` element lists a `date` attribute and a `count` of bookmarks posted on that date.

Deleting a Bookmark

```
http://del.icio.us/api/posts/delete?url=URL
```

Description

Delete a given bookmark from the collection by URL.

Parameters

- url=*URL* (required): The URL of the bookmark to be deleted

Response XML

```
<?xml version='1.0' standalone='yes'?>
<result code="done" />
```

If for some reason the bookmark deletion fails, the code attribute returned with the <result> element will be equal to something other than done — usually a description of what error condition occurred.

Posting a New Bookmark

```
http://del.icio.us/api/posts/add?url=URL& description=
DESCRIPTION&extended=EXTENDED& tags=TAGS&dt=DATE&replace=no
```

Description

This method can be used to post new bookmarks or update existing ones, defined by the parameters supplied.

Parameters

- url=*URL* (required): The URL of the bookmark to be created or updated.

- description=*DESCRIPTION* (required): Short descriptive title to post with the bookmark.

- extended=*EXTENDED* (optional): Longer text block of notes for the bookmark.

- tags=*TAGS* (optional): Space-separated tags to attach to the bookmark.

- dt=*DATESTAMP* (optional): Timestamp for the bookmark, following a profile of the ISO8601 standard (e.g., 2005-03-13T14:23:50Z). Note that the fully specified date/time value is required, including the GMT time zone of Z. This parameter defaults to the current time for new bookmarks, and the existing timestamp for existing bookmarks.

- replace=no (optional): If this parameter is supplied, and a bookmark already exists for this URL, it will not be altered by the details of this API call.

Response XML

```
<?xml version='1.0' standalone='yes'?>
<result code="done" />
```

If for some reason the bookmark posting fails, the code attribute returned with the <result> element will be equal to something other than "done" — usually a description of what error condition occurred.

Managing Tags and Tag Bundles

One of the most powerful features of the del.icio.us API is the ability to manage tags across bookmarks without the need to update items in your collection individually.

Fetching a List of Tags and Counts

```
http://del.icio.us/api/tags/get
```

Description

With a call to this method, you can get a list of all tags used in your collection along with usage counts.

Parameters

- None.

Response XML

```
<?xml version='1.0' standalone='yes'?>
<tags>
  <tag count="21"  tag="aggregators" />
  <tag count="1"   tag="business" />
  <tag count="210" tag="rss" />
  <tag count="236" tag="syndication" />
  <tag count="5"   tag="xml" />
</tags>
```

From this method, the XML returned consists of a `<tags>` element containing a number of `<tag>` elements. Each `<tag>` element has a `count` attribute indicating the number of bookmarks for which the `tag` attribute value has been used.

Renaming a Tag

```
http://del.icio.us/api/tags/rename?old=OLD&new=NEW
```

Description

Use this method to rename a tag used across your collection. This comes in handy when gardening tags, such as replacing one tag with a more appropriate one.

Parameters

- `old=TAG` (required): An existing tag found attached to bookmarks
- `new=TAG` (required): A new or existing tag with which to replace the old one

Response XML

```
<?xml version='1.0' standalone='yes'?>
<result>done</result>
```

If for some reason the bookmark posting fails, the character data returned with the `<result>` element will be equal to something other than `done` — usually a description of what error condition occurred.

Fetching a List of All Tag Bundles

```
http://del.icio.us/api/tags/bundles/all
```

Description
A list of all named tag bundles can be fetched with a call to this method.

Parameters

- None.

Response XML

```
<?xml version='1.0' standalone='yes'?>
<bundles>
  <bundle name="hackingfeeds"
          tags="aggregation aggregator aggregators" />
  <bundle name="music"
          tags="ipod mp3 music" />
</bundles>
```

This response format offers a `<bundles>` element containing `<bundle>` elements for each tag bundle in the collection. Each tag bundle described in a `<bundle>` element is named by the attribute `name`, associated with the space-separated list of tags in the `tag` attribute.

Creating or Updating a Tag Bundle

```
http://del.icio.us/api/tags/bundles/set?bundle=BUNDLE&tags=TAGS
```

Description
A tag bundle is created or updated from a list of tags using this method.

Parameters

- `bundle=BUNDLE` (required): The name of the bundle to create or update
- `tags=TAGS` (required): Space-separated tags from which to make the bundle

Response XML

```
<?xml version='1.0' standalone='yes'?>
<result>ok</result>
```

If for some reason the bookmark posting fails, the character data returned with the `<result>` element will be equal to something other than `ok` — usually a description of what error condition occurred.

Deleting a Tag Bundle

```
http://del.icio.us/api/tags/bundles/delete?bundle=BUNDLE
```

Description
This method will delete a named tag bundle from the collection.

Parameters

- bundle=*BUNDLE* (required): The name of the bundle to delete

Response XML

```
<?xml version='1.0' standalone='yes'?>
<result>done</result>
```

If for some reason the bookmark posting fails, the character data returned with the `<result>` element will be equal to something other than `done` — usually a description of what error condition occurred.

Index

How to take it to the Extreme.

If you enjoyed this book, there are many others like it for you. From *Podcasting* to *Hacking Firefox*, ExtremeTech books can fulfill your urge to hack, tweak and modify, providing the tech tips and tricks readers need to get the most out of their hi-tech lives.